L. Thomas Holdcroft

The Holy Spirit

A Pentecostal Interpretation

GⓟH

GOSPEL PUBLISHING HOUSE
SPRINGFIELD, MISSOURI

02-0554

5th Printing 1992

Printed in the United States of America
International Standard Book Number 0-88243-554-X
Library of Congress Catalog Card Number 79-54991

Contents

Charts and Maps

1

Backgrounds
of the Study

The Christian believer who studies the person and work of
the Holy Spirit is not merely concerning himself with abstract
theology but with the personal reality of the Supreme Being. In
such an enterprise, the God whom the believer worships, the
study in which he participates, the Christian experience that he
enjoys, and the doctrinal insights that he gains, may at times
seem to merge into one. For this reason, believers have not
always clearly defined the study of the Holy Spirit. But His
reality and His ministry have never been in question among
those who are truly born again by His creative power. The Holy
Spirit is not only to be experienced and permitted to beget an
experience in the believer's life, but to the degree that He has
chosen to reveal himself, He is also to be known and understood.

The Importance of the Doctrine of the Holy Spirit

The Holy Spirit is that Person of the holy Trinity whose office
it is to touch upon the believer. He is God communicating
himself. In the Holy Spirit, God ministers to those who are His,
and He relates himself to mankind in personal fellowship. In
the words of D. L. Moody: "The Holy Spirit is God at work." He
fulfills an essential role in every genuine Christian experience,
and is therefore so much more than an abstract object of theology. Apart from the Third Person of the Godhead, no one can
truly know God.

The Church Age is often called "the age of the Spirit." Such an epithet contrasts the Gospel era as the age of the Son, and the Old Testament as the age of the Father. The Pauline epistles particularly teach that the life of the believer should be in the sphere of the Holy Spirit. Paul exhorts: "Walk in the Spirit, and ye shall not fulfill the lust of the flesh" (Galatians 5:16). The Spirit validates and implements all aspects of the Christian life. The degree to which the believer has appropriated the Spirit is the degree to which he has partaken of the provisions of the Gospel of Christ. Even doctrinal truths are made understandable and alive by the Holy Spirit.

Isaiah contrasts earthly weakness with heavenly power and victory of the Spirit. "Now the Egyptians are men, and not God; and their horses flesh, and not spirit" (Isaiah 31:3). In all aspects, the qualities of the divine Spirit contrast with those of natural physical beings. Paul prayed that the Ephesians "be strengthened with might by his Spirit in the inner man" (Ephesians 3:16). Spiritual provision and power are available to the believer in and through the Holy Spirit. Every Christian should recognize that "all merit is of the Son . . . [and] all power is of the Holy Spirit." Not only is the original understanding and impulse to live the Christian life given by the Holy Spirit, but also subsequent manifestations of blessing and power for service.

The teachings of Scripture concerning the Holy Spirit are not as numerous as those that concern Father or Son. He is the Author of Scripture, and: "He shall not speak of himself" (John 16:13). Nevertheless, 88 references to the Holy Spirit may be found in the Old Testament, and 261 in the New. There is a reference to the Holy Spirit in the Bible's beginning (Genesis 1:2), and in its ending (Revelation 22:17). The Spirit is mentioned or alluded to in 22 of the 39 Old Testament Books, and in all Books of the New Testament except Philemon, 2 John, and 3 John. Every writer of the New Testament, in at least one of his books, makes repeated references to the Spirit; and each of the four Gospels contains in its introduction a promise of the Spirit's outpouring.

Jesus' teachings concerning the Holy Spirit are chiefly limited to His final discourses during His passion week. Prior to that time, there are only five references to the Spirit in His recorded utterances. It is evident that as Jesus was about to leave His followers in the custody of the Spirit, He saw to it that they were adequately instructed concerning His person and work. The final words of the resurrected Christ, just before His ascension, concerned the Holy Spirit: "Behold, I send the promise of my Father upon you: but tarry ye . . . until ye be endued with power from on high" (Luke 24:49).

The divine objective in relation to the Holy Spirit is that Jesus Christ be glorified. "He shall glorify me, because He will take the things that belong to me and tell them to you" (John 16:14, *Williams*). The understandings and appreciations that the believer receives through studying the doctrine of the Holy Spirit relate to:

1. The divine Being in general, since the Spirit is God and He is one in essence with Father and Son.
2. The Church in its nature, purposes, and mission, since the Spirit indwells it and provides its life.
3. The Christian life on earth, since it is the Spirit who conveys the total divine provision to make it a reality in the convert's experience.

The Doctrine of the Holy Spirit in the Old Testament

The Old Testament uses the specific expression "Holy Spirit" only three times (Psalm 51:11; Isaiah 63:10, 11). However, in many other instances, the word *spirit* occurs without designation, but the context indicates a reference to the Holy Spirit; these usages account for the 88 references already mentioned. The doctrine of the Holy Spirit thus receives a large place in the Old Testament, even though most aspects of the Christian doctrine of the Spirit are developed from the New. It is the case that many seed thoughts and typical implications are found in the Old Testament, but expanded, precise, doctrinal developments await the New. Turner comments: "Everything unfolded about the Spirit in the New Testament is already found in the Old Testament with one exception, that is the new word 'baptize.' "[1]

Aspects of the Holy Spirit clearly taught in the Old Testament include: His role in creation and on behalf of the physical universe: "The spirit of God moved upon the face of the waters" (Genesis 1:2); His ministry as God's moral representative: "My spirit shall not always strive with man" (Genesis 6:8); His actions in charismatic anointing: "He hath filled him [i.e., Bezaleel] with the spirit of God, in wisdom, in understanding, and in knowledge" (Exodus 35:31); His bestowment of life: "Until the spirit be poured upon us from on high, and the wilderness be a fruitful field" (Isaiah 32:15); His communication of the mind of God: "Who hath directed the Spirit of the Lord, or being his counselor hath taught him?" (Isaiah 40:13).

The portrayal of the Spirit of God in the Old Testament is unique among ancient religions. Only the Hebrews linked their God to the realm of spirit being. The English word *spirit* translating the Hebrew *ruach* is only partially adequate to convey what was represented. The Old Testament presents "spirit" *(ruach)* as God's aspects of action, power, invisibility, mind, and life. One scholar claims to have found 33 distinct connotations of *ruach*. It was not a case of just one reality, but the whole matter of "God's activity as He relates himself to His world, His creation, His people."[2] Such concepts are, of course, not different from those noted of the Holy Spirit in general. The Old Testament believer discovered just what Christians later realized (and we have already noted): "The Holy Spirit is God at work."

It is usually concluded that one limitation in the Old Testament presentation of the doctrine of the Spirit is the lack of definite information regarding His person. Griffith Thomas writes:

The Old Testament teaching may therefore be summarized thus: The Spirit is a Divine agent and energy rather than a distinct personality. God is regarded as at work, and, as in the New Testament, the Spirit is the executive of the Godhead. He is not a gift separate from God, but God Himself in and with men; a Power rather than a Person.[3]

Lloyd Neve studies significant passages in detail, and he seeks to demonstrate that Old Testament Scriptures neither establish that the Holy Spirit proceeds in His own will, nor that the Spirit himself determines His experiences or reactions.

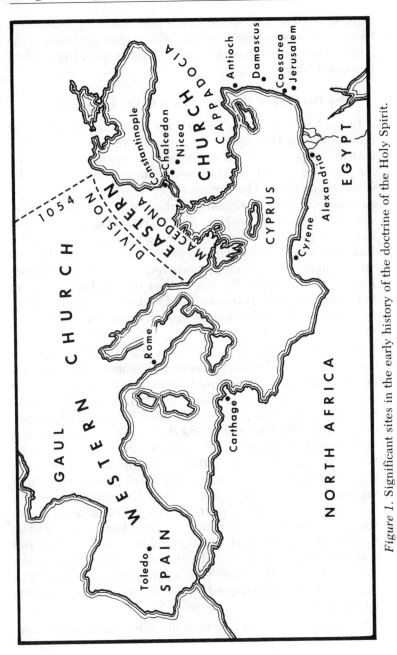

Figure 1. Significant sites in the early history of the doctrine of the Holy Spirit.

Neve says: "The final conclusion is overwhelmingly negative: there is no personalization of the Spirit within the limits of the [Old Testament]."[4] Probably many scholars would agree with this conclusion.

The Doctrine of the Holy Spirit in the Early Church[5]

In the New Testament era, and the immediate decades that followed it, the Holy Spirit was primarily an experience rather than the subject of a doctrine. Christians were satisfied to enjoy the presence of the Holy Spirit within them, and to witness His work among them. The Apostles' Creed, which is believed to have been compiled originally by the late first century, simply stated: "I believe in the Holy Spirit." When the creed took its final form in the sixth century, nothing further concerning the Holy Spirit had been added. To much of Christendom He was only a name. Fortunately, however, some of the Church Fathers or Patristics (Christian pastors and teachers in the era following the New Testament) did concern themselves with the doctrine of the Spirit, and through them some significant insights developed.

Noteworthy comments from this era include: "The grace of the Spirit brings the machinery of redemption into vital connection with the individual soul. Apart from the Spirit the cross stands inert" (Ignatius of Rome, c. 70-115); and, "The Holy Spirit is one and the same everywhere" (Clement of Alexandria, c. 155-220). Clement taught that the Holy Spirit streams upon man from heaven and enables him to behold divine things. In Tertullian's (c. 160-222) description of water baptism, a confession of faith in the Holy Spirit is required prior to the final immersion (he appears to describe a ceremony involving a threefold immersion). It was either Tertullian or a contemporary who first used "trinity" as a theological term, and he thereby placed the Spirit on an equal basis with Father and Son. Tertullian is also credited with identifying the Spirit as the "vicar of Christ," meaning "Christ's substitute in office." The expression was later adopted by the Catholic Church as a title for the pope.

In a statement meant to reflect the generally accepted doctrines of his day, Origen (c. 186-253) wrote: "The Holy Spirit is associated with the Father and Son in honor and dignity. It is not clear whether or not He was generated. He inspired the sacred writers." Elsewhere, Origen took the position that the Holy Spirit is uncreated. He also taught that the Spirit bestowed holiness, and that the doctrine of the Spirit is to be derived solely from the Scriptures.

Cyril of Jerusalem in his *Catechetical Lectures* (c. 348) discussed the Spirit, particularly in His practical work in human lives. However, he warned that concerning the nature of the Spirit the believer should "enquire not curiously," and declared: "To define accurately the hypostasis [i.e., nature] of the Holy Spirit is impossible; we must be content to guard against errors on various sides."

Along with valid insights concerning the Spirit developed in the Early Church, there were also unscriptural doctrines and outright errors. These emerged, no doubt, because of indifference to the Holy Spirit's doctrine in a church that was being rapidly institutionalized. The Homily of Clement (of Rome) (c. 95) mentions the Spirit only to intimate that He was a created being, and hence not eternal nor divine. Tertullian marred his valid insights already noted by also holding that the Holy Spirit is material substance that in some way improves the effects of the baptismal water. Groups outside of orthodoxy, such as the Monarchians in the third century, denied the distinct existence of the Spirit; the Pelagians, in the late fourth century, denied that He has a part in man's regeneration. Hippolytus, in the early third century, presented the Spirit as a force rather than a person; while late in that century, the so-called Semi-Arian school denied the Spirit's personality and also His deity.

Although the issue at the Council of Nicea (A.D. 325) primarily was the deity of Jesus Christ, the personality and deity of the Holy Spirit were relevant topics. The Nicene Creed, which emerged at this time, echoed the Apostles' Creed in asserting a single fact concerning the Spirit: "We believe also in one Holy Spirit." A little over three decades later, Athanasius produced his *Letter to Serapion* (c. 359) which, in spite of being propagandistic in approach, served to express orthodox doctrine of the Holy Spirit. Athanasius taught: 1) The Holy Spirit is exalted

above all created things, 2) The Holy Spirit is the same substance as the Father and the Son, 3) The Holy Spirit is God's
creative activity and power renewing and sanctifying man, and
4) In His ultimate being the Holy Spirit transcends human
understanding.

A much more scholarly and systematic work on the Holy
Spirit in the era of the Early Church was by Basil of Cappadocia
(330-379). (He was also known as St. Basil the Great, Bishop of
Caesarea.) Basil's work *On the Holy Spirit* (c. A.D. 374) *(De
Spiritu Sancto* in Latin) was intended to refute the Semi-Arians
(also called "Macedonians" and "Pneumatomachi"—
contenders against the Spirit). The error of the Semi-Arians has
already been noted. In his work, Basil argued: 1) The Spirit is
equal in rank to Father and Son, 2) The Spirit is the giver and
dispenser of life, 3) The Spirit is above all creation and He
exercises sovereign freedom, 4) Through the Spirit men are
able to know the Son. The Church officially endorsed the views
of Basil and his fellow Cappadocians at the Council of Constantinople in 381. This endorsement promptly led to a controversial expansion of the Nicene Creed.

The Medieval Debate Concerning the Spirit's Procession

The doctrine of the Holy Spirit was a matter of heated dispute
in the church for almost the entire medieval period. The Scripture passage: "Even the Spirit of truth, which proceedeth from
the Father" (John 15:26) became the arena of this extended
debate. At the Council of Constantinople, this passage was
incorporated into the Nicene Creed so that it declared: "We
believe in the Holy Ghost, the Lord and Giver of life, who
proceedeth from the Father, who with the Father and the Son
together is worshipped and glorified, who spake by the
prophets." Two centuries later, at the third Council of Toledo
in Spain (A.D. 589), the third clause of this statement was
expanded to read: ". . . who proceedeth from the Father and
the Son." In Latin, the expression "and the Son" is the one
word *filioque,* and on occasion this word is used as a noun or
adjective to identify the doctrine of the dual procession of the

Spirit. The word *spiration* is sometimes used as a synonym for "procession."

The claim that the Spirit proceeded from both the Father and the Son was by no means acceptable to all the Church. At first it prevailed only in Spain, and not until four centuries had elapsed from the Council of Toledo was it generally accepted in Europe. But at best, the doctrine of dual procession was limited to the Roman (or Latin or Western) church. It remained unacceptable to the Eastern (Greek or Orthodox) church which centered in Constantinople. The differences between the East and the West concerning the procession of the Holy Spirit was one of the major causes of the final division between the Roman Catholic and Eastern Orthodox churches in 1054.

Theodoret of Cyrrhus (Syria), who flourished in the first half of the fifth century, was chiefly responsible for shaping Eastern thinking in the matter of the procession of the Spirit. Unfortunately, Theodoret was thoroughly inflexible in his doctrines, and he repudiated the moderate teachings of Cyril of Alexandria that might have brought harmony between East and West. In the eighth century, John of Damascus, in the tradition of Theodoret, published his doctrines that to this day constitute the position of the Eastern church. John taught: 1) The Spirit proceeds from the Father, 2) He proceeds through the Son, 3) He rests in the Son, and 4) He is united to the Father through the Son. It was John's influence that led to the Eastern creedal statement: "We believe in one Holy Spirit, the Lord and Giver of life, who proceedeth from the Father and resteth in the Son."

The division of the Eastern and Western churches in 1054 has had enduring consequences. Before the end of the medieval period, there had been more than 30 official attempts to reconcile the dispute, but the Eastern church continued to deny that the Holy Spirit proceeds from the Son. They noted that the only scriptural reference to the procession of the Spirit relates Him exclusively to the Father—i.e., "even the Spirit of truth, which proceedeth from the Father" (John 15:26). There were, of course, other differences, but the procession controversy has been one of the basic doctrinal conflicts that has kept the Western and Eastern churches separate to this day.

Western Catholics, and most Protestants, hold that the procession of the Spirit is not a matter of a single text, but of Scripture as a whole. They note that even in John 15:26, Jesus made the point that He was to be the one who would send the Spirit. Similarly, Jesus promised: "If I go not away, the Comforter will not come unto you; but if I depart, I will send him unto you" (John 16:7). They see the Bible as teaching that the Spirit is the Spirit of Jesus Christ as well as the Spirit of the Father. Downer speaks for many when he plainly says: "The Spirit is not only sent by, but also proceeds from, the Son, as well as from the Father, since the Son can only send that which is His own."

Even though evangelical Protestants typically accept the dual procession of the Spirit, they still have the task of determining the nature of the procession relationship. In many instances, it proves easier to say what it is not. Walvoord writes:

Procession like the eternal generation of Christ is not a matter of creation, commencement of existence, or analogous in any way to physical relationships common in the human realm. It proceeds rather from the very nature of the Godhead, being necessary to its existence. Without the Holy Spirit, the Godhead would not be what it is.[6]

It would be generally agreed that the relationship of proceeding in no way subordinates the Holy Spirit, nor does it provide Him with an inferior role in the Godhead, but it simply constitutes a means of describing His unique status.

The Doctrine of the Holy Spirit in the Reformation and Thereafter

The first 14 centuries of the Christian Church had seen the development of only minimal insights concerning the Holy Spirit. The Protestant Reformation, which began in 1517, marked a turning point in this state of affairs. The leaders of the Reformation such as Luther, Calvin, and Melanchthon specifically gave place to the Holy Spirit in their doctrine and in their personal lives. They reinstated Him in His role as the author and interpreter of the Scriptures, and they saw His functioning as the basis of the "priesthood of every believer." In his *Institutes* (1536), Calvin declares that the reality of salvation is achieved through "the secret energy of the Holy Spirit, by which we enjoy Christ and all His benefits." The Protestant *Book of Concord* (1580), a doctrinal summation of German Lutheranism and the first major joint publication of the reformers, includes a complete basic theology of the Spirit. In the preface of the book, the authors set forth a fivefold acknowledgment of the Spirit.

It was, of course, not the case that the 16th-century reformers proceeded to develop the full doctrine of the Holy Spirit as we would study Him today. The Reformation was a time of laying foundations and establishing bases. Former indifferences and confusions died slowly, even in the ranks of Protestantism. The Spirit's role in sanctification and personal piety was for the most part a separate stream in the process. However, it may be noted that Sebastian Franck (d. 1542) founded the Inner Light Movement which held that the Holy Spirit may be appropriated by the believer in order to attain insights into the Scriptures. The Puritans of the 17th century gave a large place to the Spirit in His regenerating and sanctifying ministries. In the same century, the Quakers placed special emphasis on an awareness of the Holy Spirit, and in their *Confession* (official statement of faith) they named the Holy Spirit 18 times. The Pietists of the 18th century followed the Puritans in stressing the ministry of the Spirit to sanctify the believer.

The Holy Spirit was specifically involved both experientially and doctrinally in the first and second evangelical awakenings of the 18th and 19th centuries in England and the Continent, as well as the 18th-century Great Awakening in America. Starkey characterizes the first of these revivals as the event "when the Christ-like God became dynamically present and real to men as the Holy Spirit." The spiritual vitality and interest of England's John Wesley (1703-1791) and Germany's Count Zinzendorf (1700-1760) are in each case credited by Starkey to the Holy Spirit. He notes Wesley's claim that "inspiration [Wesley meant by this 'inbreathing' or 'infilling'] of the Spirit was the main doctrine of the Methodists."[7]

The publication, in England, of William Arthur's *The Tongue of Fire or The True Power of Christianity* in 1856 is usually held to be one of the bases of the second evangelical awakening which began in 1859. This book, appropriately honoring the Holy Spirit, is considered to have transformed the religious life of the English-speaking world. In North America, Methodist laypersons Walter and Phoebe Palmer enthusiastically promoted revivalism, including Arthur's views and Spirit-imparted holiness.

As the 19th century ended, the doctrine of the Holy Spirit had achieved its greatest development since the New Testament era. F. D. Bruner lists five late 19th- and early 20th-century evangelicals: A. J. Gordon, Andrew Murray, F. B. Meyer, A. B. Simpson, and R. A. Torrey. He comments: "These five formed a kind of theological fund from which the Pentecostal theology of the Spirit has drawn heavily to establish itself."[8] None of these authors was, of course, Pentecostal in the modern sense, but it is probably true that they made a contribution as Bruner claims. Those Pentecostal groups that were beginning to flourish in this era were not yet producing their own theological writings. Although a wealth of material[9] was produced pertaining to the Catholic Apostolic Church, a more or less Pentecostal denomination founded in 1832, it seems to have made little enduring contribution to the doctrine of the Spirit. And similarly, no permanent doctrinal works appear to have emerged from the Welsh revival of 1904, nor from the revival associated with the Azusa Mission which began in 1906.

Not all movements in the Protestant Church have maintained the role of the Holy Spirit. In the 17th century, Socinianism, associated with Faustus Socinus (1509-1604), revived the Arian interpretation that denied personality to the Spirit. Socinianism concluded that the Holy Spirit was nothing more than God's power and influence, and therefore not a topic for special theological emphasis. The so-called "father of liberal theology," Friedrich Schleiermacher (1768-1834), taught that the Holy Spirit is an outflow from Christ and merely a working spiritual force. His successor, Albert Ritschl (1822-1889), transformed the person of the Spirit into a concept of impersonal power emanating from God and dwelling in the church. In effect, the doctrine of the Spirit was dismissed rather than developed.

The Oxford Movement in the Anglican (i.e., Episcopal)

church, which began in the third decade of the 19th century
and was associated with Edward B. Pusey (1800-1882), denied
the Spirit's inspiration of Scripture. In general, this movement
replaced claims of supernaturalism with theories of naturalism
or humanism. In the U.S., Horace Bushnell (1802-1876) concluded that his doctrine of the development of Christian experience by social nurture gave grounds for denying that the
Holy Spirit is an Agent of man's salvation. (But paradoxically,
Bushnell wrote in defense of Edward Irving and the reality of
Pentecostal experiences within the Catholic Apostolic
Church.) Other liberal theologians in the 19th and 20th centuries similarly disposed of the Holy Spirit, so that He became
little more than good purpose in the human heart. Among
liberals, teaching concerning the Holy Spirit was im-
poverished and neglected to the degree that observers have
referred to it as the "Cinderella doctrine" and the "neglected
stepchild of Christian theology."

The teachings of neoorthodoxy give place to an inner commitment and a personal experience that appears to parallel the
genuine work of the Holy Spirit. However, the approach remains that of humanistic liberalism, and ultimately the Holy
Spirit is seen as little more than a self-induced attitude of heart.
He is equivalent to inner sensation such as a sense of despair,
conviction, or self-rebuke, or even of hope or joy. Rudolf
Bultmann, who became a spokesman for neoorthodoxy, saw
references to the Spirit as simply an allegorical way of speaking
of "the possibility of a new life which is opened up by faith." To
Bultmann, and others in neoorthodoxy, the Holy Spirit is not to
be thought of as a divine person.

In effect, the existential commitment of neoorthodoxy substitutes the enthronement of the inner self for the miraculous
regenerating power of the Spirit. Instead of living and walking
in the Spirit in the Biblical pattern, the convert is urged to
maintain a constant responsible confrontation with God.
Human effort is made to substitute for the supernatural. Similarly, in neoorthodoxy the doctrine of plenary inspiration and
the inerrancy of the Scriptures is replaced by the claim of the
subjective "inspiringness of the Bible." The Spirit's role is
reduced to the level of a personal response with the believer. In

each instance, neoorthodoxy replaces the Spirit's work with some aspect of human behavior.

The doctrine of the Holy Spirit saw only a slow development among classical Pentecostals in the first half of the 20th century. A few significant works were produced, but they were only modestly innovative. However, the rise of the charismatic movement in the 1960's brought sweeping changes. An entire school of charismatics, many out of scholarly literate backgrounds, launched a fresh wave of thinking, teaching, and writing on the subject of the Holy Spirit. Simultaneously, the classical Pentecostal movements began to be of age, and to sponsor competent Pentecostal scholars and theologians. The doctrine of the Holy Spirit has, therefore, now reached a level of development never before known in the history of the Church.

2

Titles and Symbols of the Holy Spirit

The various titles and symbols by which the Holy Spirit is depicted in the Bible convey a wealth of insights and truths concerning Him. At least 11 titles can be distinguished specifically in Scripture, and 10 different symbols is a probable minimum. Whereas Scripture may not formally expound facts concerning the Holy Spirit, it accomplishes the same results by naming Him in these diverse ways. Each title or symbol conveys its own special truths concerning the Spirit's person and work.

Titles of the Spirit and Their Significance

The Holy Spirit. A random Scripture passage illustrates this title: "How much more shall your heavenly Father give the Holy Spirit to them that ask him?" (Luke 11:13). Other similar designations include: ". . . declared to be the Son of God with power, according to the *spirit of holiness*" (Romans 1:4); and, "Ye have an unction from the *Holy One*" (1 John 2:20). The use of the adjective *holy* in the Spirit's title identifies Him as unique even in the Trinity. It is not that He is more holy than Father or Son, but it is the Spirit who is charged with executing divine holiness within mankind and throughout the universe. This title also, of course, serves to distinguish Him from all the unholy spirits that are at work in the world.

The title *Holy Spirit* effectively establishes a contrast between His spiritual essence and any kind of material substance. It is an error to consider that the Spirit is a type of material or physical substance. The medieval concept of the appropriation of the Spirit into one's life through partaking of the sacraments was confused at this point. The so-called "materialization of grace" that calls for dispensing the Spirit through the christening water or communion wafer ignores the fact that the spirituality of the Spirit is firmly established by His very name. It may be noted that the expression "Holy Ghost" found in the King James Version is a translator's variant of "Holy Spirit" that reflects usage in the era of 1611.

The Spirit of God. "Grieve not the Holy Spirit of God, whereby ye are sealed unto the day of redemption" (Ephesians 4:30). In choosing this title for the Spirit, Paul linked Him to God the Father and implied that the Spirit is particularly the Father's representative upon earth. The Holy Spirit serves the Father in drawing men to Christ (John 6:44) and through Him to the Father; He reveals truth (John 16:13), and thus directs men to the Father of all truth; He leads believers (Romans 8:14) in practical Christian living that they may more effectively serve the Father. In all, there are 11 scriptural titles which relate the Spirit to the Father: Spirit of God, Spirit of the Lord, Spirit of our God, His Spirit, Spirit of Jehovah, Thy Spirit, Spirit of the Lord God, Spirit of the Father, Spirit of the Living God, My Spirit, and Spirit of Him. The Father promised, has sent, and has given the Spirit that He might achieve His own good will and pleasure.

The Spirit of Christ. To know the Holy Spirit as the Spirit of Christ is essential to salvation. "Now if any man have not the Spirit of Christ, he is none of his" (Romans 8:9). By this title, the identification of the Spirit with Christ is emphasized, for it is as the Spirit of Christ that the Holy Spirit: imparts the Christ life (Romans 8:2); produces Christ fruits (Philippians 1:11); reveals the things of Christ (John 16:14); imparts the power of Christ (Acts 1:8; John 14:12); and takes the place of the ascended Christ (John 14:16-18).

Five scriptural titles relate the Holy Spirit to Christ: Spirit of Christ, Spirit of Jesus Christ, Spirit of Jesus, Spirit of His Son, and Spirit of the Lord. It has been well said: "The personalities of Christ, and the Spirit are never identical, their presence always is." When Jesus was incarnate, He was the subject of the Spirit's anointing, and this the Spirit did by anointing Jesus with himself. In the Church Age, the Spirit ministers to make Christ present in the Church, and to form Christ in the believer just as truly as He formed the body of the human Jesus before His birth. Jesus Christ may be seen in all the Spirit says and does, and ultimately every work of the Spirit leads to the exaltation and glory of the Lord Jesus Christ.

Comforter. There are four Biblical references to the Holy Spirit by His title *Comforter*, all of them spoken by the incarnate Jesus and recorded in John's Gospel. "And I will pray the Father, and he shall give you another Comforter, that he may abide with you for ever" (John 14:16; cf. John 14:26; 15:26; 16:7). In the fifth New Testament reference, John applied the same title to Christ, although in most versions it is rendered "advocate" (1 John 2:1). The word *Comforter* in the original is the word *paracletos* and thus it appears in its transliterated form as "Paraclete." In the 14th century, John Wycliffe chose "Comforter" as the best English translation of *paracletos*, but most scholars today would prefer to leave the word untranslated and simply speak of the Paraclete. Proposed modern synonyms include: instructor, guide, advocate, ombudsman, part taker, interpreter, advice giver, governor, assistant, helper, caretaker, attorney, and barrister.

It has been noted that the word *Comforter* belongs not in the sickroom but in the courtroom. It is a word for one who toils and strengthens and gives battle on behalf of another. As Paraclete, the Holy Spirit is ready to provide counsel, wisdom, guidance, strength, and grace in all needed ways. Writes Sanders:

> In two instances, the Comforter is identified as the Spirit of truth, who was to lead the disciples into all truth. In the third instance, His function is said to be that of remembrance of and witness to Christ. In the last instance the Spirit is seen convicting the human heart. . . . From our Lord's usage of the word, it becomes clear that, while present, the idea of consolation and comfort is distinctly secondary to that of strength and help.[1]

In speaking of the Spirit as "Comforter," Jesus conveyed the

Spirit's role in continuing His ministry upon earth. As Comforter, the Spirit is to believers what the incarnate Jesus was to His disciples. Simultaneously, the believer enjoys a heavenly Comforter (Advocate, Paraclete) in Jesus Christ: "If any man sin, we have an advocate with the Father, Jesus Christ the righteous" (1 John 2:1). The heavenly Advocate looks after the believer's interests in heaven; the earthly Comforter looks after Christ's interests in the believer. As an earthly Comforter or Advocate, the Holy Spirit represents Christ, exalts Him, and presses His claims within mankind. He does not so much minister comfort to soothe spiritual babes, but He ministers power, wisdom, and courage to arm strong warriors for the fight.

As Comforter, the Holy Spirit desires to be the believer's warm personal friend. It is of interest to note that Jesus promised not to leave His people "comfortless" (John 14:18), or in the original, *orphanos*. The gift of the Comforter assures Christians they are not "orphaned." Greek-speaking theologians of the Early Church saw the word *paraclete* as denoting that personal agency who acts toward another to empower, embolden, encourage, and comfort him. Biblical usage illustrates this understanding, for it reports the churches of the provinces of Palestine: ". . . walking in the fear of the Lord, and in the comfort [GK., *paracleis*] of the Holy Ghost, were multiplied" (Acts 9:31). One outcome of the ministry of the Spirit as Comforter is the growth in numbers and spiritual power of the church of Christ on earth.

The Spirit of Grace. Willful sinners are described in Scripture as those who have "done despite unto the Spirit of grace" (Hebrews 10:29). Such a title depicts the Spirit as the one through whom all of the provisions of divine grace become available to mankind. Comments Riggs: "The Holy Spirit presents heaven's treasures as gracious gifts to men. . . . Grace is the fundamental law of His ministry." Because grace is involved, it is evident that the Spirit's goodness toward humans is wholly independent of personal human worthiness. Historically, scholars have spoken of the Spirit's role in "prevenient" grace. Such grace is a preliminary gift to a prospective convert that is more than natural conscience, but not enough of the divine to achieve salvation. Prevenient grace permits a sinner to rise to penitent faith, and thence to actual regeneration. It is because the Holy Spirit is the Spirit of grace that humans can be transported from spiritual death to eternal life in Christ.

The Spirit of Glory. Peter assigns this title to the Holy Spirit: ". . . for the spirit of glory and of God resteth upon you" (1 Peter 4:14). The term *glory* is associated with worship. It conveys the idea of honor, esteem, praise, and the commitment of affection extended by the believer out of the sincere motive of rendering worship. The human appreciates and responds to the divine glory only to the degree that the Spirit of glory suitably il- lumines and motivates him. The Holy Spirit in this role is an essential associate in every genuine service of worship that ascribes praise and honor to the God of glory. Significantly, in Peter's reference, the glory is the outcome of persecution upon God's child. The true believer glorifies God the more in the face of worldly hostility.

The Spirit of Truth.   The Lord Jesus gave the Holy Spirit this title, and in His farewell discourse to His disciples, He referred to Him thus three times. "Howbeit when he, the Spirit of truth, is come, he will guide you into all truth" (John 16:13; cf. 14:17; 15:26). The Holy Spirit reveals truth, witnesses to or verifies truth, and He personifies truth. Since God is the author of truth, it follows that His Spirit is the Spirit of Truth. If believers are to relate rightly to the Spirit, they must exhibit lives and proclaim messages in harmony with the truth. Their commission is no longer to search for the truth, but within the Spirit to search the truth. He embraces both a perfect knowl- edge and an infinite love of all truth.

All aspects of the Father's knowledge are within the scope of the Spirit of Truth, for of course there is nothing the Father knows that the Spirit does not know. Although His specialty is spiritual truth, He embraces also truths of science, nature, and logic. When the occasion arises, the Spirit may interpret truth, or enable believers to recall particular truths. "He shall teach you all things, and bring all things to your remembrance, what- soever I have said unto you" (John 14:26). On occasion, He may choose to reveal the future: "He will show you things to come"

(John 16:13). When the Spirit reveals to the believer truths concerning the Christian walk, He is able also to empower the believer to implement these standards in his own personal life.

An outstanding example of the ministry of the Spirit is His inspiration of the writers of Scripture. He has produced a true literary record that extensively features the Father and the Son. Because the Spirit-inspired Bible is the eternal repository of divine truth, it rightly becomes the infallible rule of faith and conduct. An obedient commitment to the truth of the Book goes hand-in-hand with a commitment to the Spirit of Truth. By His very nature, the Holy Spirit is essentially committed to truth. And conversely, He must repudiate all falsehood, deceit, and error. The death of Ananias and Sapphira (Acts 5:1-11) is a solemn witness to the essential concern of the Spirit for truth.

The Spirit of Life. The Holy Spirit constitutes the believer's life. "For the law of the Spirit of life in Christ Jesus hath made me free from the law of sin and death" (Romans 8:2). He replaces the reigning law of sin and death which is man's natural heritage. At conversion, the Spirit quickens (makes alive) the one who is dead in trespasses and sins (cf. Ephesians 2:1; 2 Corinthians 5:17). The Spirit of life as a basic New Testament provision contrasts with Old Testament legalism. "The letter killeth, but the Spirit giveth life" (2 Corinthians 3:6). Marsh wrote: "The Spirit of Life leads us to the Living Stone to quicken us, to the Living God to shield us, to the Living High Priest to keep us, to the Living Bread to feed us, to the Living Word to assure us, to the Living Way to access us, to the Living Christ to satisfy us, and to the Living Water that He may assuage us."[2]

Not only is the Holy Spirit the Spirit of life in spiritual renewal in the New Testament, but in the Old Testament He is life in the sense of a physical animating principle. The various translations of the Hebrew *ruach*, spirit, breath, or wind, imply that all of life in all living organisms is dependent upon the Holy Spirit. "Thou sendest forth thy spirit, they are created: and thou renewest the face of the earth" (Psalm 104:30); "Thus saith God the Lord . . . he that spread forth the earth . . . he that giveth breath unto the people upon it, and spirit to them that walk therein" (Isaiah 42:5); "O remember that my life is wind"

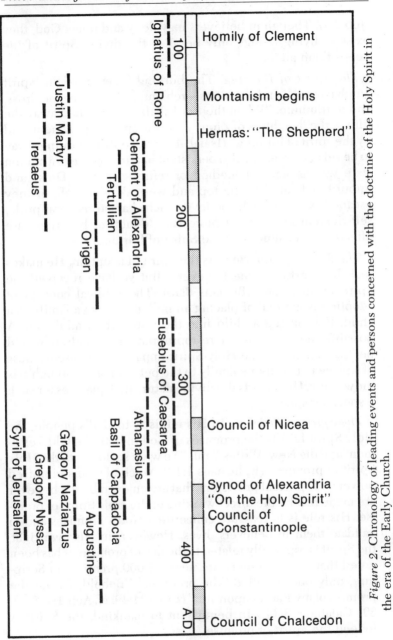

Figure 2. Chronology of leading events and persons concerned with the doctrine of the Holy Spirit in the era of the Early Church.

(Job 7:7). Though unbelievers may deny and reject God, they exist as living beings only because the divine Spirit of life keeps them alive.

The Spirit of Burning. The burning function of the Spirit emphasizes His ministry to search out, refine, consume dross, and to illumine. "When the Lord shall have washed away the filth of the daughters of Zion . . . by the spirit of judgment, and by the spirit of burning" (Isaiah 4:4). Not only is burning a way to be rid of refuse, but also persistent heating by fire to a molten state was an ancient method of refining metals. Dross and impurities floated to the top and were skimmed off, or they escaped as vapor. In the believer, such characteristics as pride, self-righteousness, mere profession, doubt, or bitterness are effectively consumed by the Spirit of burning.

The Spirit of Adoption. As the Spirit of adoption, He makes real the sonship of the believer. "But ye have received the Spirit of adoption" (Romans 8:15). The Biblical concept of adoption is not that of placing an individual into a family as a child, but placing a child into the status of an adult son. A possible alternate word more appropriate in our culture would be "partnership." The Holy Spirit imparts this consciousness of a place in the divine family to the believer, and through His indwelling, He imparts the divine nature that qualifies for such a special status.

The Spirit of Promise. In His ministry to God's people, the Holy Spirit fulfills the promises of God in both the Old Testament and the New. Writes Paul: "Ye were sealed with the Holy Spirit of promise" (Ephesians 1:13). Much of God's promised power and spiritual provisions that are enjoyed by the believer are made real by the direct working of the Holy Spirit of promise. His role is to reassure concerning God's promises and to validate them in believers' lives. However, in His own right, the Spirit is especially related to the fact of promise. It has been noted that although there are nearly 7,000 promises in Scripture, only one is called "the promise." "Behold, I send the promise of my Father upon you" (Luke 24:49; cf. Acts 1:4; 2:33, 39; Galatians 3:14). In being sent to mankind, the Spirit is indeed the Spirit of promise.

The Spirit of Wisdom. All true wisdom proceeds from the Holy Spirit who is wisdom's channel and author. "And thou shalt speak unto all that are wise hearted, whom I have filled with the spirit of wisdom" (Exodus 28:3); "That the God of our Lord Jesus Christ . . . may give unto you the spirit of wisdom" (Ephesians 1:17). It is noted that the first named of the gifts of the Spirit is "the word of wisdom." As the Spirit of wisdom He is: wise, tactful, informed, thoughtful, sensitive, relevant, and resourceful.

Other titles of the Spirit sometimes discussed include: Eternal Spirit, Power of the highest, Spirit of prophecy, Breath of the Almighty, Spirit of might, Spirit of counsel, Spirit of understanding, Spirit of knowledge, Spirit of judgment, and the seven Spirits of God.

Symbols of the Spirit and Their Significance

Most symbols of the Holy Spirit derived from Scripture are inferred rather than explicitly identified. Grounds for the inferences that follow include: parallel language that interchanges the Spirit and the symbol (e.g., spirit, breath, wind), a verb form that describes the function of the Spirit in terms of the function of the symbol (e.g., sealed, anointed), a direct identification (e.g, "This spake he of the Spirit," John 7:38), a specific association (e.g., "like a dove," Matthew 3:16), or a descriptive adjective that also names a symbol (e.g., earnest). Depending on classification and structure, as many as a dozen Biblical symbols of the Spirit may be recognized. However, some of the terms may be combined.

Wind or Breath. Job spoke in typical Old Testament parallelism: "The Spirit of God hath made me, and the breath of the Almighty hath given me life" (Job 33:4). Jesus said: "The wind bloweth where it listeth . . . so is every one that is born of the Spirit" (John 3:8). The dry bones of Ezekiel's vision were made alive by the Spirit as wind: "Come from the four winds, O Breath, and breathe upon these slain, that they may live" (Ezekiel 37:9). The operation and mode of functioning of the Spirit is thus aptly symbolized as wind or breath. The fact that the usual Hebrew and Greek terms for Spirit *(ruach, pneuma)* each translate not only "spirit" but also "breath" or "wind" further supports the symbolism. The Holy Spirit is designated as the outbreathing of God, so that He constitutes the atmosphere within which the believer lives.

Because wind is unseen but powerful, penetrating, life-giving, exhilarating, and refreshing, it especially symbolizes the redemptive work of the Spirit. On occasion, natural wind manifests great power—as in a hurricane; the Holy Spirit in the spiritual realm may do likewise. The power of the wind to cleanse away clouds, dust, fog, and vapors compares to the Spirit's power to cleanse spiritual fogs from human intellects. "The wind passeth, and cleanseth them" (Job 37:21). In their respective operations, neither the wind nor the Spirit is totally unpredictable. Solomon observed: "The wind goeth toward the south, and turneth about unto the north; it whirleth continually, and the wind returneth again according to the circuits" (Ecclesiastes 1:6). Comments Marsh:

> The Holy Spirit has a special circuit of service in relation to the redeemed. . . . He encloses us in His love, encircles us in His presence, encompasses us about with His power, and environs us through His Word.[3]

Fire. John the Baptist prophesied: "He shall baptize you with the Holy Ghost, and with fire" (Matthew 3:11). At Pentecost: "There appeared unto them cloven tongues like as of fire, and it sat upon each of them" (Acts 2:3). Since He is the Spirit of burning, fire is indeed an appropriate symbol. Men use fire to warm, illumine, purify, test, release energy, and generate power. The fiery sun provides vast outputs of power in our universe. Fire breaks down some substances (cf. Judges 16:9), and softens others (Psalm 68:2). It consumes combustible materials, and refines or purifies what cannot be consumed. "He will thoroughly purge his floor, and gather his wheat into the garner; but he will burn up the chaff with unquenchable fire" (Matthew 3:12). The touch of the burning coal was sufficient to purge the vicarious sin of the prophet (Isaiah 6:6, 7).

Fire attracts attention, for it led Moses to turn aside to see the burning bush (Exodus 3:2, 3). Fire speaks of divine endorsement and authority: Elijah's sacrifice was designated by this means (1 Kings 18:39), and so was Elisha's divine calling before his intended captors (2 Kings 1:10). God's role as a judge is set forth under the figure of "a consuming fire" (Hebrews 12:29). To the believer, the Holy Spirit, as fire, ministers warmth to the heart, illumination to the mind, and purity and cleansing to the soul. Although the carnal nature of man may survive a baptism of water, it can never survive a baptism of fire. The fiery Holy Spirit assures personal holiness that soundly validates the burning passion of the Christian soul winner.

Water. The Old Testament depicts the gift of the Spirit as the gift of water upon dry ground. "I will pour water upon him that is thirsty, and floods upon the dry ground: I will pour out my Spirit upon thy seed, and my blessing upon thine offspring" (Isaiah 44:3, 4). Jesus declared: "Whosoever drinketh of the water that I shall give him shall never thirst" (John 4:14). A later declaration by Jesus is explained by John: "He that believeth on me . . . out of his belly shall flow rivers of living water. (But this spake he of the Spirit . . .)" (John 7:38, 39). Water is that which purifies, refreshes, and cleanses; the Spirit is He who purifies from sinful habits and becomes to the soul a refreshing and cleansing fountain. The Spirit as living (i.e., running) water is meant to be a river of life that refreshes and renews and delivers from all deadness.

Growth normally requires the presence of water. "Can the flag [i.e., reed] grow without water?" (Job 8:11). Water is a common agent in washing and cleansing. "Let us draw near with a true heart in full assurance of faith, having our hearts sprinkled from an evil conscience, and our bodies washed with pure water" (Hebrews 10:22). The Psalmist noted that abundant water is essential for fruitfulness: "He shall be like a tree planted by the rivers of water, that bringeth forth his fruit in his season" (Psalm 1:3). To the thirsty soul water cheers and delights. "As cold waters to a thirsty soul, so is good news from a far country" (Proverbs 25:25). "There is a river the streams whereof shall make glad the city of God" (Psalm 46:4).

Cloud, Rain, and Dew. That which cooling clouds, rain, or dew means to the parched countryside parallels that which the Spirit means to the responsive believer. As precipitation descends, so He comes down upon the human soul with life-giving refreshment and nourishment. ("He planteth an ash [tree], and the rain doth nourish it," Isaiah 44:14.) Historically, God's Spirit ministered to mankind under the figure of various forms of precipitation. "The pillar of the cloud departed not from them by day, to lead them in the way. . . . Thou gavest also thy good spirit to instruct them" (Nehemiah 9:19, 20). "He shall come down like rain upon the mown grass" (Psalm 72:6). "I will be as the dew upon Israel" (Hosea 14:5).

Seal. Paul assured the Ephesians: "Ye were sealed with that Holy Spirit of promise" (Ephesians 1:13; cf. Ephesians 4:30; 2 Corinthians 1:22). A seal was used in Biblical times in the manner of a signature today to denote ownership and responsibility. The indwelling Holy Spirit becomes a seal within the convert's heart, and He constitutes indisputable evidence that the one He indwells indeed participates in the finished work of Calvary. The Spirit as a seal guarantees security as far as God is concerned. "The foundation of God standeth sure, having this seal, the Lord knoweth them that are his" (2 Timothy 2:19). It was by means of the seal that imperial Rome sought to assure that Christ's tomb would remain closed. God has promised to seal the 144,000 in the era of the end time (Revelation 7:2-8). It was by means of their seal that the signers of Nehemiah's covenant obligated themselves (Nehemiah 9:38; 10:1). It was the king's seal that gave Jezebel's letters to the elders of the city of Naboth the authority she desired (1 Kings 21:8).

Oil. The Holy Spirit is particularly set forth under the figure of anointing oil in His relationship to Jesus Christ. "Therefore God, even thy God, hath anointed thee with the oil of gladness above thy fellows" (Hebrews 1:9). As Jesus began His ministry He proclaimed: "The Spirit of the Lord is upon me, because he hath anointed me to preach the gospel to the poor" (Luke 4:18). However, Paul testified concerning the New Testament believer: "He which . . . hath anointed us, is God" (2 Corinthians 1:21). As the Old Testament prophet, priest, and king were each inducted into office by the sacred anointing oil, so the Holy Spirit ministers to the believer. John rejoiced that the Lord Jesus "hath made us kings and priests unto God and his

Father" (Revelation 1:6), and Peter described the Church as "a royal priesthood" (1 Peter 2:9). Because the Spirit ministers as anointing oil, the believer is legally set apart both as king and priest.

In addition to its use in anointing to special office, oil may be a food to nourish and sustain. It may also be used in healing and soothing, and it can be an aid to beauty. Burned in a lamp, it provides light, and in the process it produces warmth. In parallel ways, the Holy Spirit strengthens and empowers the believer, comforts and heals him, and imparts spiritual beauty. The Old Testament prohibitions upon substitutions or human imitations of the sacred oil (Exodus 30:32) emphasize the necessity of the Spirit's exclusive motivation and anointing as opposed to that of the flesh.

Dove. Each of the four Gospels reports the descent of the dove in the account of the baptism of Jesus. "Lo, the heavens were opened unto him, and he saw the Spirit of God descending like a dove, and lighting upon him" (Matthew 3:16). The "dove ministry" of the Holy Spirit is thus pointedly identified with the earthly life and ministry of the incarnate Christ. Among the characteristics of the dove that have application in understanding the Spirit are: gentleness, tenderness, grace, innocence, mildness, peacefulness, patience, and faithfulness. The dove is pronounced ceremonially clean in Scripture, and this accords with his nature; he is selective in his diet, swift in flight, beautiful in his plumage, gregarious and sociable in his manner of life, and monogamous in his mating practices.

It is noteworthy that the first Biblical mention of the Holy Spirit depicts Him as ministering in a dovelike manner: "And the Spirit of God moved [i.e., brooded or fluttered] upon the face of the waters" (Genesis 1:2). The believer is exhorted to allow the Spirit in His "dove ministry" to exercise His influence: "Be ye therefore wise as serpents, and harmless as doves" (Matthew 10:16). In His relationships to men, the Spirit as a dove primarily works by gentle leadings and persuasions, and He seldom demands or compels. As the heavenly dove indwelling the believer's heart, He delights in conveying the peace of God and in proclaiming the fact of peace with God.

He is most pleased when the heart in which He abides maintains those qualities of gracious godliness that best reflect His own nature.

Wine. Not everyone agrees that it is valid to portray the Spirit under the symbol of wine. J. W. Jepson writes: "It is more accurate, perhaps, to say that wine is a contrast to the Holy Spirit, rather than a type of the Holy Spirit."[4] However, there are limited scriptural intimations of this symbolism. The Old Testament prophet invited: "Come buy wine ... without money and without price" (Isaiah 55:1). Jesus' reference to the "new wine" is seen as the fulfillment of this invitation. He said of the gift of the Spirit to the Church: "Neither do men put new wine into old bottles ... but they put new wine into new bottles" (Matthew 9:17). The mocking bystanders on the Day of Pentecost spoke a greater truth than they personally recognized when they declared: "These men are full of new wine" (Acts 2:13). Certainly it is the case that God's work calls for men who are free from restraints and inhibitions, bold, willing if need be to become loquacious, and stimulated or motivated to the point of being aggressively enthusiastic. These goals are achieved within the believer by the new wine of the Spirit.

Clothing. A possible rendering of the Hebrew reads: "The Spirit of the Lord clothed Gideon" (Judges 6:34, *Jewish Version*). This relationship between the Spirit of the Lord and clothing finds repeated confirmation in the New Testament. The Spirit is He whom the believer must "put on" even as he must "put off the old nature." The acceptance of the covering of the Spirit becomes to the believer: "the armor of light" (Romans 13:12), "the whole armor of God" (Ephesians 6:11), "the breastplate of faith and love" (1 Thessalonians 5:8), and "the new man" (Ephesians 4:24). The word *endue* literally means "to clothe," and Jesus instructed: "Tarry ye in the city of Jerusalem, until ye be endued with power from on high" (Luke 24:49). In being endued or clothed with the Spirit, the believer is protected, adorned, and covered. As clothing may be a uniform identifying members of a group, so the Spirit's enduement uniformly marks the members of the body of Christ.

A quite different, and sometimes preferred translation of

Judges 6:34 reads: "The Spirit of Jehovah clothed himself with Gideon." Thus, it was not that the Spirit was Gideon's clothing, but Gideon was the clothing worn by the Spirit. As it were: "Gideon was a suit of working clothes the Spirit wore that day." This concept is seen as complementing the preceding one, rather than conflicting with it. The Holy Spirit is both that which clothes, and He who adopts the lives and persons of believers as His clothing. The believer becomes His embodiment or incarnation, and it is by this means, at least in part, that He fulfills His tasks on earth.

Earnest. Paul explained: "God hath also sealed us, and given the earnest of the Spirit in our hearts" (2 Corinthians 1:22). An earnest is ordinarily something of significance or value given to bind a contract. It is a firstfruit, a foretaste, a token, or a pledge; and sometimes it may be a partial payment or an installment. In Old Testament times, an earnest of a basket of fruit or a handful of wheat would be sufficient to seal a transaction involving the sale of an orchard or a grain field. The grapes of Eshcol were taken as an earnest of the prosperity of the Promised Land (Numbers 13:23-25). An earnest is a little that speaks of a larger reality, and when given and received between humans, it assures the binding of a contract.

The gift of the Holy Spirit is an earnest that establishes that God is rigorously binding himself to maintain forever the provision for that convert. In turn, the convert who receives the earnest of the Spirit commits himself to perpetual faith in his Lord. The measure of the Spirit bestowed to believers in this life is only an earnest, but that bestowment is reassuring proof of the certainty of future blessings. In the life to come, believers will enjoy not merely an earnest of the Spirit, but that unrestrained abundance that was the privilege of the incarnate Jesus: "For God giveth not the Spirit by measure unto him" (John 3:34). Because the earnest will someday be superseded by the totality of the Spirit, the believer may anticipate future resurrection and immortality.

3

The Personality of the Spirit

An understanding of the fact and nature of the personality of the Spirit is fundamentally essential as a basis for understanding His work and relationship to God and man. To ignore or deny the Spirit's personality is seriously to confuse and handicap the study of pneumatology. Thus, an author such as Richardson, who denies independent personal existence to the Spirit, is reduced to describing Him as "a periphrastic description of God's initiative and action."[1] One could expect a vastly different set of conclusions if the Spirit is a "periphrastic description" than if He is the divine Third Person of the eternal Godhead. Actually, belief in the personality of the Spirit is prerequisite to belief in the Trinity.

The term *personality* is typically defined: "self-conscious individuality possessing self-directing power." The task of establishing the Spirit's personality has been accomplished when it has been demonstrated that He does qualify according to the standards of a typical definition. It may be conceded: 1) Not every Biblical reference teaches the fact of the Spirit's personality (scholars debate whether the personality of the Spirit is taught in the Old Testament. Carter suggests that the Spirit's personality is: "Implicit in the Old Testament, but explicit in the New Testament."); and 2) The term *personality* has been variously defined during the passing centuries, and to this day, scholars are not in complete agreement concerning its connotation. One scholar has reminded us: "There is no Hebrew or Greek word that is a one-to-one correspondent to our word person. . . . The entire Holy Scripture was written without the word person." But these facts do not invalidate the immediate task: to show that the Bible portrays the Holy Spirit in terms that today we take as specifically identifying a person.

Hindrances to the Understanding of the Spirit's Personality

In many instances, humans find the fact of the personality of the Holy Spirit a difficult one to apprehend. It is noted that the Spirit cannot definitely be identified in theophanies as the Father, nor was He ever incarnate as the Son. Instead, He operates within the inner being, invisible in form, and mysterious in manner. Only by careful investigation can it be seen that the characteristics of the Spirit do entitle Him to be considered personal. Although humans ordinarily experience personalities in interaction with others who are corporeal and visible, neither visibility nor corporeality are essential attributes of personality. A real person is not the physical body, but the spirit and/or soul within that body. Although in human experience personalities reside in physical bodies, the Holy Spirit, in not being incarnate, has no need for such an association.

A further factor pertaining to the difficulty of recognizing the personality of the Spirit is the nature of His names. Cambron points out:

The personal name of the Holy Spirit is unknown. The title "Holy Spirit" is a designation—what He is: it is not His name. The silence of the Scriptures concerning His personal name is very significant. He withholds His own name, that the name of the Lord Jesus Christ may be exalted.[2]

Inasmuch as the name of the Spirit is unknown, He is referred to in terms of His essence and operations. Pearlman wrote:

The Spirit is often described in an impersonal way—as the Breath that fills, the Unction that anoints, the Fire that lights and heats, the Water that is poured out, the Gift of which all partake. However, these are merely descriptions of His operations.[3]

The early day believers, and many thereafter, tended to consider that the Holy Spirit was simply the spirit of Jesus Christ. Thus the separate personality of the Spirit was overlooked. Hermas (who wrote *The Shepherd* about A.D. 150) declared: "The Holy Spirit. . . is the Son of God." The Ebionites, in their concern to maintain Jewish monotheism, taught that the process of the attainment of deity by Jesus Christ (which was the particular emphasis of their doctrine) was achieved through His appropriation of the Spirit. Thus, again, the distinct being of the Spirit was merged into that of Christ. In one comment, Justin Martyr (c. 100-165) quite clearly denied the fact of the Holy Spirit's personality: "The Spirit and the Power which is from God must not be thought of as anything else than the Word, who is the first begotten God."

The Gnostics added to the confusion on the subject of the Spirit's personality by teaching that the Holy Spirit was a female principle. In answering them, Irenaeus (c. 120-200) set forth the rather strange claim: "Through the Spirit we mount up to the Son, and through the Son to the Father." To him, the Spirit was only an aspect of the divine. On another occasion, Irenaeus described the Holy Spirit as "the oil with which the Father anointed the Son." Although Arius of Alexandria (who died in 336) is chiefly remembered for denying that Christ was the same essence as the Father, he also repudiated the Spirit's personality and claimed He was merely the "exerted energy of God."

The Development of the Doctrine of the Spirit's Personality

At least two centuries passed in the life of the Early Church without any firm declaration of the fact of the personality of the Holy Spirit. Although the Fathers clearly recognized the influence of the Spirit in the life and work of the Church, they were much slower to assign Him a place in the Godhead. The earliest clear-cut statement of the personality of the Spirit was by Origen (185-254) of Alexandria: "We being convinced that there are three persons in God, the Father, the Son and the Holy Spirit. . . . The material . . . of the gifts of grace that come from God . . . exists personally in the Holy Spirit." Others who

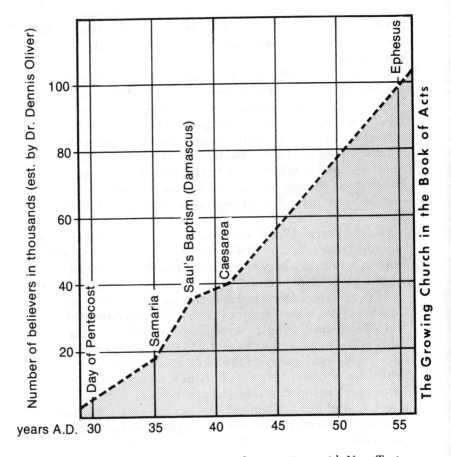

Figure 3. Correlation of Pentecostal outpourings with New Testament church growth.

clearly set forth and defended the personality of the Spirit included: Eusebius öf Caesarea (c. 260-340), "Each of those persons . . . the Father . . . the Son . . . and the Holy Spirit"; and Cyril of Jerusalem (c. 315-386), "The Holy Spirit, living and personally subsisting . . . and a personally existing being, Himself speaking and operating and exercising His dispensation." Athanasius (c. 295-373) mainly contended for the deity of the Spirit, but he also presupposed a commitment to the Spirit's personality.

It has been noted that it was in Cappadocia in Asia Minor that the first systematic efforts to understand the Holy Spirit were manifested. These theologians of the fourth century included Basil, Gregory of Nyssa, and Gregory of Nazianzus. Although this school was attached to the Eastern Church, it served as the chief center of productive thought on the subject of the Holy Spirit. In addition to that which has previously been noted from Basil's essay "On the Holy Spirit," he also argued convincingly that the Spirit was a Person on an equal basis with Father and Son.

That the East and West later should have divided on the issue of truths concerning the Holy Spirit is an irony in view of the fact that in this era what was believed in the West was limited to what had been developed in the East. The Cappadocian Fathers are considered to have laid the foundation for the thinking of Augustine, and they were basically responsible for that which was declared concerning the Holy Spirit in the Athanasian Creed. At the Council of Constantinople in 381, the issue of the personality of the Holy Spirit was permanently settled for orthodox believers in both the East and the West. Later opinions on this subject have been considered to be errors. Out of this background, the Church as a whole firmly rejected 16th-century Socinianism with its denial of the Spirit's personality.

Biblical Evidences for the Spirit's Personality

Scripture sets forth a variety of relevant facts that may be gathered and discussed.

His offices entail personality. The basic office of the Holy

Spirit, that of Comforter, as already noted, was so designated by Jesus: "And I will pray the Father, and he will give you another Comforter, that he may abide with you for ever" (John 14:16). Other offices ascribed to the Spirit or implied of Him include: Author, "All Scripture is given by inspiration [i.e., the inbreathing of the Spirit] of God" (2 Timothy 3:16); Teacher and Guide, "He shall teach you all things" (John 14:26); Witness to Christ, "He shall testify of me" (15:26); and Creator, "Thou sendest forth thy spirit, they are created" (Psalm 104:30). It is noted that His chief office, and the only one by which He is specifically designated, remains that of Comforter.

The role of Comforter is certainly that of a person. The implications and connotations of the term have already been discussed in connection with the Spirit's titles. Only a person can be an understanding, powerful assistant, a representative as an ombudsman, or a spokesman for another. Inasmuch as Jesus promised that the Spirit would replace Him on earth, none other than a personal Spirit could fulfill such a task. Authors, teachers, guides, witnesses, and the one who creates are, in each case, personal beings. Quite conspicuously and characteristically, the ministry and functioning of the Holy Spirit according to His offices, either expressed or implied, are identified with those expected of a person.

The Holy Spirit is referred to by personal pronouns. Although there are occasions in the New Testament when the Holy Spirit is referred to by a neuter pronoun (the neuter noun *spirit* would require it), whenever possible, a masculine personal pronoun is used. Christ's use of the term *Comforter*, since it is a masculine noun, permitted a masculine pronoun. The expression "Spirit of truth" is made an interchangeable synonym (John 16:13). Our Lord thus could speak of Him and declare: "He shall glorify me: for he shall receive of mine, and shall show it unto you" (John 16:14). In this 16th chapter of John, the masculine pronoun *ekeinos* is used 12 times in referring to the Holy Spirit. Elsewhere, John records the words of Jesus concerning the Holy Spirit: "But ye know him; for he dwelleth with you, and shall be in you" (14:17). It is evident that it is the spirit of Scripture to refer to the Holy Spirit by means of masculine personal pronouns, and thus the Revised Standard Version commendably renders Romans 8:16 and 26 "the Spirit himself," rather than "the Spirit itself."

The Holy Spirit is identified with other personalities. The fact that the Holy Spirit is the Third Person of the Holy Trinity is an outstanding proof of His personality. In the baptismal formula and in Biblical benedictions, He is placed on equal status with Father and Son: ". . . baptizing them in the name of the Father, and of the Son, and of the Holy Ghost" (Matthew 28:19). "The grace of the Lord Jesus Christ, and the love of God, and the communion of the Holy Ghost, be with you all" (2 Corinthians 13:14). In manner of working, the Holy Spirit and our divine Lord are one. If the Father is a person, so also is the Spirit. "Now the Lord is the Spirit: and where the Spirit of the Lord is, there is liberty" (2 Corinthians 3:17).

In many of the divine works of grace, the Spirit takes His place with the Father and Son. The redemption that is taught in the New Testament is grounded in the eternal love of the Father, provided through the sacrificial atonement of the Son, and applied in the regenerating work of the Spirit. God's insights in election are based on the work of the Spirit and the Son: "Elect according to the foreknowledge of God the Father, through sanctification of the Spirit, unto obedience and sprinkling of the blood of Jesus Christ" (1 Peter 1:2). The bestowment of spiritual gifts involves the cooperative enterprise of the triune Godhead: "Now there are diversities of administrations, but the same Lord. And there are diversities of operations, but it is the same God which worketh all in all" (1 Corinthians 12:4-6).

The Spirit is also identified with believers in making personal choices and decisions. "It seemed good to the Holy Ghost and to us" (Acts 15:28). The apostle Peter was thus directed in his behavior and in his theological understanding. "While Peter thought on the vision, the Spirit said unto him . . ." (Acts 10:19). Paul reported: "My speech and my preaching was . . . in demonstration of the Spirit and power" (1 Corinthians 2:4). The Holy Spirit ministered in the earthly life of the Lord Jesus, and under the Spirit's direction outstanding accomplishments in our Lord's earthly ministry frequently were accomplished.

"And Jesus returned in the power of the Spirit into Galilee" (Luke 4:14). Peter summarized the relationship: "God anointed Jesus . . . with the Holy Ghost and with power" (Acts 10:38). Thus, the Holy Spirit actively identified with the apostles and with the incarnate Lord Jesus and lent not only His bestowment of power, but also the gift of His presence to enrich the lives of other personalities.

Personal characteristics are ascribed to the Spirit. The commonly recognized characteristics of personality include intellect, will, and emotion, and each of these attributes is assigned to the Holy Spirit. The Spirit is described as engaging in profound intellectual activities: "For the Spirit searcheth all things, yea, the deep things of God" (1 Corinthians 2:10). "And he that searcheth the hearts knoweth what is the mind of the Spirit, because he maketh intercession for the saints" (Romans 8:27). The fact that the Spirit is concerned with the use of human language is an aspect of His intellectual activity. Language is specifically a human and a personal characteristic, but significantly, it is by language that the Spirit repeatedly conveys himself to humans: "We speak not in words which man's wisdom teacheth, but which the Holy Ghost teacheth" (1 Corinthians 2:13); "They began to speak with other tongues, as the Spirit gave them utterance" (Acts 2:4).

The Spirit exercises will: "But all these worketh that one and the selfsame Spirit, dividing to every man severally as he will" (1 Corinthians 12:11). In His operations through and in praying believers, He manifests His own desires or preferences: "And God who searches our inmost being knows what is preferred by the Spirit" (Romans 8:27, *literal rendering*). Such an independent exercise of will, or one's own mind, is a distinctive characteristic of personality. Not only does the Spirit choose according to His will, but also, in cooperation with the eternal Godhead, He effects these choices in this universe. The Holy Spirit is not merely an extension of God in His spiritual operations, but an independent Person in His own right who makes choices as He personally sees fit.

The Spirit manifests love, an emotional attribute: "Now I beseech you brethren, for the Lord Jesus Christ's sake, and for the love of the Spirit" (Romans 15:30). Where there is genuine love, there is the most basic and powerful of all emotions, and indisputable evidence of a person. It has been noted that the love of the Holy Spirit is truly worthy of acclaim, for He "has lived eighteen hundred years in this scene of sin, and this land of enemies." However, in addition to the emotion of love, the Spirit also manifests jealousy: "The Spirit which He has caused to dwell in us yearns jealously over us" (James 4:5, *Weymouth*). Downer expounds this verse and concludes: "St. James teaches the Divine Personality of the Holy Spirit as unequivocally as the most advanced Christian symbols."[4] (A symbol is a creed.)

Personal acts are ascribed to the Spirit. The Spirit is depicted in Scripture as performing such vocal operations as speaking, interceding, crying out, and testifying. "The Spirit said to Philip, Go near, and join thyself to this chariot" (Acts 8:29). "The Holy Ghost said, Separate me Barnabas and Saul for the work whereunto I have called them" (13:2). "While Peter thought on the vision, the Spirit said unto him, Behold, three men seek thee" (10:19). "And it was revealed unto him by the Holy Ghost, that he should not see death" (Luke 2:26). "He that hath an ear, let him hear what the Spirit saith unto the churches" (Revelation 2:7). "The Spirit himself maketh intercession for us with groanings" (Romans 8:26, *ASV*). "The Spirit of truth, which proceedeth from the Father, shall testify of me" (John 15:26). This variety of instances makes clear that on occasion the Holy Spirit may verbally communicate the mind of God to the mind of humans.

The Spirit acts in relation to others to perform such acts as: calling missionaries, appointing leaders to oversee churches, and teaching, leading, and directing. "The Holy Ghost said, Separate me Barnabas and Saul for the work whereunto I have called them" (Acts 13:2). "After they were come to Mysia, they assayed to go into Bithynia: but the Spirit suffered them not" (16:7). "Take heed therefore unto yourselves, and to all the flock, over the which the Holy Ghost hath made you overseers" (20:28). "The Holy Ghost . . . shall teach you all things" (John 14:26). "Thou gavest also thy good Spirit to instruct them"

(Nehemiah 9:20). "For as many as are led by the Spirit of God, they are the sons of God" (Romans 8:14).

The Spirit operates as a person to restrain and convict or reprove. "For the mystery of iniquity doth already work: only he that now letteth [hinders] will let until he be taken out of the way" (2 Thessalonians 2:7). "And when he is come, he will reprove the world of sin, and of righteousness, and of judgment" (John 16:8). In Noah's day, it was the Spirit who restrained for 120 years (Genesis 6:3). Isaiah saw God's Spirit acting as a restraint upon the enemies of God's people (Isaiah 59:19). As noted above, it was the Spirit who restrained Paul from ministering in Bithynia; the Spirit is thus portrayed as exercising His restraining ministry both toward believers and toward unbelievers. One of the means by which divine guidance is made real in the believer's life is through a system of checks or restraints, not so much against acts of sin, but simply against acts that would not conform to the divine purpose in a given situation.

These personal operations of the Spirit—His speaking, His directing and leading, and His restraint and conviction—are necessarily the operations of a person. A mere influence or emanation would not behave in this manner. Scripture pointedly distinguishes the Spirit in His person from the gifts He bestows. The gift of the Spirit (a Person sent to replace Christ on earth) is to be distinguished from the gifts of the Spirit (His divine endowments upon believers). The particular act of the personal Holy Spirit in His relationship to the believer is described as "the communion of the Holy Ghost" (2 Corinthians 13:14). The process of communion is the process of interchanging thoughts, ideas, and the feelings and affections of the heart. In all of these aspects, the Holy Spirit is acting in a personal manner.

He is susceptible to personal treatment. The Holy Spirit may be affected by the actions of persons just as any other person may be affected. He acts as a person, and reacts as a person also. The Spirit may be insulted, grieved, lied to, and blasphemed against. "Of how much sorer punishment, suppose ye, shall he be thought worthy, who . . . hath done despite [injury, insult] unto the Spirit of grace?" (Hebrews 10:29). "And grieve not the Holy Spirit of God, whereby ye are sealed" (Ephesians 4:30). "But they rebelled, and grieved his Holy Spirit" (Isaiah 63:10 *RSV*). "But Peter said, Ananias, why hath Satan filled thine heart to lie to the Holy Ghost?" (Acts 5:3). "Wherefore I say unto you . . . blasphemy against the Holy Ghost shall not be forgiven unto men" (Matthew 12:31). Similarly, the Spirit may be tempted and resisted. "Then Peter said unto her, How is it that ye have agreed together to tempt the Spirit of the Lord?" (Acts 5:9). "Ye do always resist the Holy Ghost" (Acts 7:51). In prophetic context, the Spirit, as breath, can be appealed to or invoked: "Come from the four winds, O breath, and breathe upon these slain, that they may live" (Ezekiel 37:9).

Outcomes of the Fact of the Spirit's Personality

The Holy Spirit is in himself a distinct, living, powerful, intelligent, divine Person. He is vitally and intimately associated with the Father and with the Son. Where the Father brings forth, the Son arranges, and the Spirit perfects. In Old Testament times, He revealed the Father; in New Testament times it was He by whom Jesus Christ was conceived, and by whom Jesus was constituted the Anointed One or Messiah. He is most assuredly not a mere blessing, a feeling, an influence, or simply an effulgence proceeding from the Father. When one relates to the Spirit and, as it were, is in the Spirit's company, he is in the company of a divine Person. The Spirit takes His place in the divine Godhead with all of the essential qualities and attributes of the Father and the Son. What They are as divine Persons is what He is as a divine Person.

The personal being of the Holy Spirit makes possible living companionship with Deity; it leads to the intimacy of family fellowship with God. To a very large degree, the divine work of the Spirit in the life of the believer results from the fact of the Spirit's personality. Believers who comprised the Early Church, as already noted, particularly emphasized this personal relationship: "It seemed good to the Holy Ghost and to us" (Acts 15:28). The phrase "communion of the Holy Ghost"

(2 Corinthians 13:14) was so basic to the emphasis and under-standing of the Early Church that it was chosen to comprise the reference to the Spirit in the apostolic benediction. Because the Holy Spirit is a Person, the human heart and soul, as it were, are able to gain an intelligent and conscious hold upon Deity.

A very large part of the experiences of Christian living in-volves a relationship between the personal Holy Spirit and the believer. His person is dynamically brought to bear upon those who will respond. It is frequently noted that in the first seven chapters of Romans, the Spirit is mentioned only once (cf. Romans 5:5). But in the victorious, reassuring chapter 8, He is mentioned 19 times. The believer's worship, his daily life for God, and his personal appropriation of the provisions of God all relate essentially to the personal Holy Spirit.

Practical Christian living calls for obedience to the Spirit. As a divine Person, He speaks, and when He speaks, He must be obeyed. His method of speaking may be an inner voice, an ordering of circumstances, the counsel of a fellow Christian, or the illumining of a portion of Scripture. The words of Hebrews apply to the believer: "The Holy Ghost saith, Today if ye will hear his voice, Harden not your hearts" (3:7, 8). On occasion, the Spirit may use the voice of the conscience as His instru-ment; and His voice and the believer's inner voice become merged. He is, of course, particularly concerned to maintain the credibility and overall authority of the Scriptures.

To a large degree, the believer's relationship to Jesus Christ is just that which is effected by the Holy Spirit. Without the Spirit, men would know the Lord Jesus only as a historical character. The Holy Spirit does not displace Christ, but inas-much as Christ has ascended, in today's believer, the Spirit replaces Christ. Thus, He seeks to be to this generation what Jesus on earth was to His disciples. It is often noted: "Christ is our advocate with the Father for us, while the Holy Spirit is our advocate from the Father with us." Since He is himself a per-son, the Holy Spirit is able to convey to the believer the person of the Lord Jesus, and it is the Spirit's personal being that particularly qualifies Him for this role.

In being a person, the Holy Spirit manifests attributes such as love and wisdom, and thereby He is worthy of the believer's trust and surrender. Writes Sanders: "If He is merely an influence, our constant aim will be, 'How can I obtain more of this influence?' But if He is a Divine person, our consistent attitude will be, 'How can He have more of me?' "[5] He is not to be thought of as power to be captured and contained in the human, nor merely as a principle of life, but He is specifically and uniquely a divine Person with the relevant character traits and relationships that are appropriate for a person.

4

The Deity of the Spirit

To affirm the deity of the Holy Spirit is to ascribe to Him the same attributes that characterize the Father and the Son. The one divine essence exists uniformly in Father, Son, and Spirit. Whatever may be established concerning the unique person and ministry of the Spirit, it is also true that His basic substance is one with that of the divine Father and the divine Son. The Holy Spirit must be understood as divine if He is to be identified in the triune Godhead according to orthodox belief. Even though the essential spirituality of the Spirit may complicate the human visualization of His divine attributes, the fact of these attributes must be recognized and accepted if the Godhead is to be known.

The Development of the Doctrine of the Spirit's Deity

It has already been noted that concepts concerning the Holy Spirit developed very slowly in the Early Church. For some centuries, there was no clear formulation of the Spirit's deity. Justin Martyr in one passage ranked the Spirit next in the spiritual hierarchy following the angels. He taught that the Spirit was equal to the Father in nature and essence, but inferior to Him in rank. Irenaeus did attest to the fact of the Spirit's deity, but he weakened his stand because he inconsistently denied the Spirit's personality. The Arians of the fourth century held that the Spirit was a created being and therefore not really true Deity.

At the Synod of Alexandria in 362, the Church for the first time formally discussed the deity of the Spirit. The Synod concluded that the Spirit "belongs to . . . and is indivisible from the essence of the Son and the Father." The Council of Constantinople in 381 further vindicated orthodoxy, affirming on behalf of all the Church, the deity and personality of the Holy Spirit. This Council is considered to have been an endorsement of the Cappadocian school. Somewhat paradoxically, Basil of Cappadocia, while arguing for the deity of the Spirit, nevertheless refused to call Him "God." It remained for Basil's successors, the two Gregories, to develop the doctrine of the Spirit's deity, assigning Him equality in glory and seeing Him of the same substance as Father and Son. Gregory of Nyssa declared: "He who grants that the Holy Spirit is God has granted all the rest [i.e., all relevant truths concerning the Spirit]."

A further development, and perhaps a popularization of the concept of the doctrine of the deity of the Spirit is credited to Augustine (354-430). By sound scriptural exposition, Augustine related the Spirit to Father and Son, and he established a pattern for identifying the Spirit in theological thought. Unfortunately, Augustine failed to produce a parallel exposition of the potential reality of the Spirit in one's personal Christian life. The authority of Augustine prevailed throughout the centuries, and no significant later theological school doubted the Spirit's deity. At the Council of Chalcedon in 451, the deity of the Spirit was once more affirmed. The Church had achieved scriptural orthodoxy in the matter of the Spirit's person, even though His work was being tragically neglected.

Biblical Evidence for the Deity of the Spirit

At least six distinct Biblical evidences that establish the deity of the Holy Spirit may be enumerated.

The Spirit is named and respected as God. The fact that the Holy Spirit is repeatedly identified in terms that relate Him to the Father and the Son is clear evidence of the Bible's intention to teach His deity. The basic terms *Spirit of God* and *Spirit of Christ* each have many variants, and the effect of such usage is to emphasize that the Holy Spirit is revealed in terms that denote deity and the status of equality within the Trinity. The familiar expression *the Holy Spirit,* by its very form and structure, speaks of a spiritual being that is pointedly unique. He is not just a Spirit among spirits, but that Spirit which embodies the totality of perfections, and therefore He belongs within the realm of the divine.

In a number of instances, Scripture significantly interchanges an expression identifying the Holy Spirit with the name "God" or "Lord." In explaining the bestowment of spiritual gifts, Paul writes: "Now there are diversities of gifts, but the same Spirit. And there are differences of administrations, but the same Lord. And there are diversities of operations, but it is the same God which worketh all in all" (1 Corinthians 12:4-6). Similarly, Paul makes no difference between the indwelling of God in man's temple, and the Spirit in that temple: "Know ye not that ye are the temple of God, and that the Spirit of God dwelleth in you?" (1 Corinthians 3:16). Liberty is jointly and equally credited to the Lord or to His Spirit: "Now the Lord is that Spirit: and where the Spirit of the Lord is, there is liberty" (2 Corinthians 3:17).

The words of Peter to Ananias particularly identify the Holy Spirit as one with God. Peter said: "Why hath Satan filled thine heart to lie to the Holy Ghost . . . ? Thou hast not lied unto men, but unto God" (Acts 5:3, 4). The narrative explicitly sets forth the divine dignity of the Spirit and the tragic error of failing to grant Him the respect that is His due. The Scripture passages that speak of blasphemy against the Spirit similarly confirm His deity, and they teach that in this matter, the Spirit's person and name must be taken as absolutely inviolable. "And whosoever speaketh against the Holy Ghost, it shall not be forgiven him, neither in this world, neither in the world to come" (Matthew 12:32).

The Spirit possesses divine attributes. Either directly or indirectly, the various natural attributes of Deity are set forth in the Bible as applying to the Holy Spirit. *Omnipotence:* "Through mighty signs and wonders, by the power of the Spirit of God . . . I have fully preached the gospel of Christ" (Romans

15:19); "The Holy Ghost shall come upon thee, and the power of the Highest shall overshadow thee" (Luke 1:35; cf. Mark 2:7). *Omniscience:* "But the Comforter, which is the Holy Ghost . . . shall teach you all things, and bring all things to your remembrance" (John 14:26); "The Spirit searcheth all things, yea, the deep things of God. . . . Even so the things of God knoweth no one but the Spirit of God" (1 Corinthians 2:10, 11). *Omnipresence:* "Whither shall I go from thy Spirit? or whither shall I flee from thy presence?" (Psalm 139:7). *Eternity:* "How much more shall the blood of Christ, who through the eternal Spirit offered himself without spot to God . . . ?" (Hebrews 9:14).

Within His own being, the Holy Spirit, in the pattern of Deity, enjoys self-existent life: "For the law of the Spirit of life in Christ Jesus . . ." (Romans 8:2); "It is the Spirit that quickeneth" (John 6:63). Life as an attribute is essentially His, and for this reason He is able to transmit life to the universe: "Thou sendest forth thy spirit, they are created: and thou renewest the face of the earth" (Psalm 104:30). In the angel's announcement of the conception of Jesus (Luke 1:35 as cited above), it should be noted that the parallel construction establishes that the Holy Spirit is no less omnipotent and self-existent God than the Father.

Divine works are ascribed to the Spirit. Many tasks and works performed by the Spirit could be performed only by a divine Being. *Creating:* "The Spirit of God moved upon the face of the waters" (Genesis 1:2); "The Spirit of God hath made me" (Job 33:4); "By his spirit he hath garnished the heavens" (Job 26:13). *Raising the dead:* "But if the Spirit of him that raised up Jesus from the dead dwell in you, he that raised up Christ from the dead shall also quicken your mortal bodies by his Spirit that dwelleth in you" (Romans 8:11). *Regenerating:* "Except a man be born of water and of the Spirit, he cannot enter into the kingdom of God. . . . That which is born of the Spirit is spirit" (John 3:5, 6). *Convicting:* "And when he is come, he will reprove the world of sin, and of righteousness, and of judgment" (John 16:8). *Casting out demons:* "But if I cast out [demons] by the Spirit of God, then the kingdom of God is come unto you" (Matthew 12:28). *Directing the divine harvest:* The Spirit ministers as "Lord of the harvest" (cf. Matthew 9:38) and sends forth missionaries: "So being sent forth by the Holy Ghost" (Acts 13:4).

As the divine principle of life, the Holy Spirit works actively throughout the universe. Adam became alive because of the divine work of the Holy Spirit in implanting life: "And the Lord God formed man . . . and breathed into his nostrils the breath [literally, spirit] of life" (Genesis 2:7). In the traditional Nicene Creed, since 381, the Spirit has been identified as "the Lord and giver of life." The believer can anticipate the Spirit as God's life principle to achieve promised resurrection: "When I have opened your graves, O my people, and brought you up out of your graves, And shall put my spirit in you, and ye shall live" (Ezekiel 37:13, 14; cf. Romans 8:11). The believer's present spiritual life, as one born of the Spirit, is imparted solely as a work of the Spirit. "The spirit giveth life" (2 Corinthians 3:6). Humans begin their regenerate life only when they come under His influence. "He saved us by . . . the renewing of the Holy Ghost" (Titus 3:5).

The Spirit's role in relation to the Scriptures specifically establishes His deity. The heritage of the written Word exists because the divine Spirit acted to provide it: "Holy men of God spake as they were moved by the Holy Ghost" (2 Peter 1:12). Martin Luther especially related the Holy Spirit to Scripture when he wrote: "The Bible is the special, very own book, writing, and Word of the Holy Spirit." Today's Christians know Him not only as the Author of the Book, but also as He who illumines and interprets. The Holy Spirit validates the divine Word because He is himself divine.

An important aspect of the work of the Spirit relates to His ministry in conveying holiness. The title *Holy Spirit* which occurs in Scripture no less than 95 times, emphasizes this work. When it is recognized that primary, basic holiness is found only in God, the divine status of the Spirit is seen as essentially manifest in this, His characteristic work. As a divine Agent, He conveys the holiness of God and causes it to be reflected and reproduced in created moral intelligences. The "sanctification of the Spirit" mentioned by Peter (1 Peter 1:2) and Paul (2

Thessalonians 2:13) can be achieved in believers only by Deity himself. The task of indwelling the believer and in him reproducing the spotless life of Jesus Christ is a task fit for a God, and it is precisely because the Holy Spirit is God that He can attempt a project so challenging.

The Spirit is depicted as coordinate with Father and Son. Scripture explicitly identifies the Holy Spirit with the Father and Son, and depicts Him as sharing the activities of the Godhead on the basis of equality. He participated in the events involving the baptism of Jesus: "Jesus also being baptized, and praying, the heaven was opened, and the Holy Ghost descended in a bodily shape like a dove upon him, and a voice came from heaven, which said, Thou art my beloved Son" (Luke 3:21, 22). The importance of this event is emphasized by the fact that it is recorded in all four Gospels. The Spirit shares in the Great Commission and baptismal formula: "Go ye therefore, and teach all nations, baptizing them in the name of the Father, and of the Son, and of the Holy Ghost" (Matthew 28:19). Similarly, He shares in the apostolic benediction: "The grace of the Lord Jesus Christ, and the love of God, and the communion of the Holy Ghost, be with you all. Amen" (2 Corinthians 13:14).

The believer's salvation is provided and implemented as a cooperative effort by the coequal Trinity. The Spirit participated in Christ's sacrifice on Calvary: "Christ . . . through the eternal Spirit offered himself without spot to God" (Hebrews 9:14). The believer's election is made a fact of experience through the particular sanctifying ministry of the Spirit: "Elect according to the foreknowledge of God the Father, through sanctification of the Spirit" (1 Peter 1:2). Assurance and confidence in the Christian life result through the Spirit's ministry: "The Spirit itself beareth witness with our spirit, that we are the children of God" (Romans 8:16). Only because the Holy Spirit is divine is He able to share in so vital a work as that involved in the salvation of mankind.

Christian practice sees no subordination in the relation and role of the Spirit in the Trinity; in Christian prayers and songs He is both the channel, and at least on certain occasions, the

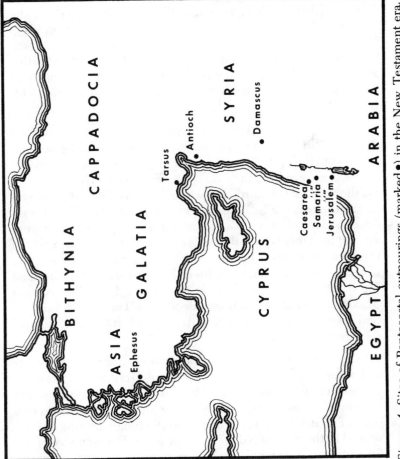

Figure 4. Sites of Pentecostal outpourings (marked •) in the New Testament era.

object of worship. "But ye, beloved, building up yourselves on your most holy faith, praying in the Holy Ghost; Keep yourselves in the love of God" (Jude 20, 21). In a multitude of details of worship and service, the believer relates to the Spirit in the manner of the prophet Isaiah who testified: "Now the Lord God, and his Spirit hath sent me" (Isaiah 48:16). Even the incarnate Christ was dependent upon the Spirit's anointing: "The Spirit of the Lord God is upon me; because the Lord hath anointed me to preach good tidings" (Isaiah 61:1). The Spirit's role as set forth in Scripture may be less conspicuous than that of Father or Son, but it is nevertheless a coordinate role befitting one who is likewise divine in essence.

Scripture interprets the Holy Spirit to be God. On various occasions, the New Testament, in quoting the Old Testament, ascribes to the Holy Spirit deeds or outlooks that in the original incident are credited to "God" or to the "Lord." In Isaiah 6:8 it is "the voice of the Lord" but when this verse is quoted in Acts 28:25, the text reads: "Well spake the Holy Ghost." Hebrews 3:7-9 declares that Israel's protestations in the wilderness were against the Holy Ghost, while Exodus 17:7, where the report of the incident is cited, clearly indicates that the "Lord" was the one offended. Jeremiah credited the Lord with declaring that He would implant His law "in their inward parts" (Jeremiah 31:33); the writer of Hebrews declares: "The Holy Ghost . . . had said before . . . I will put my laws into their hearts" (Hebrews 10:15, 16).

In general, the writers of Scripture freely interchange historical references between God and the Holy Spirit. Genesis quotes the divine decision: "My Spirit shall not always strive with man" (Genesis 6:3). However, when Peter describes this state of affairs he says: "When once the long-suffering of God waited in the days of Noah" (1 Peter 3:20). The ministry of the Spirit to strive, or God's procedure to wait, are seen as simply two ways of describing the same event. In Acts, Luke quotes Peter and Paul who credit the Spirit with inspiring and speaking through the prophets: "The Holy Spirit by the mouth of David spake . . ." (Acts 1:16); "Well spake the Holy Ghost by Isaiah the prophet" (Acts 28:25). In the Gospel, Luke quotes

Zechariah who attributes the speaking to God: "Blessed be the Lord God of Israel. . . . As he spake by the mouth of his holy prophets" (Luke 1:68, 70).

On occasion, the Biblical instructions and encouragements for the living of a practical Christian life make no effort to distinguish the ministry of the Spirit and the ministry of the Father. Both are portrayed as accomplishing the same goal. "And the Lord make you to increase and abound in love one toward another" (1 Thessalonians 3:12); "The love of God is shed abroad in our hearts by the Holy Ghost which is given unto us" (Romans 5:5). Scripture encourages each believer to sense an indwelling by God and, simultaneously, an indwelling by His Spirit: "Know ye not that ye are the temple of God, and that the Spirit of God dwelleth in you?" (1 Corinthians 3:16). One who is led of the Spirit is necessarily a son of God: "For as many as are led by the Spirit of God, they are the sons of God" (Romans 8:14).

The Spirit is said to proceed from the Father. The obvious intention of the Scripture in describing the Spirit as "proceeding" is to identify the essence of the Spirit to be one with that of the Father. "But when the Comforter is come, whom I will send unto you from the Father, even the Spirit of truth, which proceedeth from the Father, he shall testify of me" (John 15:26). Other versions render "proceedeth" as "issues from" or "goes forth from." The term is distinctively different from "creation," for it avoids any concept of a beginning of existence. In relation to the Spirit, procession is analogous to generation in Christ. Walvoord notes: "While the nature of procession is largely inscrutable, it is an expression in human words based on the Scriptural revelation of the relationship of the persons of the Trinity to each other."[1]

The fact that the Spirit proceeds, on the one hand establishes Him as divine in essence, but on the other hand, confirms His obedient commitment to the Father. The status of the proceeding Spirit compares to that of the "begotten" Christ who cheerfully submits to the divine will. "Thou art my Son; this day have I begotten thee" (Psalm 2:7); "I delight to do thy will, O my God" (Psalm 40:8). The Spirit whom the Son sends, proceeds from the Father, and He thereby takes His place in obedient subordination to the overall will of the Godhead. The term *procession* thus serves to convey meaningful insight into the relationship between the persons of the holy Trinity.

One of the traditional understandings of the Church concerning the term *proceeding* is that it connotes a continuous or perpetual relationship. The word is in the present tense in the original, and thus continuous action is implied. Long ago, the Athanasian Creed (c. 430) declared: "The Holy Ghost is of the Father and of the Son, neither made, nor created, nor begotten, but proceeding." In comparatively modern times, the Westminster Confession (1646) described the Spirit as "eternally proceeding from the Father and the Son." The concept of eternal procession permits the Spirit to be seen as coequal and coeternal in the Godhead, while at the same time, He is seen as fulfilling His specific role.

Outcomes of the Fact of the Spirit's Deity

Because the Holy Spirit is God, the believer's relationship with Him follows appropriately. The ministry of the Spirit must be accepted as God communicating himself to mankind; just as the ministry of the Son is accepted as God manifesting himself to mankind. The characteristics of the Spirit must be seen as precisely those that can be asserted of God himself. He is to be understood as the inmost principle of God and, thereby, the agent and executor of the divine purpose. He is the Father at work in creation and providence, and in reaching unto and acting upon the spirits of humans. He is the Son at work in effecting and applying salvation, and in witnessing of abundant saving grace to whomsoever will.

The total fullness of the omnipotent God becomes available to the believer exclusively in and through the divine Spirit. Bickersteth writes: "This ever present One with whom we have to do is God, in whose hand our breath is, and whose are all our ways."[2] In seeking to relate to the Spirit, the believer is not thereby seeking a serving assistant; rather, he is seeking to place himself into the hands of a powerful Someone who is to assume total control and direction of his being. The potential of the indwelling Spirit is identical with the potential of the eternal God. The glory, the power, the sovereignty that so mightily characterize Father and Son, likewise inhere without restriction in the divine Holy Spirit who indwells the believer's heart.

Whatever the Spirit does in and for the believer, He does in the manner of Deity. He does not merely observe or influence the human heart from without as an angel, but from within as true Deity. His role is to "search" the heart. He understands and knows every inner thought and intention. The believer must recognize that his innermost being is exposed to the Spirit, and that all hypocrisy and efforts to impress or to bargain are totally without warrant. The one plausible human response is submission and commitment to the divine Spirit, so that the Believer becomes truly a vessel or channel in His hand. The divine Spirit simply confirms and implements whatever may be true for the believer in his relationship to Father and Son; for Father, Son, and Spirit are, after all, one in essence.

5

The General Work and Ministry of the Spirit

The Holy Spirit is the executive or active agent of the Godhead. In this capacity, He is committed to achieving God's purpose and will for the universe that the glory of God may thereby result. Kuyper describes the Spirit's role: "The Father brings forth, the Son disposes and arranges, the Holy Spirit perfects."[1] The actual bringing into being of that which Deity intends and has provided for the universe is particularly the work of the Holy Spirit. Although He may be seen at the beginning to relate to the physical universe, by far the greater scope of His ministry concerns the spiritual realm.

The Spirit's Work in the Physical Universe

It is evident that the Holy Spirit participated in the original creation: "By the word of the Lord were the heavens made; and all the host of them by the breath [i.e., spirit] of his mouth" (Psalm 33:6). The Spirit is introduced in the second verse of the Bible: "The Spirit of God moved upon the face of the waters" (Genesis 1:2). The Vulgate uses *incubat* and conveys the image of a bird incubating a nest of eggs into active life. Job reports: "By his Spirit he hath garnished [decorated or beautified] the heavens" (Job 26:13). The special function of the Spirit in Creation appears to have been to give order and organization to that which was created. He was commissioned to bring forth hidden beauty, to achieve form out of the formless, to bring all things to fulfillment, and to rouse into activity that which was dormant and slumbering. While not everyone agrees the Spirit himself created, it does seem clear the Spirit perfected that which the Father originated.

The discussion of the "Spirit of Life" has noted that the Bible teaches that the Spirit is the fundamental principle of all life in the universe—human, animal, and plant. Bible scholars declare: "The Holy Spirit, who in regeneration kindles the spark of eternal life, has already kindled and sustained the spark of natural life."[2] "The Holy Spirit, then is . . . the Giver of life to all Nature. . . . The beginnings of life, its transmission, and all its subsequent developments and communications, are from Him."[3] The Spirit constitutes this life principle by virtue of His original creative impulse. Man's spirit is in no sense to be considered a fragment of the divine Spirit, but simply a particular product or entity which He has seen fit to create in order to give life to human flesh. Although this spirit is in the image of the divine, it is not the same substance as the divine Spirit. It is this fact that makes the new birth so essential: "Except a man be born of . . . the Spirit, he cannot enter into the kingdom of God" (John 3:5).

From the time of the original creation until the present, the Spirit has ministered to sustain the physical universe. "Thou sendest forth thy spirit, they are created: and thou renewest the face of the earth" (Psalm 104:30). In succeeding generations, the Spirit has preserved and renewed the entire physical universe in general, and the life principle in particular. Writes Walvoord:

> Creation is ordered by God in such a way as to be self-sustaining to some extent, the design of animal and plant life being such that species are self-perpetuating. Behind the outward phenomena, however, is the work of the Holy Spirit, sustaining, directing, and renewing.[4]

It is undoubtedly this ministry of the Spirit that makes possible the Psalmist's testimony: "O Lord, thou preservest man and beast" (Psalm 36:6).

The Spirit's Work in Unregenerate Men

Deity makes His first contact with mankind by an act proceeding from the Holy Spirit rather than from the Father or Son.

It has been said that though the Son touches man outwardly, only the Spirit touches him inwardly. Thus, the Spirit strives to lead all men to seek and to know God in spite of the resistance of man's carnal nature and the active opposition of the Adversary. Jesus acknowledged these problems when He described the Spirit as He "whom the world cannot receive" (John 14:17; cf. 1 Corinthians 2:14). At his fall, man chose carnality, and thus he disqualified himself as the dwelling place of the Holy Spirit. Scripture describes the absence of the Holy Spirit in the sinner's life by the expression "dead in trespasses and sins" (Ephesians 2:1). To the sinner, the Spirit relates only to reprove and convict: "And when he is come, he will reprove the world of sin, and of righteousness, and of judgment" (John 16:8).

The Holy Spirit reproves (i.e., convinces unto salvation and convicts unto condemnation) the world of sin (as distinct from *sins*) by His ministry of conviction. As our Lord's "Prosecuting Attorney," the Holy Spirit works in the lives of men with even more severity than human conscience or Biblical law. The function of these two media is to reveal particular sins. The Spirit, on the other hand, specifically convicts of the sin of rejecting the atoning work of Jesus Christ. In effect, He places the human life beside the standard of the Scriptures so the need of a Saviour becomes apparent. The sin of not believing on Christ has been said to "summarize all other sins." It is not merely a matter of identifying particular shortcomings as sins, but a matter of recognizing the overall sin of unbelief. This sin would not be known if judged by otherwise available standards.

The Spirit reproves the sinner of righteousness in the sense that He exhibits the spotless righteousness of Jesus Christ in His total life and works beside the silenced sinner's shortcomings. Negatively, the claims of self-righteousness are thus effectively denied, and false excuses are rejected. Positively, the divine provision of the imputed righteousness of Jesus Christ becomes apparent. The sinner is made aware of the possibility of the bestowment of righteousness provided divinely through Calvary's atonement. In relation to society in general, the Spirit's work in convicting of righteousness maintains the sensitivity to righteousness that civilized life requires. Scripture implies that the presence of the Spirit on earth withholds the unrestrained exercise of evil: "The mystery of iniquity doth already work: only he who now letteth [hinders] will let [hinder], until he be taken out of the way" (2 Thessalonians 2:7). On earth today, lawful moral life in civilized countries remains dependent on this ministry of the Spirit.

The Holy Spirit convicts of judgment insofar as He directs men to a decision either to accept or to reject God and His Christ. On the one hand, He leads men to what is known as "evangelical repentance," that is, the submission of their lives to God and the achievement of a state of hope. And on the other hand, He becomes the occasion of further obstinacy and hardness, and the achievement of a state of despair. John Owen commented: "It is the work of the Spirit to harden and blind obstinate sinners, as well as to sanctify the elect; and his acting in the one, is no less holy than in the other."[5] Usually, the pronouncement of God: "My Spirit shall not always strive with man" (Genesis 6:3), is linked with this concept. The process of the conviction of judgment results in either further hardness or in conversion. The Spirit particularly seeks a responsive chord relating to the gospel presentation or to some background experience.

The Christian worker cannot impart internal conviction, but he can seek to present with telling effect the data that will become the sinner's basis of decision. Peter balances the role of the Christian's witness and that of the Spirit: "We are his witnesses of these things: and so is also the Holy Ghost" (Acts 5:32). R. A. Torrey once remarked: "The Holy Ghost has no way of getting at the unsaved world except through us who are already saved." By the mode of his life and by the message of his lips, the Christian believer becomes the Holy Spirit's channel, and the sinner's response to that worker is simultaneously his response to the Holy Spirit. Above all, God chooses to use Spirit-anointed preaching to bring about Holy Spirit conviction (1 Corinthians 1:21).

The Spirit's Work in the Old Testament

The contrast between the believer's relation to the Spirit in

Old Testament as compared to New Testament times is stated by Jesus: "For he [i.e., the Spirit] abideth with you and shall be in you" (John 14:17). (When Jesus spoke these words the disciples were still technically in the Old Testament era.) In Old Testament times the Spirit moved upon mankind in abundant ministry, but it was not provided that by faith humans might receive the Spirit. On those few occasions when the Spirit indwelled a man, He did so, not basically because the man was a believer, but to empower him for a particular task or mission. Thus: "Take thee Joshua the son of Nun, a man in whom is the spirit" (Numbers 27:18). Within this qualification, Cambron correctly points out:

The Holy Spirit [in the Old Testament] is never represented as indwelling the believer. The Holy Spirit filled them but never took His abode within them. No Old Testament saint was ever baptized with the Holy Ghost. That initial baptism came at Pentecost, fifty days after Christ arose from the dead.[6]

In general, the Spirit's relation to God's people in the Old Testament era concerned externals such as qualifications for office, skills for a task, or motivation to behavior. Michael Green comments: "The first thing that strikes us as we come to the Old Testament is the tremendous emphasis on the Spirit of God as a violent, invading force."[7] In that era the Spirit *came upon men* (e.g., Balaam, Numbers 24:2; Jephthah, Judges 11:29; Gideon, Judges 6:34; Saul, 1 Samuel 11:6, 7; David, 1 Samuel 16:13; Azariah, 2 Chronicles 15:1, 2); *He filled men* (e.g., Bezaleel, Exodus 31:2, 3; Micah, Micah 3:8; Moses, Isaiah 63:11; Joshua, Deuteronomy 34:9); and *He rested upon men* (e.g., 70 elders, Numbers 11:25; Eldad and Medad, Numbers 11:26).

The Spirit's Old Testament ministry is very appropriately symbolized by a physical transaction such as Elijah's mantle resting upon Elisha (1 Kings 19:19). David seems to have enjoyed the Spirit's anointing, particularly when he composed the Psalms. He reported: "The Spirit of the Lord spake by me, and his word was in my tongue" (2 Samuel 23:2). During this period, the ministry of the Spirit appears to have been restricted to the sovereign works of God rather than in fulfillment of a promise to be claimed by a believer.

The temporary aspect of the Spirit's enduement is especially evident in the Old Testament. Samson was under the control of the Spirit for some time (cf. Judges 13 to 16), but the Spirit withdrew and did not return until the end of his life. This relationship is described in a typical instance. "The Spirit of the Lord came mightily upon him, and he rent him [a young lion] as he would have rent a kid" (Judges 14:6). Saul suffered the departure of the Spirit from his life (1 Samuel 18:12; 16:14), and Ezekiel only periodically experienced spiritual enduements (cf. Ezekiel 2:2; 3:24). One author describes the relationship of the Old Testament believer to the Spirit as typically "a seizure of the Spirit." In the New Testament era, believers are not limited to such temporary occasions.

The Holy Spirit in Old Testament times reserved His greater ministry for the prophets. He was much more likely to identify with prophetic proclamations than with the routine service of the priests. He is mentioned repeatedly in the lives of Isaiah and Ezekiel, and His anointing is inferred in the ministry of Jeremiah. This latter's experience when "His word was in mine heart as a burning fire shut up in my bones" (Jeremiah 20:9) parallels the Spirit-anointed New Testament prophet. Ezekiel experienced the special ministry of the Spirit to transport him bodily from place to place (cf. Ezekiel 3:12, 14; 8:3; 11:1, 24; 37:1; 43:5). Zechariah spoke of "the words which the Lord of hosts hath sent in his spirit by the former prophets" (Zechariah 7:12). Whatever irregularities existed in the life of King Saul, Scripture reports: "The Spirit of God was upon him also, and he went on, and prophesied. . . . Wherefore, they say, Is Saul also among the prophets?" (1 Samuel 19:23, 24).

Concerning the Spirit's relationship to Old Testament believers, Kuyper wrote: "He used their personal life, conflict, suffering, and hope as the canvas upon which He embroidered the revelation of redemption for us."[8] The value of Old Testament events as examples is certainly to be noted. Scripture passages that illustrate the close relationship between Old Testament believers and the Spirit include: "Cast me not away from thy presence; and take not thy holy spirit from me"

(Psalm 51:11); "See, I have called by name Bezaleel.... And I filled him with the Spirit of God, in wisdom, and in understanding, and in knowledge, and in all manner of workmanship" (Exodus 31:2, 3); "And the woman bare a son, and called his name Samson.... And the spirit of the Lord began to move him at times in the camp of Dan" (Judges 13:24, 25). At least some Old Testament believers enjoyed a very real personal relationship with the Spirit. Moses sincerely desired: "Would God that all the Lord's people were prophets, and that the Lord would put his Spirit upon them" (Numbers 11:29).

Much that the New Testament believer knows concerning the tender warmth of the Spirit and His concern for the refinement of character through spiritual fruit seems to have remained unrevealed in Old Testament times. Nevertheless, there are significant parallels. The Old Testament clearly tells of the Spirit's work to convict or strive (Genesis 6:3; Nehemiah 9:30), and of His susceptibility to being grieved (Isaiah 63:10). In the penitential Psalm 51, David prayed, "Take not thy Holy Spirit from me" (v. 11), and he indicated that to him the presence of the Spirit was vitally important. Similarly, each of the administrators and prophets of Israel enjoyed a genuine relationship with the Spirit, and trouble arose when His influence was rejected. In a very real sense, to the degree that men gave place to Him, He ministered as leader of the nation and the executive agent of the divinely ordered theocracy.

The Spirit's Work in the Lord Jesus

The Holy Spirit was identified with all crucial points of Christ's life on earth. The same Spirit who in Old Testament times had inspired scores of prophecies pertaining to Christ acted to provide for the fulfillment of these prophecies through the conception of Christ. "The Holy Ghost shall come upon thee [i.e., Mary] . . . and the power of the highest shall overshadow thee" (Luke 1:35; cf. Matthew 1:18, 20). Traditionally, the Spirit has been described not as the father of the manhood of Jesus, but as the creator of His manhood. However, this creative role of the Spirit is not that of bringing something out of nothing, but that of uniquely ordering and arranging previously existing material. The participation of the Spirit in Jesus' conception in Mary enabled the incarnate Christ to be sinless on the one hand, and truly man on the other. In being conceived by the Spirit's intervention, the sanctification of Jesus' humanity was assured. Paul said of Him, "[He] knew no sin" (2 Corinthians 5:21), and Peter noted: "[He] did no sin" (1 Peter 2:22).

The Holy Spirit freely baptized the incarnate Lord with His own power and anointing: "It came to pass, that Jesus also being baptized, and praying, the heaven was opened, and the Holy Ghost descended in bodily shape like a dove upon him" (Luke 3:21, 22). "God anointed Jesus of Nazareth with the Holy Spirit and with power" (Acts 10:38). Walvoord comments: "While it is not possible to produce evidence beyond question, it is a matter of reasonable inference that Christ was filled with the Holy Spirit from the very moment of conception."[9] If there be uncertainty concerning the time of the Spirit's baptism in Jesus' life, at least there is no uncertainty concerning the fact of it. Jesus declared of himself: "The Spirit of the Lord is upon me, because he hath anointed me to preach the gospel" (Luke 4:18). The Greek word *Christ* and the Hebrew *Messiah* each mean "anointed one." It is significant that repeated references describe the Spirit as being "upon" Christ (cf. Matthew 3:16; Mark 1:10; Luke 3:22; John 1:33).

The emphasis in the account of the Spirit as a dove descending upon Jesus (Luke 3:21) is on the visibility of the Spirit. John the Baptist had said: "He on whom ye see the Spirit descend and remain, this is he who baptizes with the Holy Spirit" (John 1:32). The significance of this event was not that Jesus was being endued with the Spirit for the first time, but rather that, for the first time, openly and publicly, God was confirming the fact that Jesus related to the Spirit in a distinctive manner.

The temptation of Christ took place under the direction of the Spirit: "The Spirit driveth him into the wilderness" (Mark 1:12); and at the conclusion of this experience it is reported: "And Jesus returned in the power of the Spirit into Galilee" (Luke 4:14). (It should be noted that the Judean ministry, recorded only in John, intervened between these two incidents.) Jesus was personally conscious of the Spirit's anointing as He began His Galilean ministry: "The Spirit of the Lord is upon me, because he hath anointed me" (Luke 4:18). Consistently thereafter, Jesus saw himself as the host of the Spirit, and His body as the Spirit's temple: "Destroy this temple and in three days I will raise it up" (John 2:19).

Throughout His life and ministry, the incarnate Christ remained dependent on the Holy Spirit. His works of power were achieved in and by the Spirit: "Jesus Christ our Lord . . . declared to be the Son of God with power, according to the spirit of holiness" (Romans 1:3, 4). Our Lord's ministry was not in the power of the Second Person of the Trinity, but in the power of the Third Person. The Holy Spirit made possible the casting out of demons: "But if I cast out devils [lit. demons] by the Spirit of God . . ." (Matthew 12:28). Jesus taught by the Spirit's enabling: "After that he through the Holy Ghost had given commandments unto the apostles" (Acts 1:2). That which Jesus taught and proclaimed was altogether based on the Spirit's anointing, for He was no mere spokesman for God's Word, but the Word of the Father made incarnate. Although there are parallels between Jesus' relationship to the Spirit and that of today's believers, in His case there was an important difference. "God giveth not the Spirit by measure unto him" (John 3:34). Only God's Anointed One received an unlimited bestowment of the Spirit.

Calvary was achieved through the ministry of the Spirit. Jesus "through the eternal Spirit offered himself without spot to God" (Hebrews 9:14). The Holy Spirit made possible the commitment that enabled Him to submit himself as a sacrifice. That same Spirit made possible the Resurrection: "Christ . . . being put to death in the flesh, but quickened by the Spirit" (1 Peter 3:18). In the Resurrection, the Spirit was the quickening agent (i.e., He who caused to be alive. See Romans 1:4; 8:11). Even after the Resurrection, Jesus acknowledged His continuing dependence on the Holy Spirit (cf. Acts 1:2, quoted above). In the heavenlies, He promptly fulfilled His promise to send the Holy Spirit upon the waiting disciples (cf. Acts 2:33; Revelation 5:6).

In the present age, the Holy Spirit would not be said to work in the Lord Jesus, but for Him. Traditionally, He has been known as the "vicar of Christ," for He is indeed Christ present in the Spirit. (A "vicar" may be thought of as a delegated representative rather than a mere substitute.) Jesus promised: "If I depart, I will send him unto you" (John 16:7). Downer writes:

The Holy Spirit did not come to take the place of an absent Christ, but to cause that Christ should be ever present with us. . . . Because [Christ] is present by the Spirit, He can be present with all the assemblies of His people and with every holy soul everywhere, without . . . restriction.[10]

Today's believers have testified: "The Spirit is other than Christ; yet the presence of the Spirit is not other than the presence of Christ," or more concisely: "The Holy Spirit is Christ's other self," or, "The Holy Spirit is the other unlimited Jesus."

In His personal influence on individual believers, the Holy Spirit ministers to reveal the person of Christ, and to reproduce the Christ-life within. Although the Ascension took place centuries ago, He continues to fulfill the ministry of Jesus Christ on earth. The believer rightly counts Christ as the sole object of his faith, but he counts the Holy Spirit as the sole power that validates and implements that faith. The work of the Holy Spirit is not independent, but in every aspect it relates to Christ, and translates His promises and provisions into actual experience. Jesus declared: "He shall not speak of himself. . . . He shall glorify me: for he shall receive of mine, and shall show it unto you" (John 16:13, 14). Any true work of the Holy Spirit ultimately magnifies the Lord Jesus Christ.

The Spirit's Work in the Insufflation

The historical incident when Jesus enacted the bestowment of the Spirit as the exhaling of a breath is known as the "insufflation," or by some as: the "afflation," the "Pascal Gift," or the "Johannine Pentecost." The event is described in Scripture:

Then said Jesus to them again, Peace be unto you: as my Father hath sent me, even so send I you. And when he had said this, he breathed on them, and saith unto them, Receive ye the Holy Ghost: whosesoever sins ye remit, they are remitted unto them; and whosoever sins ye retain, they are retained" (John 20:21-23).

It is noted that the expression "receive ye" translates the Greek *labete,* and this identical word is used to instruct the disciples to accept the elements of the Lord's Supper (Matthew 26:26). Jesus' exhortation, "Receive ye the Holy Ghost," appears to call for a participatory response. Stanley Horton comments: "The language used in John 20:21-23 does not fit the idea that nothing happened. . . . The command to receive indicates that the Spirit was actually then being given."[11]

However, the manner in which Jesus intended the disciples to participate in the receiving of the Spirit remains undecided. Two common views seek to explain the Spirit's role in the insufflation:

1. *This event was a symbolic portrayal of Pentecost.* According to this view, the Spirit did not especially move on this occasion, but hearts were prepared for His soon-to-occur Pentecostal bestowment. The Lord used this rather dramatic procedure as an audiovisual lesson to impress His followers to seek a specific experience of receiving the Holy Spirit. In thus announcing the divine provision of the Spirit, Jesus neither denied the relationship of the Spirit that already existed, nor did He encroach upon the greater relationship that was to come at Pentecost. Palma supports this view when he writes: "There are several links . . . which suggest that what happened on Easter Sunday was a foretaste, or a reinforcement, of the promise of the Spirit that was fulfilled in Acts 2."[12]

Many who support this viewpoint probably do so out of default, for they see no adequate pattern of events that infer far-reaching consequences for the insufflation. The whole incident seems rather casual and informal, and there simply is not enough made of it to attach dispensational significances. Palma defends his position by noting that this could not be the occasion when the disciples were made regenerate because unsaved people are never commanded to receive the Spirit. He argues that Jesus' breath at this time would simply serve to prepare the disciples for the rushing mighty wind of the Day of

Pentecost, and that, in context, the disciples were being prepared for service and not for salvation.

2. *The event was the occasion of the disciples' new birth.* Since Jesus was now resurrected from the dead, this view suggests that His promise concerning the Spirit could be fulfilled. Jesus had said: "He dwelleth with you, and shall be in you" (John 14:17). The indwelling of the Spirit is a necessary condition of regeneration. Jesus extended the privilege of the indwelling Spirit to achieve the new birth to His disciples the first evening following His resurrection. Riggs writes:

> This Spirit of the resurrected, glorified Christ was not available for human hearts, and Jesus hastened to impart this life to His disciples. The Spirit of God's Son, the Spirit of Christ, as the Spirit of conversion, came into their hearts on that occasion.[13]

MacDonald says:

> He breathed out from himself unto them the Holy Spirit. . . . Thus they became united with Christ in a new way in the experience of receiving Christ's Spirit; this may properly be called their Christian "regeneration."[14]

To accept the insufflation as the occasion when the disciples were born again in the manner of all Christians in the Church Age is, in the opinion of the supporters of this position, to solve a number of problems. It allows today's seeking believer to identify more completely with the 120 awaiting Pentecost. Those baptized on the Day of Pentecost were also regenerated, Spirit-indwelt believers, awaiting only the added experience of being Spirit-filled. The consequences of the divine breath— the capacity to declare the remission of sins—are more understandable if there was an actual spiritual transaction in the disciples' hearts. Because the disciples were spiritually changed on this occasion, they were prepared for a new commission and a new authority.

However one decides in relation to the foregoing views, there are some general conclusions accepted by most Bible scholars: 1) The disciples were not regenerated prior to this time. A few days previously Jesus had said to Peter: "I have

prayed for thee, that thy faith fail not: and when thou art con-
verted, strengthen thý brethren" (Luke 22:31, 32). 2) Our Lord
considered that it was of great importance that all disciples
should receive the Spirit (cf. "Receive ye the Holy Ghost"). 3)
By the third hour of the Day of Pentecost (Acts 2:15), not only
the disciples, but also all the 120 had been both regenerated
and baptized in the Holy Spirit.

The Spirit's Work in the Church

Apart from the Spirit, the Church would not exist. The life
principle that characterizes the Church as a living body is
provided solely by the Spirit. It may be said that the Holy Spirit
is incarnate in the Church, just as the Second Person of the
Godhead became incarnate in the human Jesus. One may
rightly consider the Day of Pentecost as a "birth event" paralleling that which had taken place in Bethlehem 33 years before.
However, scriptural limitations upon this concept must be observed, for the relationships of the Spirit are exclusively
spiritual. Insofar as the Church is a spiritual entity working
toward the evangelization of the world, it is directed, ener-
gized, and equipped by the Spirit.

It has been said: "The amount of God's power flowing out
into the world is in direct proportion to the opportunity given
the Holy Spirit to dwell in His church." This indwelling officially began on the Day of Pentecost when the Holy Spirit was
freely bestowed upon and within each member of the apostolic
band. Cumming says of this occasion: "That day was the Instal-
lation of the Holy Ghost as the Administrator of the Church in
all things, which office He is to exercise, according to circumstances, at His discretion."[15] At the very outset, there was a new
power and courage that was evident in Peter and his sermon:
"The same day there were added unto them about three
thousand souls" (Acts 2:41). Shortly afterward, there was the
healing of the lame man at the temple gate. The Holy Spirit had
launched His role as "Producer of Church history."

So many of the accomplishments and characteristics of the
Church in the Book of Acts are credited to the Holy Spirit. He
has been called: "The Executor of the Great Commission and

the Administrator of the missionary enterprise." It was by His enabling that conversions were achieved, unity prevailed in the Church, dynamic new administrative leadership was provided, and miracles were accomplished. Either by direct action, or through an angel or a vision, the Spirit proceeded to send Philip to Gaza (Acts 8:26), to direct Ananias to pray for Saul (9:10), and to call Saul and Barnabas as the first missionaries (13:2-4). He led in the rejection of the limitations of exclusive Jewish nationalism, and in the breaking down of racial prejudices and discrimination (cf., "For it seemed good to the Holy Ghost, and to us," Acts 15:28). One author writes: "The Church of New Testament days is a running river. The influences of the Spirit are the pure water of life by which that river is supplied."

The overall upbuilding of the Church throughout the Christian era continues to be the work of the Spirit. He is engaged in making real in the corporate body of regenerated humans that which Christ potentially provided for His redeemed Church. Paul spoke of the multitude of converts which as a building fitly framed together "groweth unto an holy temple in the Lord: In whom ye also are builded together for an habitation of God through the Spirit" (Ephesians 2:21, 22). Jesus had promised several ministries of the Spirit to the Church: to teach (John 14:26); to guide (16:13); to show forth the glory of Christ (16:13, 15); and to bring to remembrance (14:26). In these ministries He would confirm the truth concerning Jesus Christ, and authenticate our Lord's person and mission in the lives of men. Without doubt, the work of God whereby He "giveth the increase" (1 Corinthians 3:7), is brought about on this earth through the Holy Spirit.

In general, the administration of the Church on earth is intended ultimately to be the Spirit's prerogative and ministry. "Take heed therefore unto yourselves, and to all the flock, over which the Holy Ghost hath made you overseers" (Acts 20:28; cf. 15:28). The headship of the Holy Spirit assures a thriving Church. Though humans may be elected to offices of leadership in the Church, such elections are not a rejection of the Spirit; they are merely the provision of appropriate channels through whom the Spirit may work. The chief issue in church leadership is not the skill and talent of human leaders, but the degree to which they place themselves under the control of the Spirit's will and purpose. It has been noted: "The Holy Spirit has never abdicated His authority nor delegated His power. The Church that is man-managed instead of God-governed is doomed to failure." The Spirit's method, characteristically, is to bestow divine gifts to enable humans to be His channels to accomplish His work.

The Spirit's indwelling assures that the Church is essentially an organism rather than an organization. Union with the Church is not merely a matter of a horizontal relationship with other humans (as in a nominal church), nor is it a matter of exclusively vertical relationship (as in solitary mysticism), but a matter of both relationships in wholesome balance. The Protestant view holds: "Where the Spirit is, there is the Church," and rejects the traditional: "Where the Church is, there is the Spirit." Thus, there is a vital interrelationship between the person and ministry of the Holy Spirit and the existence and function of the Church. The Spirit elevates the assembly of believers into a true living, serving, worshiping body under the headship of Jesus Christ.

The unity of the Church is the work of the Holy Spirit. He provides not mechanical uniformity, but unity with diversity; it is a spiritual unity and not a unity of organization. It has been said: "The Church in which the Holy Ghost abides is no meager sectarian fragment, but the whole body of believers united in Christ, the living Head." The Spirit knits believers together: "For by one Spirit are we all baptized into one body" (1 Corinthians 2:13); "Endeavoring to keep the unity of the Spirit. . . . There is one body, and one Spirit" (Ephesians 4:3, 4). In its fundamental nature, the Church is a fellowship of the redeemed; it is a fellowship of those who are made regenerate before God by the work of the Holy Spirit. The need of the Church is not a greater emphasis on the externals of unity, but a greater yieldedness to the Holy Spirit. It is in sharing Him that believers share a common divine life and rightly take their place in the one body of Christ.

It has been previously noted that the Spirit's role as "Spirit of Truth" directly involves Him in the sacred Scriptures. He thus acts to impress the believer with the divine authorship of the Bible and the authoritative nature of its teachings. The Protestant stand holds that it is the Holy Spirit rather than the Church that confers authority on Scripture. He gave the Word (cf. 2 Peter 1:21; 2 Timothy 3:16), and He confirms and corroborates that Word in the heart of believers: "Which things also we speak, not in the words which man's wisdom teacheth, but which the Holy Ghost teacheth; comparing spiritual things with spiritual" (1 Corinthians 2:13). Throughout the Christian era, the Holy Spirit has continued to operate to make the Bible real, vivid, and understandable to all responsive readers. He ministers to seal the Word to the believer, and to impel him to receive it and follow it in daily living.

In having prepared and preserved the Scriptures, the Spirit deserves special credit for their existence. Through this medium the Spirit has mastered the problem of communicating the divine message to mankind in terms of intelligible human language. The Scriptures have been called: "A child of the Holy Spirit, the first among the divine works of art produced by the Holy Spirit, and the literary masterpiece of the Holy Spirit." Apart from the large and significant role of the Spirit, the Scriptures would be merely "the letter that killeth." He now uses the Scriptures as an instrument to work on the heart of man, both in leading him to reject sin and carnality, and in leading him into all the positive works of righteousness that eventually constitute full Christian adulthood, which is the standard of perfection of Jesus Christ.

6

The Spirit's Ministry and Work in the Believer

The Holy Spirit ministers to be the believer's empowering and enablement for all spiritual operations and functions. For a godly believer to be "spiritual" demands the presence and ministry, for "what He does is what He is." Nevertheless, the impartation of spirituality is not the Spirit's promotion of himself, but His directing to a right relationship to the Lord Jesus. The Spirit operates within to touch man's inner being, and through His presence and power He motivates to a living consciousness of the divine Christ.

He Regenerates or Makes Spiritually Alive

The Holy Spirit ministers the beginning of all spiritual life. "Except a man be born of water and of the Spirit, he cannot enter into the kingdom of God" (John 3:5). In His own mysterious manner, the Holy Spirit causes those who were spiritually dead to become alive, and thus the convert is begotten of the Holy Spirit. "Now if any man have not the Spirit of Christ, he is none of his" (Romans 8:9). The process is a complete re-creation and no mere fanning into flame of the divine spark; it is not a matter of developing a higher nature but creating a new nature. "According to his mercy he saved us, by the washing of regeneration and renewing of the Holy Ghost" (Titus 3:5). Being born of the Spirit is the only possible way of becoming spiritually alive: "That which is born of the Spirit is spirit" (John 3:6). The actual process of regeneration is exclusively the work of the Spirit, and is a divine and not a human work.

74

Someone has counted 85 distinct New Testament references emphasizing this ministry of the Spirit to impart new life.

Historically, generations of theologians have asked the question: "When does the work of the Holy Spirit begin?" This problem was widely discussed during the era of the Reformation. Martin Luther taught that men made the first move when they accepted God's Word, and as a second action the Holy Spirit proceeded to impart faith in order that regeneration might be achieved. Philipp Melanchthon and John Calvin contended that the first process is a move of the Spirit, and only then is repentance made possible. However, both Lutheran and Calvinistic schools placed Spirit-imparted faith ahead of repentance. The 18th-century Methodists were even more emphatic about the essential role of the Spirit in bringing converts to God. The founder of Methodism, John Wesley, taught that the Spirit works within man from birth in what he called "prevenient" or preliminary grace. It is this gift of grace, conveyed by the Spirit, that works on the human faculties to guide men to penitence and subsequent conversion.

An excessive emphasis on the role of the natural human in conversion characterizes the theology of Congregationalist Horace Bushnell. In his doctrine of "Christian nurture," Bushnell taught that the unaided natural human spirit has in itself the capacity to grow into the state of regeneration. According to Bushnell, the mission of the church is not to preach the gospel to accomplish miraculous conversions, but to promote the elevation of character on a natural plane. He felt that excessive emphasis on the role of the Spirit in conversion denies man his proper involvement in becoming a Christian, and it errs in making the Spirit responsible for all outcomes. In his opinion, to overstress the power of the Spirit is to deprive man of his legitimate involvement. The outcome would be that man won't improve himself, and if man won't, then the Spirit cannot. Bushnell was, of course, overly optimistic about the potential of the nature of natural man to achieve righteousness.

Errors arise when scholars attempt to divide the acts of men from the acts of God, for in many cases they are inseparable. Believing, on the one hand, is an act of man; but it also constitutes a gift of God. For man to claim independent freedom in achieving salvation is only to impose bondage on himself. There is a sense in which all that is achieved in the life of the believer is the work of the Holy Spirit, and another sense in which all that is achieved is by man's personal effort. In no instance can one be regenerated except he personally moves toward God; in no instance can one be regenerated except God personally moves toward him. In the pattern of the typical paradoxical God-human relationship, both God and man are credited with launching the process of regeneration. The paradox may not be understandable, but it is consistent with the teachings of Scripture.

The quickening ministry of the Spirit is set forth in Scripture as equivalent to regeneration. "You hath he quickened who were dead in trespasses and sins" (Ephesians 2:1). The word *quicken* is an archaic English word meaning "to make alive." However, the Bible also uses this word to describe the end-time resuscitation of the body at the second coming of Christ. Thus, the provision to the believer of a glorified body is also a quickening: "He that raised up Christ from the dead shall also quicken your mortal bodies by his Spirit that dwelleth in you" (Romans 8:11). This aspect of the ministry of the Spirit is yet future, and it awaits the return of Christ. However, on occasion, some believers enjoy a foretaste of the Spirit's quickening as He ministers to strengthen and empower them for God's service.

The Holy Spirit Indwells

The indwelling of the Spirit is so basic to Christian experience that the believer is described as the Spirit's temple: "Your body is the temple of the Holy Ghost which is in you" (1 Corinthians 6:19); "Know ye not that ye are the temple of God, and that the Spirit of God dwelleth in you?" (1 Corinthians 3:16). The indwelling Spirit confirms the believer's sonship: "And because ye are sons, God hath sent forth the Spirit of his Son into your hearts" (Galatians 4:6). Pearlman wrote: "One of the most comprehensive definitions of a Christian is that he is a man in whom the Holy Spirit dwells." Talbot once wrote: "You show me a man who is not indwelt by the Spirit of God, and I

The
Spirit's Ministry and Work
in the Believer

Regenerates or Makes Spiritually Alive

Indwells

Grants Assurance

Sanctifies or Achieves Holiness

Empowers Spiritually

Leads and Guides

Assists in Worship and Prayer

Implements Adoption

Communes and Fellowships

Anoints

Seals

Teaches and Reminds

Figure 5: The Spirit's ministry and work in the believer.

will show you a man who is not a child of God." Scripture affirms: "If any man have not the Spirit of Christ, he is none of his" (Romans 8:9).

Much that is unique about the Christian experience is the outcome of the Spirit's indwelling. Scofield comments: "That impartation of the Spirit as indwelling the believer simply and only because he was a believer marked the tremendous transition from the age of law to the age of grace." Jesus assured His disciples that their relationship to the Spirit would change following Calvary: "He dwelleth with you, and shall be in you" (John 14:17). He had noted that this was to be a permanent relationship: "That he may be with you forever, even the Spirit of truth" (John 14:16). It has been said concerning the permanency of the Spirit's indwelling: "He so inheres in and cleaves to us that, though we were thrown into the hottest crucible, He and we could not be separated. The fiercest fire could not dissolve the union."

The indwelling of the Spirit is rightly a source of joy and power to the believer. He was that even in Old Testament times to those chosen ones who particularly related to Him. Pharaoh testified of Joseph: "Can we find such a one as this is, a man in whom the Spirit of God is?" (Genesis 41:38). Paul repeatedly reminded New Testament believers of their privileged status in the Spirit (cf. 1 Corinthians 3:16, 17; 6:19; 2 Corinthians 13:5). The Spirit's indwelling begins at the moment of conversion: "And hereby we know that he [ie., Jesus] abideth in us, by the Spirit which he hath given us" (1 John 3:24). Although there are future experiences relating to the Spirit, no later attainment is necessary to qualify for the Spirit's indwelling. The indwelling of the Spirit precedes all other relationships that the believer has with Him.

The Spirit Grants Assurance

Paul reported: "The Spirit himself beareth witness with our spirit, that we are the children of God" (Romans 8:16). In a parallel statement John says: "And it is the Spirit that beareth witness, because the Spirit is truth" (1 John 5:6). As it were, the Spirit provides a spiritual perception that expands the natural senses. Thus, the believer is made aware of the eternal realm, and he clearly perceives his status as a justified child of God who is at peace with his Father. When the Holy Spirit has granted assurance, the believer is able calmly to appropriate God's promises. Thus: "To be spiritually minded is life and peace" (Romans 8:6). Many new converts undergo severe misgivings, or even open doubts, concerning their newfound faith. The impartation of assurance is an essential and welcome ministry of the Spirit.

The Spirit may be understood to minister to grant assurance by fulfilling His function as a seal. He is the gift of God: "Who hath also sealed us, and given the earnest of the Spirit in our hearts" (2 Corinthians 1:22). An earnest or foretaste of the Spirit's provision is just what is needed to provide confidence and certainty to the new believer. His ministry bestows faith based on eternal spiritual reality rather than mere transient feelings. In the Spirit, the new believer enjoys just what he needs to grow in the Christian life in confident assurance. Nevertheless, at no time does the Spirit's assurance permit careless living. The believer is exhorted: "Grieve not the Holy Spirit of God, whereby ye are sealed unto the day of redemption" (Ephesians 4:30). Even while the Spirit is reassuring the believer of his stability and security in God, He is simultaneously imposing conformity to His holy nature.

The Holy Spirit Sanctifies or Achieves Holiness

The Spirit achieves sanctification or personal holiness in the believer as He brings him under the control of the living Christ. Negatively, He imparts an awareness and aversion to sin: "Woe is me! for I am undone; because I am a man of unclean lips, and I dwell in the midst of a people of unclean lips" (Isaiah 6:5). Positively, He exerts a moral creative power that is described in Scripture under the figure of the fruit of the Spirit (cf. Galatians 5:22, 23). Spiritual fruit is identical with the expression of the Christ-life, and the bearing of such fruit is an enthroning of Jesus Christ. The Holy Spirit represents to the believer the inner life of Jesus with all the richness of His divine-human holiness. The believer experiences "sanctification of the Spirit unto obedience and sprinkling of the blood of Jesus Christ" (1 Peter 1:2).

In achieving the believer's sanctification, the Spirit begins by purging out the deeds of the flesh: "Ye have purified your souls in obeying the truth through the Spirit" (1 Peter 1:22). He thereupon replaces the inner vacuum with himself so the believer is given strength to walk in righteousness in a world filled with temptations. The Christian is, thus, "strengthened with might by his Spirit in the inner man" (Ephesians 3:16). It is the Spirit and not the flesh which makes possible the life of genuine godliness. "Are ye so foolish? having begun in the Spirit, are ye now made perfect by the flesh?" (Galatians 3:3). It is His intention that the life that is Spirit-filled is also "Spirit-lived" (i.e., lived in the Spirit). It is His desire that the soul be emptied of self-righteousness and the old nature be rejected: "Seeing that ye have put off the old man with his deeds" (Colossians 3:9).

In effect, the Holy Spirit makes Christ the believer's sanctification. "But of him are ye in Christ Jesus, who of God is made unto us . . . sanctification" (1 Corinthians 1:30). As it were, the Spirit seeks to direct the convert to bow his head to the Lord Jesus and acknowledge Him as King. Roy Hession writes concerning the Spirit's ministry: "He does not convict us of sin as something merely unethical or contrary to the ten commandments, but as that which has dethroned the Lord Jesus and caused His death upon the Cross."[1] The Holy Spirit seeks always to lead the Christian into new areas of submission in his growth into Christlikeness. It is a case of being dead to sin and alive unto Jesus Christ: "Reckon ye also yourselves to be dead indeed unto sin, but alive unto God through Jesus Christ our Lord" (Romans 6:11).

The believer appropriates "sanctification by the Spirit" through submitting to divinely imparted power within, rather than attempting to conform to external rules. The Spirit sanctifies as He sets the believer free from the law of sin and death, and as He enables the believer to produce spiritual fruit. "For the law of the Spirit of life in Christ Jesus hath made me free from the law of sin and death" (Romans 8:2). The ministry of the Spirit does not cancel the believer's responsibility, but it does give him opportunity for spiritual and moral growth. He increasingly strives to foster the expression of the attitudes and sense of personal values represented by Jesus Christ. God has personally chosen that the process of sanctification should operate in the believer: "God hath from the beginning chosen you to salvation through sanctification of the Spirit" (2 Thessalonians 2:13).

The Holy Spirit ministers in sanctifying man's total being; He implements the divine intention: "I pray God your whole spirit and soul and body be preserved blameless unto the coming of our Lord Jesus Christ" (1 Thessalonians 5:23). "Sanctify them through thy truth: thy word is truth" (John 17:17). His program in sanctifying is not the improvement of the old nature, but that of building within the believer a life that is totally new. The old nature is to be seen as crucified with Christ (cf. Romans 6:6); He develops the new nature as the life of the new creature in Christ Jesus unfolds (cf. 2 Corinthians 5:17). What has traditionally been called "experimental sanctification" (and which preferably may be called "experiential sanctification") is thus a matter of degree among believers, and its growth and perfection continue throughout the believer's life on earth.

Although the role of the Spirit in sanctification appears generally acceptable to most Christians today, in the past the subject has often been a matter of dispute. In the late medieval period, the Roman Catholic church had developed its "works-righteousness" doctrines whereby personal conduct was held to be vitally identified with salvation. Sanctification was not a matter of pleasing God and growing in Christian usefulness, but a burdensome attempt to attain salvation. One achieved the sanctified life by fulfilling a set of legal requirements, and what particularly counted was legal rather than actual approval. The payment of fines or the fulfillment of petty penances were frequently the roads to holiness. It was against these extremes that Martin Luther reacted in the 16th-century Protestant Reformation.

In the name of "justification by faith," Luther rejected the medieval Catholic "works-righteousness" doctrines. He also rejected other doctrines calling for good works, including the perfectionism of certain early-day Protestant contemporaries. Thus Lutheranism, as a movement, took a stand against sanctified living or "pietism." The Calvinists also rejected pietism, although they did support the doctrine that the convert is to grow toward Christlikeness. The Reformers agreed in teaching that human behavior, regardless of its motivation, did not govern one's standing before God. Therefore, good works, including the works of holy living, were counted as mere "alien righteousness."

Although the Pietists represented a righting of the extreme reactionism of the early Reformers, it was not until the time of the Methodists in the 18th century that Protestants in significant numbers began to practice personal sanctification. The evangelists and theologians of the Methodist revival, including John Wesley, George Whitefield, Francis Asbury, and John Fletcher, were vitally concerned for practical holiness. They believed that the Holy Spirit ministered in the believer's life by purging all sin from the heart in order to accomplish this holiness. Methodists believed that their special mission was to convey to the Church their doctrine as their unique "depositum." Most evangelical Christians today enjoy at least some measure of the Methodist legacy, and for the most part, faith in Christ and commitment to the Holy Spirit are related to the life of holiness.

The Spirit Empowers Spiritually

As Christ departed in person from His earthly followers, He set forth a firm promise relating to the Holy Spirit: "Ye shall receive power, after that the Holy Ghost is come upon you" (Acts 1:8). Since the Lord's promise is without qualification, it may be concluded that the degree to which the believer is empowered by the Spirit is determined by the degree of his commitment. Wuest has written: "It is not that the believer uses the power of God but that God's power uses him. . . . The power of the Holy Spirit is potentially resident in the saint by virtue of His indwelling presence, but it is operative in that believer when he is yielded to and dependent upon the ministry of the Spirit."[2] Even in His ministry of power, the Holy

Spirit does not thrust himself on the human. He can only begin to operate powerfully when the believer has achieved the emptying of himself and his natural powers.

In at least some sense, every significant spiritual attainment is by virtue of the Spirit's empowering. Louis Evans once wrote: "Whenever we say, 'I believe,' it is because He has been our Tutor." Paul reported: "Our gospel came not unto you in word only, but also in power, and in the Holy Ghost, and in much assurance" (1 Thessalonians 1:5); and he prayed: "That he would grant you, according to the riches of his glory, to be strengthened with might by his Spirit in the inner man" (Ephesians 3:16). The imparted power of the Holy Spirit equips the believer to perform his ministry (1 Peter 1:12), to witness concerning his faith in the proclamation of the gospel of Christ (John 15:26, 27; cf. Acts 1:8), and to act authoritatively in the line of Christian duty (cf. "Behold, I give you authority . . . over all the power of the enemy," Luke 10:10, literal translation).

The Spirit Leads and Guides

The Spirit ministers to direct the believer in making decisions and solving problems, particularly those related to the service of God. He fulfills God's promise: "I will instruct thee and teach thee in the way which thou shalt go: I will guide thee with mine eye" (Psalm 32:8). He offers deliverance from distractions, including the carnal self. "For as many as are led by the Spirit of God, they are the sons of God" (Romans 8:14; cf. John 16:13). To be led of the Spirit, one must set aside dependence on self and natural wisdom, although the Spirit's leading may not be contrary to these. Paul exhorted: "If we live in the Spirit, let us also walk in the Spirit" (Galatians 5:25). Comments Gutzke: "To be led by the Spirit involves self-denial but it brings great blessing." Being sensitive to the Spirit's leading is a mark of Christian maturity.

The Spirit's ministry in guidance has been described as operating in the believer by the "intuitions of our sanctified judgment." In discussing this subject, George Flattery writes:

The Holy Spirit leads us much as a father leads his sons or as a master executive leads his work force. At times He delegates decisions to us;

at other times He influences our decisions; finally, there are times
when He very directly reveals God's will to us.[3]

Flattery makes the point that one who proceeds to decisions
prayerfully, submissively, and with the sincere and humble
desire to achieve God's will, can be confident of His leading.
An exciting aspect of the Spirit's leading is the personal involvement of the believer, and this contrasts with legalism. "If
ye be led of the Spirit, ye are not under the law" (Galatians
5:18).

On occasion, the Spirit's guidance is negative and preventa-
tive. Thus, in the case of Paul and his party: "When they had
gone through Phrygia and the region of Galatia, and were
forbidden of the Holy Ghost to preach the word in Asia, after
they were come to Mysia, they assayed to go into Bithynia: but
the Spirit suffered them not" (Acts 16:6, 7). Edmund Tedeschi
comments on this incident:

> The Holy Spirit leads, and the result is that Christ is presented to an
> individual, a family, or a whole region of the world. And the checking
> of the Spirit in effect withholds the gospel, perhaps to protect His
> messengers, perhaps in judgment of the region, perhaps to speed the
> message to some other more ready people, or perhaps because He is
> leading some other apostle (sent one) to that place.[4]

In the lives of believers today, the guidance of the Spirit
frequently consists of His illumination of Scripture. Jesus said:
"He shall bring all things to your remembrance, whatsoever I
have said unto you" (John 14:26). A specialty of the Spirit is
making clear the mysteries of God depicted in Scripture. "The
things of God knoweth no man, but the Spirit of God" (1 Corinthians 2:11). In personal cases, He sometimes informs in
greater detail than the general principles of Scripture in order
to provide individual guidance. Thus, at the outset of His
ministry, Jesus was "led by the Spirit into the wilderness"
(Luke 4:1); Philip was sent to the Gaza desert where he might
win the Ethiopian (Acts 8:39); and Simeon was directed into
the temple to meet the infant Jesus (Luke 2:27). Jesus promised
His disciples that in times of persecution, when before hostile
authorities: "It shall be given you in that same hour what ye

shall speak. For it is not ye that speak, but the Spirit of your Father which speaketh in you" (Matthew 10:19, 20).

The leading of the Spirit must not be confused with personal human desires and opinions. It is usually suggested that Paul went to Jerusalem and was imprisoned wholly in the will of God in spite of the warning by the disciples at Tyre. The Spirit's role was to warn Paul to prepare him for the imprisonment that awaited him; it was the disciples' personal judgment that sought to discourage the journey (cf. Acts 20:22-24). While opinions concerning these matters may differ, the principle of distinguishing divine leading from human response and application definitely stands. It is important to note that some directions that are said to be the Spirit's leading actually are the product of human opinion or reasoning.

The Spirit Assists in Worship and Prayer

Paul wrote: "We are the circumcision who worship by the spirit of God" (Philippians 3:3, literal trans.). The New Testament Christian is privileged to enjoy the ministry of the Holy Spirit to give him direction and provide efficacy in the process of worship. Jesus promised concerning the Spirit: "He shall glorify me" (John 16:14). The Holy Spirit ministers to conduct the worshiping believer, who is justified by the shed blood of Christ, into the presence of the King. In this connection, Pentecostals typically apply Paul's words: "Where the Spirit of the Lord is, there is liberty" (2 Corinthians 3:17). P.S. Brewster writes: "The Holy Spirit is supreme when the Church is at worship. He magnifies and glorifies the Christ."[5] A. W. Tozer described the Spirit's power at work in the worshiping church as conveying "a heightened sense of the presence of Christ."

The Spirit's ministry particularly assists the believer in prayer: "Praying always with all prayer and supplication in the Spirit" (Ephesians 6:18). Wisloff writes: "Prayer is a miracle of the Spirit. Without the Spirit, no prayer, and without prayer, no Spirit. . . . It is the Spirit who has called us to prayer every time we have prayed."[6] This statement accords with Luther's slogan: "Without the Holy Spirit, no prayer is prayed." Paul wrote: "Likewise the Spirit also helpeth our infirmities: for we know not what we should pray for as we ought: but the Spirit himself maketh intercession for us with groanings which cannot be uttered" (Romans 8:26). The believer may be thought of as praying under the tutorship of the Spirit. It is preferable to say the believer goes to God through the Spirit (one step), rather than through the Spirit the believer goes to God (two steps).

Specific instruction concerning the believer's worship is given by Paul: "Be filled with the Spirit; speaking to yourselves in psalms and hymns and spiritual songs, singing and making melody in your heart to the Lord" (Ephesians 5:18, 19). The divine Spirit is provided to constitute the spirit of our response to God.

The expression "spiritual songs" has occasioned considerable discussion. While it would seem plausible to conclude that the reference is simply to human musical compositions, with words that convey a spiritual theme, some Pentecostal authors have concluded otherwise. Larry Hurtado summarizes his study of this subject: "Spiritual songs are truly unpremeditated words sung in the Spirit. . . . They are the direct utterance through us of the aspiration of the Paraclete."[7] J. Rodman Williams writes of "the moment when not only is the melody given by the Spirit but also the language, as words and music sung by the assembled worshippers blend into an unimaginable, humanly impossible, chorus of praise."[8] It is usually understood that to speak of "singing . . . in your heart" identifies the manner rather than the place of singing.

The Holy Spirit Implements Adoption

Scripture specifically identifies the Holy Spirit as the "Spirit of adoption": "For ye have not received the spirit of bondage again to fear; but ye have received the Spirit of adoption, whereby we cry, Abba Father. The Spirit itself beareth witness with our spirit, that we are the children of God" (Romans 8:15, 16). Since Biblical "adoption" is equivalent in Western society to recognition of adult sonship, it is correct to say the Spirit's voice is the "voice of sonship." He witnesses that the believer possesses both the status and the heart of an adult son, and a period of probationary growth is not necessary. Through the Spirit, the believer proceeds to immediate adulthood. He appropriates the firstfruits of his eternal legacy as an adult son, and he shares with the Father the task of administering the Kingdom. There is complete deliverance by the Spirit from the bondage of the flesh and of the Law (cf. Galatians 5:16-18).

The Holy Spirit Communes and Fellowships

Since the Holy Spirit is a divine Person, He ministers to extend personal communion and a sense of fellowship to the believer. Actually, the one Greek word *koinonia* is variously translated either "fellowship" or "communion." "If there be any consolation in Christ, if any comfort of love, if any fellowship [*koinonia*] of the Spirit . . ." (Philippians 2:1); "The grace of the Lord Jesus Christ, and the love of God, and the communion [*koinonia*] of the Holy Ghost, be with you all" (2 Corinthians 13:14). The Holy Spirit and the regenerate believer share many things in common and, in a very real sense, He offers friendship and fellowship to God's people. He shares with the believer His love for the Father and the Son, and He leads each one whom He indwells into a growing relationship with God through His divine person. He becomes the channel through whom believers enter the Church which is the fellowship that He has created.

The Holy Spirit Anoints

The Greek word *chrisma** is translated by "anointing" or "unction," and it means "a rubbing in or spreading on of oil." The New Testament references recall the Old Testament procedure of pouring oil on candidates for appointment as prophet, priest, or king. In the Church, the Holy Spirit anoints every believer for all three of these offices. John wrote: "Ye have an unction [*chrisma*] from the Holy One. . . . But the anointing [*chrisma*] which ye have received of him abideth in you" (1 John 2:20, 27). According to John, the Holy Spirit's anointing: 1) abides, 2) assures spiritual knowledge, 3) conveys teaching,

---

* To be distinguished from *charisma* which means: "given as a gift."

4) imparts truth, 5) relates to abiding in Christ. The anointed believer is more competent to communicate God's message, not merely because his mind is stimulated, but because there is a divine accuracy, authority, honesty, and efficiency to his words.

Scripture tends to merge the Spirit's role in anointing with the role of the Father. "Now he which . . . hath anointed us, is God" (2 Corinthians 1:21). The will of the Spirit, and the will of the Father and the Son are one, and that with which the Spirit anoints the believer is himself. He does not anoint to bestow material blessings or gifts of power as such, but to bestow His own person. It has been said: "The Holy Spirit has himself laid hands on the anointed believer." This anointing is not a special favor, but the ordinary outcome of His presence and indwelling. Because the believer is anointed, he may undertake the Great Commission, and whatever personal calls to service may be his as well.

The Holy Spirit Seals

The Holy Spirit, in taking up His residence within, sets His seal or mark of ownership on the convert: "In whom ye also trusted, after that ye heard the word of truth . . . in whom also after that ye believed, ye were sealed with that holy Spirit of promise" (Ephesians 1:13); "[God] hath also sealed us, and given the earnest of the Spirit in our hearts" (2 Corinthians 1:22). The use of the aorist (i.e., past) tense for the verb *seal* in each of these passages implies that the sealing is a one-time act. The Holy Spirit seals with himself, just as He anoints with himself. The Spirit thus communicates His character and image, He authenticates the believer's inheritance, and He implants a new purpose and a new motivation. It is not that the sealed Christian is necessarily a perfect Christian, but his sealing identifies him with a perfect Saviour and a perfect salvation. The sealing process establishes ownership and assures authenticity.

The Holy Spirit Teaches and Reminds

Jesus said: "The Holy Ghost . . . shall teach you all things, and bring all things to your remembrance, whatsoever I have said unto you" (John 14:26). The Spirit's teaching clearly involves, among other things, providing tangible solutions to practical problems. "The Spirit of truth . . . will guide you into all truth" (John 16:13). Since He sets teachers in the Church, He teaches both by direct impression, illumination of Scripture, and through human instruments. One outcome of the Spirit's ministry in teaching and reminding of Jesus' message was the production of the New Testament by the apostles. In this generation, every believer can anticipate the Spirit's ministry to teach and remind in the hour of trial and legal examination: "When they shall lead you, and deliver you up, take no thought beforehand what ye shall speak, neither do ye premeditate: but whatsoever shall be given you in that hour, that speak ye: for it is not ye that speak, but the Holy Ghost" (Mark 13:11).

In teaching and reminding, the Spirit is not limited to human intellect or to the conventional logical operation of the mind in reasoning and recall. He simply communicates a measure of the divine understanding, and this is different in kind from that which is conventionally human. "Ye need not that any man teach you: but . . . the same anointing teaches you of all things and is true" (1 John 2:27). The Holy Spirit is God's unique provision to the Christian to make the revealed truths of the mind of God understandable. In many cases, the natural human mind would not otherwise be an appropriate instrument for understanding the spiritual truths that are to be known: "The things of God knoweth no man, but the Spirit of God" (1 Corinthians 2:11). In His ministry, the Spirit specializes in spiritual understanding as contrasted with mere everyday intellectual understanding, but this is not to say that He is unconcerned about necessary practical matters.

The ministry of the Spirit to baptize is an important aspect of His work in the believer. The chapters that follow deal with this matter in depth.

7

Historical Backgrounds of Spirit Baptism

The doctrines of the Holy Spirit that are popularly known as "Pentecostal" are those that apply to contemporary experience that is in the pattern of Acts chapter 2 and subsequent New Testament practice. Within the sequence of events that launched the gospel era, those that occurred on the Day of Pentecost are specifically unique. Writes Sanders:

> It required the dynamic of the Spirit as well as the sacrifice of the Saviour to bring the benefits of salvation to a waiting world, for all Christian experience revolves around the twin centres of Calvary and Pentecost. . . . Pentecost made available to men all that Calvary made possible.[1]

Today's Pentecostals believe that it is their privilege to participate in spiritual phenomena wholly equivalent to that of Biblical times.

The fact that the day in which the Holy Spirit was outpoured on the waiting disciples was also a Jewish national holiday, humanly speaking, was somewhat coincidental. Any other day would have done as well so far as the spiritual transaction was concerned. However, God especially selected the Day of Pentecost for the sake of the witness that it permitted. The name *Pentecostal* means "fiftieth" and it identified the "feast of the fiftieth day" counted from the Feast of the Firstfruits which was the second day of the Feast of Unleavened Bread (Mazzoth) at the Passover. Another name for the Feast of Pentecost was the "Feast of Weeks," since it came at the end of 7 weeks after Passover (actually 7 weeks plus 2 days). On the

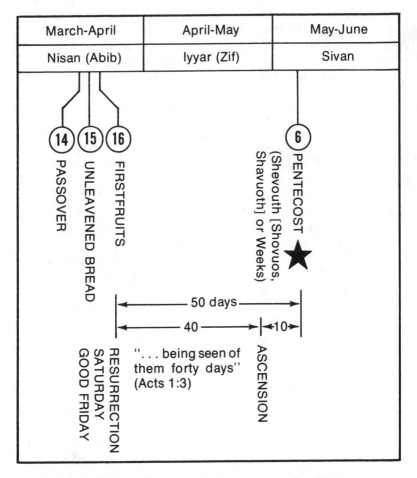

March-April	April-May	May-June
Nisan (Abib)	Iyyar (Zif)	Sivan

Figure 6. Schema of the chronology of events relating to the Day of Pentecost of Acts 2.

occasion of the Feast of Pentecost, two loaves of bread baked from the newly harvested wheat were waved before the Lord in ceremonial dedication and thanksgiving. All male Israelites were to appear before the Lord in pilgrimage on this day, but otherwise it was a day of rest (Leviticus 23:21); and for the people in general it was prescribed: "Thou shalt rejoice before the Lord thy God" (Deuteronomy 16:11).

Spirit Baptism in Biblical Times

John the Baptist had declared that the Messiah who was to come would minister the baptism in the Spirit: "I indeed baptize you with water. . . . He shall baptize you with the Holy Ghost and with fire" (Luke 3:16); "Upon whom thou shalt see the Spirit descending and remaining on him, the same is he which baptizeth you with the Holy Ghost" (John 1:33). During His ministry, Jesus predicted the Pentecostal outpouring on as many as eight separate occasions: "I will pray the Father, and he shall give you another Comforter, that he may abide with you forever" (John 14:16); "It is expedient for you that I go away: for if I go not away, the Comforter will not come unto you; but if I depart, I will send him unto you" (John 16:7). Just before His ascension, Jesus "commanded them that they should not depart from Jerusalem, but wait for the promise of the Father. . . . Ye shall be baptized with the Holy Ghost not many days hence" (Acts 1:4, 5; cf. John 7:37-39; 14:26; Luke 11:13; 24:49; Mark 16:17).

The Pentecostal bestowment upon the waiting group, presumably in the Upper Room (cf. Acts 1:13), included the sound as of a mighty rushing wind, cloven tongues as of fire, and speaking with other tongues. The wind spoke of the power of the Spirit and His rapidity in moving on human hearts; the fire, since it rested on each of them, spoke of the universality of His distribution; and the tongues were evidence that He, indeed, had come. The disciples did not "receive" the wind and the fire; these were simply visible and audible phenomena that accompanied the giving of the Spirit and the fulfillment of the promise of the Father (Luke 24:49). The disciples did "receive" tongues, for in the language of Scripture, they all "began to speak with other tongues." Before long, the newly baptized group poured forth into the streets of Jerusalem, and there they testified to the wonderful works of God. The bystanders were attracted and impressed, not by theological arguments, but by the enthusiasm and conviction of the 120 and, above all, by the miracle of diverse tongues.

Peter called the Pentecostal experience "the gift of the Holy Ghost" (Acts 2:38). He declared that these events were the fulfillment of the prophecies of Joel in the Old Testament era eight centuries earlier:

> This is that which was spoken by the prophet Joel; And it shall come to pass in the last days, saith God, I will pour out my Spirit upon all flesh: and your sons and your daughters shall prophesy, and your young men shall see visions, and your old men shall dream dreams (Acts 2:16, 17).

Decades later, Paul commented on the relationship between tongues in his day and those mentioned in Old Testament prophecies: "In the law it is written, With men of other tongues and other lips will I speak unto this people.... Wherefore tongues are for a sign" (1 Corinthians 14:21, 22; cf. Isaiah 28:11). Events on the Day of Pentecost in Jerusalem embodied far-ranging historical roots, as well as a definitive pattern for the future.

On the Day of Pentecost, the disciples who had tarried in prayer were filled or baptized with the Holy Spirit of God. In them was fulfilled Jesus' promise: "He dwelleth with you, and shall be in you. I will not leave you comfortless" (John 14:17). The bestowment of the indwelling, baptizing Spirit implemented the anticipated Church Age, and from that time until now, Jesus Christ is correctly described as: "He which baptizes with the Holy Spirit" (cf. John 1:33). On this occasion the Church began its outreach, and 3,000 converts to the gospel of Jesus Christ were made. While Jesus was on earth "the Holy Ghost was not yet given; because that Jesus was not yet glorified" (John 7:39). His bestowment, both to indwell and infill, meant the Messiah had completed His redemptive work and had assumed His intercessory ministry in glory.

Experiences according to the pattern of Acts chapter 2 were basic in the New Testament church. There are at least four instances in the Book of Acts that describe a Pentecostal outpouring similar in kind to the original on the Day of Pentecost. In the reports of Acts 10 and thereafter, the Spirit was bestowed without specific delays: "While Peter yet spake these words, the Holy Ghost fell on all them which heard the word" (10:44). Peter later noted that the phenomena duplicated the original Pentecost: "The Holy Ghost fell on them, as on us at the beginning" (11:15). The final Biblical record of a Pentecostal outpouring is the baptism of the disciples at Ephesus (Acts 19), some 21 years after the original Day of Pentecost. Within the New Testament, the Pentecostal pattern appears to have been well authenticated and stabilized in form. The occasions of Pentecostal baptism will be considered in more detail later in connection with the investigation of the role of tongues.

Spirit Baptism in the Early and Medieval Church

It has been noted that the Early Church produced only limited doctrinal statements concerning the Holy Spirit. However, the reality of Spirit baptism and Pentecostal phenomena is reflected in many sermonic references and personal testimonies. Dr. Ron Kydd found 11 out of 39 post-Biblical Christian authors prior to A.D. 200 who included references to Pentecostal experiences in the church of their day. In most cases, there was no marked distinction between the topics of Spirit baptism and the gifts of the Spirit. Thus, most of the citations will be reserved for the section "Spiritual Gifts in History," but a few can be reported here.

Both Justin Martyr (c. 108-168) and Irenaeus (c. 130-202) wrote of those who talked in tongues, and Clement of Alexandria (c. 155-220) referred to "the full outpouring of the Holy Spirit." Hippolytus, in about 217, committed a prayer to writing: "O Lord God, who didst count these thy servants worthy of deserving the forgiveness of sins by the washing of regeneration, make them worthy to be filled with the Holy Spirit." Gregory Nazianzen (330-390) wrote to extol the Holy Spirit, and to declare that He was "after baptism [in water] to be sought as a separate gift."

In the decades between 130 and 160, the movement that was known as Montanism arose in central Asia Minor. Montanus, the founder, apparently was a reformer who reacted against the growing secularism of Christianity. Although Montanism is usually considered a heresy, there is evidence that many of its beliefs and practices were in the pattern of today's Pentecostalism. Bruner declares that Montanism was "the prototype of almost everything Pentecostalism seeks to represent."[2] Eusebius, in his *Ecclesiastical History,* reports an orthodox observer's account of an encounter with Montanus: "Being suddenly in a sort of frenzy and ecstasy, he raved, and began to babble and utter strange things, prophesying in a manner contrary to the constant custom of the Church handed down by tradition from the beginning."

As matters worked out, Montanism ultimately lost its struggle, and institutionalism took over. It is sometimes suggested that in rejecting Montanism, the Church simultaneously rejected orthodox charismata and Pentecostalism in general. Historical accounts convey the impression that Montanism blended a legitimate commitment to the infilling of the Spirit with various extreme practices, the subordination of Scripture to prophecy, a misguided legalism, and a stern asceticism. However, it should be noted that accounts of Montanism are chiefly by its enemies, and it is possible that more sympathetic reporting would have evaluated it differently. It was probably early in the third century when Tertullian (c. 120-222) threw in his lot with Montanism, and became its chief spokesman. It was this identification that resulted in Tertullian's title "The Pentecostal of Carthage."

By the time Augustine (354-430) emerged as a theological leader, the profession and practices of Pentecostalism were no longer in evidence. Augustine spoke of tongues and similar evidence as signs "adapted to the time." He considered such events to be limited to centuries prior to his own, but he did teach that the reception of the Holy Spirit was intended to be a spiritual event subsequent to conversion and water baptism. He wrote: "This distinction between the reception of baptism and the reception of the Holy Spirit shows us clearly that we should not think that those whom we do not deny to have received [water] baptism forthwith have the Holy Spirit." The evidence that one had received the Holy Spirit does not appear to have been stated by Augustine, but it is clear that he would deny that the evidence would involve any tangible miraculous aspects such as tongues. Augustine's rejection of the super-natural was endorsed by his contemporary, Pope Leo I (or Leo the Great) (c. 400-461).

The developing Roman Catholic Church made Spirit baptism increasingly a matter of outward ritual. However, it is interesting to note that some churches of the late fifth century included a special chapel behind the baptistry as a place for receiving the Spirit. Upon being baptized in water, candidates would proceed to the chapel and there the bishop would lay hands on them, anoint them with oil, and pray that the Holy Spirit might be given them. The formality of the arrangement sooner or later displaced any evident spiritual phenomenon. The ordinance of confirmation in today's Catholic Church is, in part, a modification of this ancient practice, and at least some schools of Catholic theology hold that at confirmation the candidate receives the baptism in the Spirit. Stephen Clark quotes a typical Catholic tract which describes the ordinance of confirmation as "a strengthening through the power of the Holy Spirit; it is a gift of God for our growth as Christians; it gives power to be soldiers, witnesses of Christ."[3]

In the Eastern or Orthodox Church, the doctrine and practice of Spirit baptism, and speaking in tongues, seems to have survived much more generally than in the West. Kelsey comments as follows:

The East developed a mystical, individualistic, other-worldly, in-troverted Christianity. In this tradition the individual gifts of the Spirit flourished. The door was never closed to experiences like tongues. . . . While historical evidence of tongues within the Greek tradition has not been compiled, it is a fair inference that tongues speaking, being no more bizarre than other Eastern monastic practices, has simply continued within the tradition of Greek monasticism without attract-ing much notice.[4]

It appears that the Eastern church neither denied nor re-jected Spirit baptism, nor did they develop a doctrine to explain and support the experience. In general, the pursuit of charismata appears to have been limited to the occasional believer whose devotion or information exceeded that of his peers. Relationships between believers and the Holy Spirit survived in the East, but just barely.

Backgrounds of Pentecostalism in the Modern Era

From approximately A.D. 1000, the Catholic Church generally took the position that speaking in tongues was demonic. It was held that the "other tongues" of the Bible consisted of the gift of languages whereby one could be divinely assisted in learning a foreign tongue. Such views effectively dismissed any doctrine of baptism in the Holy Spirit in a Pentecostal context. However, the church simultaneously maintained a doctrine of miracles, and occasional exceptions to the hostility against tongues are recorded. Abbess Hildegard (1098-1179) is credited with a divine enduement that enabled her to speak and interpret various languages, and she testified of personal experiences that today would be classified as charismatic or Pentecostal. She produced a manuscript *Lingua Ignota* which lists and defines (in Latin mainly) 900 words of an unknown language that she believed had been given to her supernaturally. The Franciscan monk, Antony of Padua (1195-1231) was reputed to be able to preach in diverse tongues. His gift was so widely acclaimed that in 1227 he was called before the pope and his cardinals to demonstrate the ministry of tongues. In Europe, Vincent Ferrer (1357-1419) traveled from region to region, and professedly was given the gift of tongues to minister to various peoples; in the Far East, Francis Xavier (1506-1552) similarly ministered in languages he had not learned.

It is held by almost all Pentecostals that there is no Biblical basis to conclude that "other tongues" are intended to equip a worker to preach to people of a different language. Thus, what is reported concerning Ferrer and Xavier is not necessarily a contribution to the topic of Pentecostal backgrounds. However, dogmatic conclusions are not possible, since records are incomplete and not totally reliable. The biographer of Xavier notes that "the gift of tongues was a transient favor." This reference might imply that Xavier's gift was, after all, in the Biblical pattern. A somewhat later manifestation of tongues and Pentecostalism in general appears within the Catholic Church in the Jansenites of France in the 18th century (1730-33). When these reformers were expelled from church institutions in France, they responded with heightened spiritual concern. The scene of their most fervent Pentecostal worship was at the St. Medard Cemetery of Paris. Pascal became one of their converts.

Many of the pre-Reformation reforming parties that separated from the Catholic Church were in some measure Pentecostal. The general name of "Paulicians" (i.e., followers of the apostle Paul) is given to these, and such groups were identifiable as early as the eighth century. Some of the better known groups in the Paulician tradition included: the Petrobrusians, the Beguine, the Cathari or Albigenses, the Waldenses, the Euchites, the Bogomils, and the Apostolici. It would probably be held today that, although these groups were alert to errors within the Catholic Church, they fell short of complete truth. However, they all had in common that they sought to be "vehicles of the Holy Spirit." It is recorded, for instance, that the Apostolici imposed as a qualification for membership in their highest order that one should have received the baptism of the Holy Spirit.

Among the Protestant reformers, beginning in 1517, tongues and other phenomena associated with Pentecostal Spirit baptism are often mentioned. The historian, Eric Sauer, ascribed all of the spiritual gifts, including tongues to Martin Luther (1483-1546). However, the reference may be intended to be metaphorical. In Luther's own writings, tongues and miraculous spiritual manifestations in general are assigned to the apostolic era. He took the position that Acts 2:4 is intended to teach that God provides that ordinary people may be divinely anointed to preach the gospel. However, it is interesting to note that among the Anabaptists of Luther's century, Spirit baptism with the evidence of tongues appears to have been a familiar phenomenon. In discussing the baptism of adult believers in water, Menno Simons (1496-1556) wrote: "You are plainly taught that Peter commanded that those only should be baptized who had received the Holy Ghost, who spoke with tongues and glorified God, which only pertains to the believing, and not to minor children." Today's followers of Menno Simons are the Mennonites, and they are in the tradition of the Anabaptists of the Reformation era.

The ministry of the Holy Spirit to baptize, and to divinely empower to serve, was the special emphasis of a group of Protestants in France known as the Camisards or Cevenal Prophets (also spelled Cevennol, Chevennol, Cevenol). Under Louis XIV, who from 1685 sought to bring all France under Catholicism, the Camisards were fiercely persecuted. As adult Christians were destroyed, banished, or forced to recant, leadership of the movement, on a charismatic, mystical, prophetic basis, fell upon youths and even little children. In the final decade of the 17th century, some 8,000 followers were designated as Pentecostal prophets, and since most were youthful, they were known as the "little prophets." Speakers sometimes remained in ecstatic trances for hours, prophesying both in vernacular and in classic and foreign languages. Although by 1710, the Camisards were almost annihilated by their persecutors, a remnant took refuge in England, and they are thought to have become recruits for George Fox and his Quakers. It is noted that the Camisard movement was marred by excesses and non-Biblical behavior and beliefs.

In the 17th century, a branch of the Dutch Baptists known as Collegiants or Rhynsburgers reacted against what they took to be excessive clerical leadership. They developed the ministry of "prophetic openings" which involved the pursuit of a personal infilling and empowering of the Spirit in Pentecostal fashion. Driven from Holland as heretics, they too contributed to the development of the Quakers and also the Ranters and the Seekers. The Quakers, founded by George Fox and arising about 1650, freely manifested aspects of Pentecostalism as they sought the guidance of God through the "inner light." Both the Quakers and the Ranters expected to undergo experiences in which "the power of the Lord" compelled them "to weep, sing, or speak." A Quaker named Burrough reported a meeting of the Society of Friends: "We spake with new tongues as the Lord gave utterance, and as His Spirit led us."

The Shakers emerged from the Camisards and the Quakers beginning about 1758. Under the leadership of Mother Ann Lee (1736-1784), they migrated to North America and established a colony in New York State in 1774. Tongues became a normal part of Shaker religious experience, and on one occasion under formal examination by learned critics, Mother Ann demonstrated the ability to speak in 72 different languages. An eye witness, visiting a Shaker meeting in 1780, reported that in worship some sang "without words, and some with an unknown tongue . . . and some with a mixture of English." Unfortunately, there was a good deal in Shakerism that was unbiblical, and the sect has virtually died. However, also in the 18th century, even some of the conservatively orthodox Moravians, the followers of Count Nikolaus von Zinzendorf, appear to have come under the sway of Pentecostalism. History notes that in 1722, a group of Moravians in England were formally charged with reviving the "ancient Montanist heresy of tongues."

Historic Methodism, arising in 1739 under the leadership of John Wesley, gave definite support to a doctrine of Spirit baptism. It was Wesley's view that believers could enjoy a definite experience subsequent to conversion; he spoke of a "second blessing." Although Wesley did not clearly identify the second blessing with the baptism of the Holy Spirit, nor did he designate tongues as evidence of the baptism, the fact that he dealt with these topics and accepted them as part of Christian belief constitutes a vital step forward in Pentecostal backgrounds. Wesley defended the spiritual experiences of the Camisards, and he wrote of his own pursuit of stirring spiritual experiences. Methodist history tells of a prayer meeting involving John and Charles Wesley and George Whitefield in which all three of them were cast to the floor in a dramatic visitation of divine power.

Probably the greater emphasis in Wesley's Methodism was on the Holy Spirit in His role as sanctifier and producer of spiritual fruit, rather than on His role as baptizer in the Pentecostal sense. Wesley once wrote: "The Holy Ghost enables men to speak in tongues," but it was his personal preference to avoid conspicuous physical manifestations. Not all of his followers were equally as conservative. In 1750, Thomas Walsh, a well-known Methodist preacher, wrote: "This morning the Lord gave me a language that I knew not of, raising my soul to Him in a wonderful manner." Such breadth of understanding and scope of achievement made Methodism a seedbed of Pentecostalism, even though, in itself it never was a Pentecostal movement. One observer comments: "The Pentecostal movement is Methodism brought to its ultimate consequences." Kerr writes: "If we cannot hear tongues in the noises of the Wesleyan revivals, we can hear the murmurs which will soon put the Pentecostal experience back into the picture."[5]

Spirit Baptism in the 19th and 20th Centuries

In the 19th century, a distinctively Pentecostal denomination known as the Catholic Apostolic Church emerged. It was founded in 1832 by the followers of Edward Irving (1792-1834), and although he was not an accepted leader of the denomination, he was certainly its most illustrious member. The Catholic Apostolic Church was committed to Pentecostalism, but it allowed unbiblical doctrines and practices and, by most standards, it gave undue respect to ceremony and formality, and it developed an unrealistic concept of church government. Only a remnant of its churches survived into the 20th century, but it is likely that some of its adherents became recruits for other Pentecostal denominations that emerged. Many scholars are convinced that the Catholic Apostolic Church had a far greater impact in its day, and also upon subsequent history, than is popularly recognized.

By his writings and preaching, Edward Irving did a great deal to popularize Pentecostalism in the 19th century. In 1828, Irving published a work titled *On the Restoration of Spiritual Gifts*. The message of this publication is credited with launching what could be considered a Pentecostal revival in Scotland. The *Glasgow Herald*, June 18, 1830, spoke of "miracles of speaking in unknown tongues . . . the miraculous healing of the sick, and the attempt to make the lame walk without crutches." These events emboldened Irving to begin promoting Pentecostalism in his Regent Square Church in London, England. He proceeded to teach that the "standing sign" of the baptism in the Holy Spirit was speaking in tongues. Irving's ministry was cut short by denominational censure and expulsion (he had been a minister of the Church of Scotland), followed by his premature death, but he may be counted an influential 19th-century Pentecostal.

In the United States, the Presbyterian-sponsored Kentucky camp meetings encouraged a wide variety of spiritual demonstrations and manifestations in the early 19th century. It was in this setting that James McGready and Charles G. Finney first became known. Surviving accounts seem to portray an exceptionally vigorous practice and belief in matters concerning the Holy Spirit. Beginning in 1824, a branch of Seventh-Day Adventists, known as "Gift Adventists," flourished in New England with a commitment to Pentecostal phenomena. And around the world, in Russia, there was a stirring revival beginning in 1855 that led to a Spirit-baptized, tongues-speaking community in the region of the Black Sea. The followers of this movement were known as Molokans. Many of these Russian-Armenians later emigrated to North America and brought their Pentecostal beliefs with them.

A further impetus to denominational Pentecostalism was provided by Congregational "perfectionism" in the early 19th century, and the Holiness movements that emerged out of Methodism following midcentury. In 1867, a total of 67 national camp meetings under Holiness auspices were reported in the United States. The expression "baptism of the Holy Spirit" was popularly used, and it was taken to be a definite experience subsequent to salvation. However, this baptism was generally seen as a sanctifying rather than an empowering experience, and there was no particular role for tongues; but at least Spirit baptism was an experience to be sought as a "second blessing."

The testimony of evangelist-educator Charles G. Finney (1792-1875) may be taken as typical of 19th-century interpretations. He wrote of events that occurred in his life in 1825 and declared: "I received a mighty baptism of the Holy Ghost." Finney's associate at Oberlin College, Asa Mahan, in 1870 published a volume titled *The Baptism of the Holy Ghost*, which depicted Spirit baptism as a life-changing experience subsequent to conversion. After a careful scholarly review of this era, Donald Dayton concludes:

One can find in the late nineteenth century holiness thought and life every significant feature of pentecostalism. The major exception would be the gift of tongues, but even there the ground had been well prepared.[6]

By 1900, there were at least 23 Holiness denominations in North America. A number used the word *Pentecostal* in their denominational name. As already noted, by "Pentecostal" or "Spirit-baptized" they meant "committed to holiness," but so much talk about Spirit baptism inevitably led to other applications. The account by evangelist D. L. Moody (1837-1899) telling how he was filled with the Spirit in answer to prayer, or the report by the widely read devotional author, Samuel Chadwick, telling how in 1882 God led him to Pentecost, parallel the testimony of many of today's denominational Pentecostals. Although it was not the case that Holiness denominations as such became Pentecostal, they served significantly in encouraging Christian thinking and practice in a manner that made Pentecostalism more acceptable to many whom they influenced. In the words of Samarin: "Pentecostalism is a daughter of the holiness movement, but an errant one. . . ." It should be noted that in the 20th century, Holiness groups have sometimes constituted Pentecostalism's most confirmed foes.

Local church groups committed to Pentecostal belief and practice began appearing in North America in the late 19th century. In some cases, old-world immigrants with Pentecostal commitments added to the trend. However, the majority of 19th-century Pentecostal churches that arose in North America were from previously existing groups that simply added Pentecostalism. Among them were occasional Holiness, Methodist, Baptist, and Swedish Mission groups, but many had been independent and interdenominational. Centers in which a Pentecostal-style church was operating in the 19th century include: an unnamed community in Maine, 1873; Adelaide Grove and Providence, Rhode Island, 1875; Delaware, Ohio, 1890; Moorland, Minnesota, 1892; Greenville, South Carolina, 1894; Windsor, North Carolina, 1895; Murphy and Cherokee

County, North Carolina, 1896; Greenfield, South Dakota, 1896; Audubon, Minnesota, 1897; Grafton, North Dakota, 1898; Benah, Tennessee, 1899; and Lake Eunice, Minnesota, 1899.

By the beginning of the 20th century, the stage had been set to respond to a pivotal event that would elevate Pentecostalism from a local and personal experience to an overall basic theological system. Such an event occurred on New Year's Day, 1901, in the Bethel Bible School of Topeka, Kansas. The students, numbering about 40, had been assigned by their principal, Rev. Charles Fox Parham, (1873-1929), a Holiness evangelist, to determine the Biblical evidence for the baptism in the Holy Spirit. They had concluded that tongues were the evidence, and the Pentecostal experience of a coed student, Miss Agnes N. Ozman (later Agnes LaBerge), in the New Year's prayer meeting confirmed their conclusions. Other students received also, and classes were suspended while the entire school set forth to proclaim the new message. It is noted that while the school was interdenominational, most of the students were from Holiness backgrounds.

In the next few years, Parham and his students experienced varying results in their Pentecostal outreach. However, significant revivals occurred in Galena, Kansas, and Alvin, Texas. In this latter community, in a few weeks, 134 persons received a Pentecostal experience and spoke in tongues. Thus, Texas became a Pentecostal stronghold, and—according to one estimate—by 1905 there were scores of preachers and hundreds of Pentecostal believers in the state. Nevertheless, in these years, revivals also occurred in Ohio and Missouri and other central and southern states.

The celebrated Azusa Mission of Los Angeles, California, was an outgrowth of the Topeka revival that was transmitted by way of Texas. Although the Los Angeles outpouring began in the home of a Baptist minister, it soon moved to the nondescript meeting place known as the Azusa Mission—a former stable and one-time Methodist church. Leadership in the Azusa Mission was by William J. Seymour, a black ex-Holiness preacher, and more recently a student under Parham in Texas. The mission began in 1906 and operated in that capacity for only about 3 years (someone has counted "1,000 days"), but in that period it served as a center in which numerous future Pentecostal leaders received their personal Pentecost. The schedule provided three meetings each day, with an emphasis on worship, prayer, and seeking the baptism of the Spirit rather than on preaching.

Today, at least 26 Pentecostal denominations, out of approximately 40 in North America whose origins are available for study, trace their beginnings to the Azusa Mission. The revival at the mission was encouraged by correspondence with Evan Roberts of the Welsh revival during the same era. Indirectly, events in Los Angeles led to the acceptance of Pentecostalism by N. J. Holmes of the "Altamont Bible School" of Greenville, South Carolina. The school, later named for Holmes, became a bastion of the Pentecostal Holiness denomination.

The message of the baptism in the Holy Spirit was chiefly directed to existing churches and believers, and therefore its spread was a matter of proselytizing. Not surprisingly, tensions and hostility often developed. In many cases, existing congregations and denominations rejected those of their number who accepted Pentecostalism. The World Christian Fundamental Association, meeting in Chicago in 1928, formally went on record as denying any connection with the "tongue-talkers." Pentecostals, of necessity, proceeded to found new churches and Christian institutions to replace those that were no longer available to them. By 1909, there were Pentecostal churches in widely scattered places in North America, plus various centers in England, the Netherlands, India, and Scandinavia. In the second decade of the 20th century, most of the larger Pentecostal denominations were founded. By 1970, according to P. S. Brewster, on a worldwide basis there were well over 20 million Pentecostals.

A new stream of latter-day Pentecostalism emerged in 1960 from St. Mark's Episcopal Church in Van Nuys, California. The Episcopal rector, Dennis J. Bennett, had quietly encouraged Pentecostal prayer groups for some months. By the time the movement came into the open in April 1960, it included eight Episcopal ministers and nearly 100 laymen. Denominational opposition scattered the principals, and further expanded the movement, so that followers were recruited in many of the historic denominations, including the Roman Catholic Church. The term *charismatics* typically is used for these Christians who have embraced Pentecostalism, but who have remained in their historic denominations. In the early 1970s, an investigator reported charismatics in at least 40 different denominations.

Leadership for some charismatics is primarily in the hands of their denominational society (e.g., Presbyterian Charismatic Communion), but most identify with interdenominational societies, leaders, and publishing houses. Until 1966, Jean Stone and the Blessed Trinity Society gave general leadership. Since that time a variety of groups have become rallying centers. These include: Full Gospel Business Men's Fellowship International, Oral Roberts University, Christian Growth Ministries, Fountain Trust, and Melodyland Christian Center. Publishers include some of the above plus Logos International and Charismatic Renewal Services.

Catholic Pentecostals comprise the largest charismatic group in one denomination. Catholic charismatic renewal is associated with Duquesne University beginning in 1966, and Notre Dame University beginning in 1967. By the mid 1970's there were an estimated 300,000 American Catholic Pentecostals, and significant numbers elsewhere around the world. Annual Catholic Pentecostal conferences at Notre Dame University have seen scores of thousands in attendance.

The charismatic movement has greatly enlarged the circle of those committed to the baptizing ministry of the Spirit with Pentecostal signs following. However, most charismatics remain in their denominations rather than join classical Pentecostal churches. Some charismatics identify with theological schools of the Calvinist-Reformed camp. They differ significantly from traditional Wesleyan-Holiness convictions of most classical Pentecostals. Some charismatics hold reservations in regard to classical Pentecostalism's commitment to literal fundamentalism. Thus, fellowship and identification between charismatics and classical Pentecostals is on the basis of what they hold in common. At least to the present, it is by no means a matter of overall theological and practical agreement.

8

The Nature and Evidence of Spirit Baptism

The expression "baptism in the Spirit" is today freely associated with Pentecostalism, and even many of those who reject the doctrine understand what this term means to Pentecostals. Nevertheless, there is something of a controversy involving these words, since Christians define them differently. A review of scriptural intimations and the direct teaching of the Bible concerning the baptism in the Holy Spirit becomes necessary.

The Nature of Spirit Baptism

Pentecostals generally understand the word *baptism* to be derived from a root that connotes a complete overwhelming or an enveloping on all sides which is the result of being dipped or plunged into a suitable medium. The use of the word to describe the state of a ship that is sinking is a historical usage that is typically cited. Thus, when the word *baptism* is associated with the believer's experience in his relationship to the Holy Spirit, it conveys the idea of a saturation of the inner being of a human by the heavenly divine Being. The believer yields himself to the unhindered operation of the Spirit, so that he is motivated and controlled by One beyond himself. As a believer, he is already indwelt by the Spirit, now in Spirit baptism he allows the Spirit to take complete control. Holder describes Spirit baptism as the occasion when "one is immersed and soaked in the environment, influence, power and essence of the Spirit of God. It is an experience of the coming upon one of the Spirit, filling the being, and taking possession of the yielded life."[1]

When one is baptized in the Spirit, he experiences a foretaste of God's overshadowing that one day will transfer him into the pattern of the divine: "[God] hath also sealed us, and given the earnest of the Spirit in our hearts" (2 Corinthians 1:22); "That holy Spirit of promise . . . is the earnest of our inheritance until the redemption of the purchased possession" (Ephesians 1:13, 14). The believer has thus attained a vital milestone in his progress in granting full ascendancy to the Spirit. "If ye live after the flesh, ye shall die: but if ye through the Spirit do mortify the deeds of the body, ye shall live" (Romans 8:13).

Spirit baptism has been called "the beginning of a great adventure in the Christian living called 'life in the Spirit.' " Frequently, Spirit baptism is the opening of the door to a whole new Christian experience, particularly in relating the believer to the living Christ. Although the merits of Christ's sacrifice on Calvary are judicially reckoned to the believer as a sovereign act of divine grace, the ultimate earthly experience of these provisions especially relates to Spirit baptism. It is always recognized, of course, that this remarkable personal experience is based and founded upon Christ's victory on Calvary.

Pentecostals hold that when the Spirit baptizes, He so completely overwhelms that He takes control of the subject's tongue. Scripture depicts the tongue as "an unruly evil" (James 3:8); implying that it is the bodily organ that most expresses man's rebellion against God. Neurosurgeons note that the speech centers are the dominant areas of the brain, and if God is to control man's brain, He must control the speech centers. The events that occurred on the Day of Pentecost are held to be the pattern for centuries to come. The "Golden Text of Pentecostalism" reports: "And they were all filled with the Holy Ghost, and began to speak with other tongues, as the Spirit gave them utterance" (Acts 2:4). Jesus had promised: "He that believeth on me, . . . out of his belly [innermost being] shall flow rivers of living water. (But this spake he of the Spirit)" (John 7:38, 39).

The experience of Spirit baptism is designated by various names in the New Testament: "the promise of the Father" (Luke 24:49); being "baptized with the Holy Ghost" (Acts 1:5);

"the gift of the Holy Ghost" (2:38); God's act to "pour out of my Spirit upon all flesh" (2:17); an occasion when believers "received the Holy Ghost" (8:17); when "the Holy Ghost fell on . . . them" (10:44); when they "were all filled with the Holy Ghost" (2:4); and, "the Holy Ghost came on them" (19:6; cf. 1:8). Because God's people "have received the Holy Ghost" (10:47), according to God's promise they are "endued with power from on high" (Luke 24:49). God has acted and He "hath shed forth this" (Acts 2:33). The many scriptural formulas make very clear that Spirit baptism is truly a divine visitation, and not a self-induced emotional state.

But there is often an emotional quality to Spirit baptism. For many, it is an occasion of stirring personal rapture that transports from the earthly realm to the heavenly. The fact that the Spirit is said to "fall upon" recipients suggests the possibility of being forcefully seized. The frequent emphasis on the fullness of the Spirit underscores the liberality of God's bestowment. As the human reacts to such spiritual abundance, the physical is often pressed to the limits of its endurance. However, most Pentecostals are quick to point out that the reactions of the flesh are not in themselves manifestations of the Spirit. Some charismatics deliberately minimize emotional aspects of Spirit baptism. It has been said: "When the Holy Spirit moves, the destination is more important than the emotion."

It is noted that the Greek word *ecsistanto* (i.e., ecstasy) is twice used in Scripture (Acts 2:7, 12) to describe those who reacted to speaking in tongues, but it is never used to describe those who spoke in tongues. In strict usage, the word *ecstasy* denotes "a human mood of high elevation," and it is not wholly appropriate to describe the spiritual transport of the Spirit-filled believer.

Evangelical theologians who do not accept the Pentecostal position, nevertheless frequently hold definite opinions concerning the infilling of the Spirit. Talbot wrote: "Does the man who is filled with the Spirit have more of the Spirit than the man who is not? No; rather, the Spirit has more of some Christians than He does of others."[2] Cambron states:

A better word or thought for "filling" is "controlled by" the Spirit.

Thus, the Christian is admonished to be controlled by, to be possessed by, to be dominated by the Spirit. . . . It is not how much of the Holy Spirit one has, but how much of one the Holy Spirit has.[3]

It is evident that Bible believers in general recognize that to be full of God's Spirit is to leave no room for the individual's assertion of himself.

The Biblical Precedents of Spirit Baptism

Although some critics of Pentecostalism (e.g., James D. G. Dunn) try to limit relevant Scripture passages by attempting to trace a course of "salvation-history" in the Gospels, Pentecostals typically reject such restrictions. The whole New Testament is relevant as the theological and experiential foundation for those who comprise the Christian Church. Thus, five events in the Book of Acts become the Biblical precedents of Spirit baptism:

1. *The Day of Pentecost* (Acts 2:1-13). The 120 were filled with the Holy Spirit after having been together for a week or longer in prayer and Christian fellowship. External signs included "a sound from heaven as a rushing mighty wind," "cloven tongues like as of fire," and "they . . . began to speak in other tongues, as the Spirit gave them utterance" (Acts 2:2-4). The outcome of the Pentecostal experience was an enthusiastic witnessing service among the Jerusalem pilgrims. Peter's sermon on the occasion led to the conversion of 3,000. He declared that the Pentecostal experience was intended to be shared and participated in by all believers:

Repent, and be baptized . . . and ye shall receive the gift of the Holy Ghost. For the promise is unto you, and to your children, and to all that are afar off, even as many as the Lord our God shall call (Acts 2:38, 39).

Those who were gathered in one place with one accord did not receive the Holy Spirit until the Day of Pentecost because that was the day God had chosen to launch the new phase of the redemptive ministry of Christ foretold by the prophet Joel (cf. Acts 2:16-21). There is some evidence that the Day of Pentecost was considered to commemorate the giving of the Law at Sinai and the establishment of the old covenant with Israel. Whereas tongues as a sign were repeated in later outpourings of the Spirit, the signs of the sound as of a wind and tongues like as of fire were not. The wind and fire were preludes to the continuing evidence of tongues. It was warranted that special events accompany the inauguration of a new era in the Church, but the long-range normative sign that was always repeated was tongues. Peter noted that at Caesarea "the Holy Ghost fell on them, as on us at the beginning" (Acts 11:15).

2. *The outpouring in Samaria* (Acts 8:14-19). The ministry of Philip, the recently appointed deacon (he is also known as Philip the evangelist), resulted in "miracles and signs." However, the bestowment of Spirit baptism in Samaria awaited the ministry of the apostles, Peter and John. These commissioned senior workers personally traveled to Samaria and proceeded to pray for the converts. "Then laid they their hands on them, and they received the Holy Ghost" (8:17). The descriptive language and procedures are consistent with other reports of the Holy Spirit's outpouring. Tongues are not mentioned, but they certainly are inferred. Simon's action in offering money to buy the gift of laying on of hands is evidence that the effect of the procedure was outwardly demonstrable.

3. *The baptism of Saul of Tarsus* (Acts 9:17, 18). This incident, though often cited, is inconclusive. Ananias' ministry was to assure that Saul should "be filled with the Holy Ghost" (v. 17), but it is not clear that, when he "arose and was baptized" (v. 18), this baptismal event was a baptism in the Spirit. However, for Ananias' prophesied mission to be complete it was necessary for Saul to be Spirit-baptized. It is certainly known that Saul (or Paul) did receive (cf., "I thank my God, I speak with tongues more than ye all," 1 Corinthians 14:18), but when and how the event occurred is not specifically reported.

4. *The outpouring in Caesarea* (Acts 10:44-46). The "kinsmen and near friends" of Cornelius listened responsively to Peter's report of the ministry and commission of Jesus Christ. "While Peter yet spake these words, the Holy Ghost fell on them which heard the word" (10:44). On this occasion, Gentiles

received the gift of the Holy Spirit, and the Jewish believers who were with Peter "heard them speak with tongues and magnify God" (10:46). Apparently these Caesareans received Jesus Christ as their Saviour during the course of Peter's sermon, and by the time the sermon was over they were also baptized in the Holy Spirit. It is noted that Cornelius was not baptized in water until after he had received the Spirit and spoken in tongues.

5. *The baptism of the Ephesians* (Acts 19:1-7). The disciples of Apollos, the Alexandrian Jew, knew only John's baptism until Paul came with the Pentecostal message. Although these disciples were believers, their information concerning Christian truth was incomplete. Following water baptism "in the name of the Lord Jesus" (no doubt preceded by appropriate teaching), "Paul . . . laid his hands upon them, the Holy Ghost came on them; and they spake with tongues, and prophesied" (19:6). This event took place approximately 23 years after the original Pentecost, and it was near the end of Paul's missionary ministry. Conn comments: "The nations were different; the habitudes were different; the preachers were different; the circumstances were different; but the blessing was the same."[4]

An overall pattern from these individual reports relates to the number of a given group who can expect to be baptized in the Spirit. At Pentecost they were all filled (Acts 2:4); at Samaria those received who submitted to the laying on of hands (8:17); at Caesarea the Spirit "fell on them which heard the word" (10:44); and at Ephesus the inference is that there were 12 men, and all 12 received. The Biblical pattern thus encourages all members of a group to expect to receive Spirit baptism. The groups of Biblical times were already specially selected and specially prepared, but within these limitations, it can be said that Scripture minimizes qualifying conditions for receiving Spirit baptism. The emphasis is on receiving a Gift, not on measuring one's personal worth.

The Purposes and Results of Spirit Baptism

The baptism in the Holy Spirit constitutes the candidate's first experience of entire yieldedness to God. The believer thus

Occasion	Tongues reported?	Preceding prayer?	Laying on of hands?	Chief minister	Type of subjects
Day of Pentecost Acts 2:1-13	yes	yes	no	The ascended Christ	Christian Jews
Samaria Acts 8:14-19	no, but inferred	yes	yes	Peter and John	Samari- tans
Saul of Tarsus Acts 9:17, 18	not at this time	yes	yes	Ananias	Christian Jew
Caesarea Acts 10:44-46	yes	no	no	Peter	Gentiles
Ephesus Acts 19:1-7	yes	no	yes	Paul	Christian Jews

Figure 7. A summary of five Spirit baptisms reported in the Book of Acts.

learns the degree of yieldedness to which God responds. This experience is meant to be the beginning of the believer's deeper spiritual life, and it marks the occasion when he is "possessed by a master passion." God is granted admission to His temple in the human soul, and He is invited to pervade every chamber of it. There is an unrestrained reciprocal relationship between personalities, providing a new sense of intimacy between God and the believer. In a very real sense, Spirit baptism is not Spirit-centered, but God-centered and Christ-centered. The door is now opened to the highest attainments of the Christian life, including the gifts of the Spirit (1 Corinthians 12:7-11). The fruit of the Spirit (Galatians 5:22, 23) ought to become increasingly dominant in the life of the Spirit-filled believer.

Among the particular results of being baptized in the Spirit and learning to submit one's life to His presence and ministry are:

1. *A new relationship with Jesus Christ:* "He shall glorify me: for he shall receive of mine, and shall show it unto you" (John 16:14); "No man can say that Jesus is the Lord, but by the Holy Ghost" (1 Corinthians 12:3).

2. *A new enthusiasm to glorify God:* "We do hear them speak in our tongues the wonderful works of God" (Acts 2:11; cf. 10:46).

3. *A new effectiveness in witnessing:* "They were all filled with the Holy Ghost, and they spake the word of God with boldness. . . . And with great power gave the apostles witness of the resurrection of the Lord Jesus" (Acts 4:31, 33); "But ye shall receive power, after that the Holy Ghost is come upon you: and ye shall be witnesses . . ." (1:8).

4. *An expanded prayer life:* "I will pray with the spirit" (1 Corinthians 14:15).

5. *New insights into Biblical truth:* "The things of God knoweth no man, but the Spirit of God" (1 Corinthians 2:11); "But the Comforter, which is the Holy Ghost . . . shall teach you all things, and bring all things to your remembrance" (John

14:26); "Howbeit when he, the Spirit of truth is come, he will guide you into all truth" (16:13).

6. *New Christlikeness:* "But we . . . beholding in a glass the glory of the Lord, are changed into the same image . . . by the Spirit of the Lord" (2 Corinthians 3:18); "Great grace was upon them all" (Acts 4:33).

7. *A new assurance:* "God . . . hath also sealed us, and given the earnest of the Spirit in our hearts" (2 Corinthians 1:33).

8. *A new spiritual usefulness:* "The manifestation of the Spirit is given to every man to profit withal" (1 Corinthians 12:7).

9. *New freedom in worship:* "Where the Spirit of the Lord is, there is liberty" (2 Corinthians 3:17).

10. *Power for miracles:* "Through mighty signs and wonders, by the power of the Spirit of God" (Romans 15:19).

The value of baptism in the Spirit particularly emerges as the walk in the Spirit follows. Hathcoat points out concerning Spirit baptism: "It is not a goal we have reached, but a gate we have entered. It is not graduation in the Spirit's knowledge, but matriculation in his school."[5] The experience transformed lives in Biblical times, and it still does so today.

Receiving the Baptism in the Holy Spirit

Most evangelical believers agree:1) Christians ought to be filled with the Spirit, and 2) God is eager to bestow the Spirit. R. A. Torrey once wrote: "We are abundantly warranted in saying that every child of God is under the most solemn obligation to see to it that he definitely receives the Holy Spirit . . . as a definite enduement with power."[6] According to Scripture, God bestows the infilling Spirit in a variety of ways: He gives Him (Luke 11:13); He sends Him (John 14:16); He ministers Him (Galatians 3:5); He pours Him out (Proverbs 1:23); and He puts Him upon believers (Isaiah 59:21). Clearly, the fullness of the Holy Spirit is meant to be God's gift to believers, for Scripture says more about how the Lord will give than how seekers should receive. Nevertheless, the Gift is a divine Person, who in effect intends to possess the recipient. Thus, from the human point of view, one may speak of conditions and procedures that relate to the Spirit's infilling. One or more of the following is suggested:

1. *Repentance.* "Then Peter said unto them, Repent, and be baptized every one of you . . . and ye shall receive the gift of the Holy Ghost" (Acts 2:38). The Spirit baptizes no one without that person's consent and, for many, repentance is an important evidence of that consent. In one of its aspects, repentance involves a change of mind. A seeker may need to be appropriately instructed before he knows how to repent and how to open his heart and life before God. Jesus said of the Holy Spirit: "Whom the world cannot receive" (John 14:17). One evidence of thoroughgoing repentance in the convert is water baptism, and this fact was noted by Peter. It is not that water baptism is set forth as a condition for receiving Spirit baptism, but the same change of heart and will that motivates the convert to be baptized in water also prepares him to receive the baptism in the Holy Spirit.

2. *Faith.* "That the blessing of Abraham might come on the Gentiles through Jesus Christ; that we might receive the promise of the Spirit through faith" (Galatians 3:14). Peter had said: "The promise is unto you, and to your children, and to all that are afar off" (Acts 2:39). The baptizing Holy Spirit is not an object of faith, but rather faith is the process by which that which Christ has promised is possessed by the believer. It is not a matter of earning or meriting the Holy Spirit, but simply receiving Him. The disciples were instructed: "Wait for the promise of the Father, which saith he [i.e., Jesus], ye have heard of me" (Acts 1:4). It is significant that there are many promises to the believer, but only one is called "the promise." For the Christian, it is always ultimately true that the object of faith is Jesus Christ, and in receiving Spirit baptism He is received as the divine Baptizer. Before Paul laid hands on the disciples at Ephesus, he took care to explain: "That they should believe on . . . Christ Jesus" (Acts 19:4). In effect, the condi-

tions necessary to salvation—repentance and faith—are also the conditions for Spirit baptism.

3. *Obedience.* ". . . the Holy Ghost, whom God hath given to them that obey him" (Acts 5:32). Within the scope of obedience is included not only externals such as water baptism, but also the inner attitudes of the heart in submissive obedience, and death of the self-life. In one sense, obedience is an effect more than a cause. When one totally submits his heart, then he is obedient and at the same time he is a candidate for the Spirit's fullness. The exhortation: "Be filled with the Spirit" (Ephesians 5:18), is a passive imperative that indicates there is One to whom believers must submit. Mary's words to the servants apply to those seeking the infilling: "Whatsoever he saith unto you, do it" (John 2:5). Mooth writes: "When the self-life expires, the fullness of the Spirit comes in as naturally as air rushes into a vacuum. . . . This 'death of self' is the gateway to the Spirit-filled life."[7] It should be noted that the desired submissive obedience is not identical with passivity. Actually, the seeker should actively cooperate with the direction and control of the Spirit. A favorite Pentecostal text is: "Open thy mouth wide, and I will fill it" (Psalm 81:10).

4. *Personal purity.* Paul emphasizes that defiling sin or worldliness is not compatible with the indwelling Spirit of God: "The Father . . . shall give you . . . the Spirit of truth; whom the world cannot receive" (John 14:16, 17); "Know ye not that ye are the temple of God, and that the Spirit of God dwelleth in you?" (1 Corinthians 3:16; cf. 6:19). It has been well said: "God does not require golden vessels, neither does He seek for silver ones, but He must have clean ones." However, it should also be realized that the personal purity God requires is not mere human works, but His gift of holiness to the surrendered and obedient life. Christians are intended to be "partakers of his holiness" (Hebrews 12:10), and with Isaiah they can testify: "He hath clothed me with the garments of salvation, he hath covered me with the robe of righteousness" (Isaiah 61:10). Thus, the seeker for the Spirit's infilling is not prescribed a regimen of works as a qualification for receiving, but rather encouraged to validate faith by a repudiation of his

carnal self and the immediate appropriation of Christ's righteousness and holiness. "Of him are ye in Christ Jesus, who of
God is made unto us wisdom, and righteousness, and sanctification, and redemption" (1 Corinthians 1:30).

5. *Wholehearted desire.* One expresses desire by asking.
Thus, Jesus taught: "How much more shall your heavenly
Father give the Holy Spirit to them that ask him" (Luke 11:13).
As a background to this promise, He had given the parable of
the importunate (i.e., one who asks persistently) friend, and
had exhorted: "Ask, and it shall be given you; seek, and ye shall
find; knock, and it shall be opened unto you" (Luke 11:9). In
similar vein, on the occasion of the ceremony at the Feast of
Tabernacles: "Jesus stood and cried, saying, If any man thirst,
let him come unto me and drink. . . . But this spake he of the
Spirit" (John 7:37, 39). The term *thirst* is a common Biblical
term to describe the heart attitude that the seeker is encouraged
to manifest (cf. Psalm 42:1-3).

The original 120 were "with one accord in prayer and supplication [i.e., humble petition]" (Acts 1:14) while they awaited
the promised enduement of power from on high (Luke 24:49).
The fact that they persisted for several days is clear evidence of
their wholehearted desire. Because seekers prayerfully desired Spirit baptism at Samaria (Acts 8:15, 17), and at Ephesus
(19:6), they sought the laying-on-of-hands ministry of the apostles. At Caesarea, Peter "went in, and found many that were
come together" (10:27). Here were people specifically seeking
something from God under the leadership of Cornelius who
"prayed to God alway" (10:2), and even while Peter preached,
their desire was satisfied in Spirit baptism.

6. *The Spirit of praise.* In preparing their hearts for the Day
of Pentecost, the disciples "were continually in the temple,
praising and blessing God" (Luke 24:35). At Caesarea, the
Jewish observers "heard them speak with tongues, and magnify God" (Acts 10:46). The outpouring of the Spirit there was
clearly related to an audible verbal expression of praise to God.
Praise is the special sacrifice-gift that all Christians, including
those seeking Spirit baptism, can offer God. "Let us offer the

sacrifice of praise to God continually, that is, the fruit of our lips giving thanks in his name" (Hebrews 13:15). Pentecostal writers often speak of "the gates of praise," for they see heartfelt praise to God as a gateway to an unhindered relationship with Him. Seekers of the baptism in the Holy Spirit are advised first to pray until prayer is a joyfully free communication with God, and then to continue to pray until prayer becomes praise that is natural, wholehearted, and spontaneous.

The Role of Laying on of Hands

The practice of the laying on of hands, or the "imposition" of hands upon those seeking Spirit baptism has ample scriptural precedents. It has already been noted that imposition is associated with three of the five instances of Spirit baptism in Acts. Twice in writing to Timothy, Paul mentions the laying on of hands (1 Timothy 4:14; 2 Timothy 1:6), although these references refer to spiritual gifts rather than to Spirit baptism. In all, there are 30 New Testament references to imposition, and it is named among the basic principles of Christian doctrine: "Therefore leaving the principles of the doctrine of Christ, let us go on unto perfection; not laying again the foundation of repentance from dead works, . . . of the doctrine of baptisms, and of laying on of hands" (Hebrews 6:1, 2).

Since two of the five instances of Spirit baptism in Acts did not involve imposition, it is clear the practice lacks exclusive approval as a rite to accompany the receiving of Spirit baptism. Imposition is seen by most Protestants as ceremonial and external rather than functionally operative. There is no actual transmission from the officiant to the subject. Mooth notes: "The laying on of hands is simply a gesture of prayer man can make; the baptism in the Spirit is an interior work of grace which only God can perform."[8] Another writes: "The laying on of hands is valid only if God lays hands on the candidate also." The New Testament portrays all believers as priests, and no human is a necessary third party in conveying the blessing of God. Even when Peter and John at Samaria exercised the ministry of imposition, they first "prayed for them, that they might receive the Holy Ghost" (Acts 8:15).

The Evidence of Spirit Baptism: Tongues

Pentecostal believers hold that speaking in tongues is the uniform, initial, outward or physical evidence of having received the baptism in the Holy Spirit. The fact of the baptism in the Holy Spirit is not uniquely a Pentecostal belief; what is unique in Pentecostalism is that tongues are the evidence of that baptism. The Biblical bases for this view are, first, the three instances in Acts when tongues are specifically associated with Spirit baptism. Added to these are the other two instances: tongues are inferred at Samaria because of Simon's eagerness to buy the gift of imposition (Acts 8:18-24); Paul's experience is inconclusive, but it is stated that the Lord Jesus sent Ananias that he might "be filled with the Holy Ghost" (Acts 9:17), and Paul later testified: "I speak with tongues more than ye all" (1 Corinthians 14:18).

At the house of Cornelius, it was tongues, and tongues only, that convinced the observers that the gift of the Spirit had been poured out in baptism:

And they of the circumcision which believed were astonished . . . because that on the Gentiles also was poured out the gift of the Holy Ghost. For they heard them speak with tongues (Acts 10:45, 46).

At the Jerusalem conference, Peter reported this event:

And as I began to speak, the Holy Ghost fell on them, as on us at the beginning. Then remembered I the word of the Lord, how that he said . . . ye shall be baptized with the Holy Ghost (11:15, 16).

Tongues, as a sign of Spirit baptism, were similarly manifested at Ephesus: "And when Paul had laid his hands upon them, the Holy Ghost came on them; and they spake with tongues, and prophesied" (19:6). Whatever other events marked the Spirit's bestowment, such as wind and tongues that looked like fire, it was only vocal tongues that these outpourings had in common.

The expressions "other tongues" or "unknown tongues" in older Bible versions, or "strange languages" or "ecstatic utterances" in contemporary versions, are all translations of the

Greek original. The word *glossolalia* is widely used as the technical equivalent of the Biblical identification, although until recently, the word often denoted an abnormal or pathological state. The prefix *glosso* (or *glossa*) means tongue, word, or language; the verbal root *lalia* means to talk, to speak, or classically, to chatter or babble. As such, the word *glossolalia* is not strictly Biblical, for in the Greek New Testament, the prefix and root are not combined, but they stand side-by-side as two words. In its connotation, "glossolalia" identifies the use of a language different from that normally used, and it constitutes "the ability to speak in a foreign language not previously learned by the tongues-speaker." The word gives scope for heavenly languages as well as earthly. Its secular counterpart, xenolalia (or sometimes xenoglossia, or xenoglossolalia) means simply foreign languages.

Evidence that Biblical tongues embody potential for actual communication, and that they are neither "nonsense syllables" nor "nonlinguistic sound hash" includes: 1) Tongues on the Day of Pentecost were understood by visitors from 15 foreign countries. These bilingual visitors inquired: "How hear we every man in our own tongue [*dialektos*] wherein we were born?" (Acts 2:8); and then they reported: "We do hear them speak in our tongues [*glossa*] the wonderful works of God" (2:11). The free interchange of *dialektos* and *glossa* in Scripture establishes their equivalence. *Dialektos* is defined as a "language of a nation or region." 2) The content of what was uttered in tongues at Caesarea was intelligible to the observing Jews: "For they heard them speak with tongues, and magnify God" (Acts 10:46). 3) Tongues must be languages that communicate, for Paul declares that they can be used to sing, pray, bless, and give thanks (1 Corinthians 14:14-17). 4) Paul teaches that prophecy is not greater than tongues if tongues are interpreted (1 Corinthians 14:15). Since the word *interpret* means "to translate a language," tongues must communicate if they are to be interpreted with a message equivalent to a prophecy.

The fact that Paul mentions "tongues of angels" (1 Corinthians 13:1) might indicate that some tongues given by the Spirit are from a realm beyond this earth. But even if a particular tongue is extraterrestrial, it is not hindered from communicating. Alice Shevkenek, discussing tongues of angels, once noted: "Isn't it fitting that we should speak to God in pure and holy language that cannot be spotted by the world with vile curses." Actually, Paul did not say he spoke with tongues of angels, but he affirmed that even though it were so, he was still responsible to exercise love. Scripture chooses not to develop further the doctrine of tongues of angels.

Carl Brumback has compiled "Seven Reasons Why God Chose Tongues"[9]: 1) It is an external evidence constituting a visible symbol of spiritual reality, 2) It is a uniform evidence since tongues are recognizable by all cultures, 3) It properly recognizes the personality of the Spirit, 4) It is a symbol of the Spirit's complete control of the believer, 5) It manifests the Holy Spirit as the believer's source of truth and utterance, 6) It signifies the honor that God has placed upon human speech, and 7) It is a foretaste of heavenly speech. William Arthur observes concerning Biblical instances of glossolalia: "Here we see the Creator taking to himself the language of every man's mother; so that in the very words wherein he heard her say, 'I love thee,' he might also hear the Father say, 'I love thee.' " The fact of other tongues in Spirit baptism reinforces the command of the Great Commission to reach all nations for Christ.

Pentecostals hold that speaking in tongues is not itself the Baptism, but only the sign or evidence. Seekers are not to seek tongues, but to seek God, and His Son, and the presence of the personal Holy Spirit. When the quest is successful, tongues are a sign both to the seeker and to those about him. The human organs of speech are at this time being controlled by the Spirit. Typically, the seeker utters coherent statements that are praises to God in a language he has not learned. On this occasion, God supernaturally tames the human tongue which God calls an "unruly evil" (James 3:8). Because speaking in tongues is the evidence, receiving Spirit baptism is a definite, deliberate, certain event. It is not a matter of "receiving the Spirit by faith," with neither evidence nor sign, but a matter of "by faith receiving the Spirit."

On Biblical grounds, tongues are a necessary and essential evidence of the baptism in the Spirit. Believers may enjoy various remarkable experiences with God and His Spirit, but if they do not speak in tongues, their experience is not the baptism in the Holy Spirit. God promised that the Biblical pattern was the standard for future times: "The promise is unto you, and to your children, and to all that are afar off" (Acts 2:39). What was true at the Day of Pentecost, and on subsequent occasions in Scripture, must continue to be true throughout the age.

However, to say that tongues are a necessary sign of Spirit baptism is not to say that in the practical long-range outcome, tongues alone are a sufficient sign. Pentecostals would insist that the Biblical pattern for spiritual virtue and growth applies to all believers, and that Spirit baptism neither conflicts with nor replaces the responsibility for overall goodness. One who has yielded to God to receive the baptism in the Holy Spirit ought from that time forth to yield to God in all that He requires and desires for His dedicated children. An experience of Spirit baptism that does not lead to a deeper walk with God is disappointing. Spirit baptism most certainly is meant to endorse and implement in the Christian's life the entire Biblical pattern of fruitful godly Christian living "unto a perfect man, unto the measure of the stature of the fulness of Christ" (Ephesians 4:13). Peter specifically related Spirit baptism to Jesus Christ: "This Jesus hath God raised up. . . . He hath shed forth this, which ye now see and hear" (Acts 2:32, 33).

9

Spirit Baptism Related to Other Spiritual Experiences

The Pentecostal view sees Spirit baptism as a distinct experience subsequent to conversion. It is a supernatural work that is highly personal and subjective. Notwithstanding, that which the believer experiences relates specifically to the overall eternal plans and program of God. Spirit baptism is not merely an occasion of special happiness or blessing, but a step in the unfolding divine purpose. By no means is Spirit baptism an end in itself. It is a means to an end; a gateway rather than a goal. No sooner is the believer baptized in the Spirit, than he must proceed to ask what the experience means in relation to his total Christian life and standing.

Spirit Baptism and Power for Service

The resurrected Christ set forth the basic promise concerning the outcome of Spirit baptism:

Ye shall receive power, after that the Holy Ghost is come upon you: and ye shall be witnesses unto me both in Jerusalem, and in all Judea, and in Samaria, and unto the uttermost part of the earth (Acts 1:8).

The enduement of power resulting from Spirit baptism was declared to be for the purpose of enabling the apostles to accomplish their evangelistic mission. Scripture reports concerning the exciting days that followed: "With great power gave the apostles witness of the resurrection of the Lord Jesus" (Acts 4:33). It was only as Spirit-baptized believers that the disciples proceeded to minister effectively. Thereafter, preaching became forceful and bold, God was honored and worshiped, and evangelism to the unsaved proceeded. They now possessed power in the sphere of the souls of humans. In a later era, Paul testified: "God has not given us the spirit of fear; but of power" (2 Timothy 1:7).

The most conspicuous immediate example of the new spiritual power of the apostles was Peter's ministry on the Day of Pentecost. Peter, who had denied his Lord less than 2 months before, now stood in the shadow of the temple and proclaimed boldly that the people had executed their long-looked-for Messiah. The sermon that Peter preached (at least as recorded by Luke) contained approximately 1,000 words, mentioned 15 major doctrines, was comprised chiefly of selected Old Testament quotations, and resulted in a harvest of 3,000 souls.

Elsewhere in Scripture, one may trace various aspects of spiritual power: power to witness (Acts 1:8), power to speak boldly and persuasively (4:8-14), power to proclaim the deity of Christ (9:17-20), power to magnify God (10:46), and power in general to work that which is profitable (1 Corinthians 12:7). The seven men who are considered the first deacons were qualified for service because they were "full of the Holy Ghost" (Acts 6:3). Although we should distinguish the Spirit's anointing power from His miracle-working power, Paul noted that Christ's enabling to him that he might reach the Gentiles was: "Through mighty signs and wonders, by the power of the Spirit of God" (Romans 15:19); and in Corinth his "speech and ... preaching was ... in demonstration of the Spirit and of power" (1 Corinthians 2:4).

Spirit baptism leads to a variety of practical results in overall Christian living. One cannot yield to receive the Spirit to indwell in His fullness without at the same time achieving a new passion for souls, a new determination to separate from the world, a new impetus for prayer, a new devotion to Scripture, and a new life of worship and praise. Cumming describes the effect of the Pentecostal experience upon believers reported in the Book of Acts:

The new life stood the test of daily duties, petty cares, and real sacrifices. The Holy Spirit had come into the home as well as into the upper room and temple court. Great grace, gladness, singleness of heart, steadfastness, liberality, sacrificing all they had and giving up their possessions—these were the features which marked the actions of the converts in daily life.[1]

Interestingly, in Old Testament times, Micah testified that the Holy Spirit gave power to deal with sin: "I am full of power by the spirit of the Lord, and of judgment, and of might, to declare unto Jacob his transgression, and to Israel his sin" (Micah 3:8).

The Pentecostal experience constitutes a "charismatic dimension," for He introduces a new supernatural economy into human life. In anticipation of the Pentecostal enduement, Jesus promised: "He that believeth on me, the works that I do shall he do also; and greater works than these shall he do; because I go unto my Father" (John 14:12). The Spirit does not impose a negative suppression on true manhood or true womanhood, but He makes it possible to fulfill the highest hopes and aspirations of God's people. Following the Day of Pentecost, the Book of Acts reports: the healing of the lame man at the temple gate (3:1-8), Peter's supernatural knowledge of the deception of Ananias and Sapphira (5:1-10), general miracles of healing (5:12-16), and the angel's release of Peter and the apostles from prison (5:17-21).

As the long-term outcome of the Spirit's outpouring in Biblical times, the disciples of Christ moved from a mere circle of comrades to an organically related body that even went so far as to hold all goods in common: "But the multitude of them that believed were of one heart and of one soul . . . but they had all things common" (Acts 4:32). A whole new missionary impetus resulted, including the setting aside of national prejudices, and culminating in the commissioning of Saul and Barnabas to an extensive international ministry. Philip's ministry in Samaria (Acts 8:5), together with that of Peter and John, represented the first of many striking triumphs over human bigotry. Spiritual power resulting from Spirit baptism was expressed, not only in the world of outsiders, but also within the Church and its people to orient and motivate them in the true outlooks of Jesus Christ.

Spirit Baptism and New Testament Terminology

The expression "baptism in the Holy Spirit" occurs a total of seven times in the New Testament: six in the Gospels and Acts, and once in the Epistles. It is not directly used to identify events on the Day of Pentecost. On these grounds, some have concluded that what happened in Acts chapter 2 was not an instance of the baptism in the Holy Spirit. However, the conventional Pentecostal outlook affirms the identity of "Spirit baptism" and being "filled with the Spirit" of Acts two on at least two grounds: 1) The ascending Jesus promised: "Ye shall be baptized with the Holy Ghost not many days hence" (Acts 1:5). Only the events in the Upper Room satisfy this promise. 2) Peter, in describing events at the house of Cornelius, recalled the Lord's promise: "John indeed baptized with water; but ye shall be baptized with the Holy Ghost" (Acts 11:16). He thus applied these words to an occasion when: ". . . they heard them speak with tongues, and magnify God" (10:46).

As Pentecostals see the Scriptures, there is a definite spiritual experience identified as the baptism in the Spirit. This experience is to be distinguished from conversion and from water baptism. It is legitimately, however, a baptism. The Pentecostal position permits no compromise with those who attempt to embrace Spirit baptism in a single redemptive process completed on the occasion of salvation, or those who deny that the experience is correctly identified as a baptism. What is meant by the baptism in the Holy Spirit is not simply a touching of the life by the Spirit, but a complete and saturating overwhelming.

At least seven New Testament passages that speak of the experience of "receiving the Holy Spirit" appear clearly to refer to the events of the Day of Pentecost (cf. John 7:39; 20:22; Acts 2:38; 8:17; 10:47; 19:2; Galatians 3:2). Parallel expressions with the same connotation include: "descending" and "coming upon" (Matthew 3:16), "descending and abiding upon" (John 1:33), and "falling upon" (Acts 8:16; 10:44; 11:15). Certain non-Pentecostal scholars affirm that the filling, outpouring, or receiving of the Spirit on the Day of Pentecost was indeed an experience of the baptism in the Spirit. Huffman has written:

"The statement 'they were all filled with the Holy Spirit' (Acts 2:4), is a historical report of the promise, 'Ye shall be baptized in the Holy Ghost not many days hence.' (Acts 1:5)."[2] Hoekema cites: "He shall baptize you with the Holy Ghost and fire" (Luke 3:16), and comments: "The obvious reference here is to the outpouring of the Spirit which is to come on the Day of Pentecost."[3]

Paul's exhortation: "Be not drunk with wine, wherein is excess; but be filled with the Spirit" (Ephesians 5:18), may be taken as an encouragement to seek either the initial baptism in the Spirit or, as a baptized believer, to practice increasing submission to the Holy Spirit. The implied subject of the exhortation is plural, and it extends to all Christians; the construction is passive and therefore the action is performed by Him and not by human effort; and it is in the present tense which implies continued action. The results of being filled with the Spirit are specifically tabulated: a spirit of joyful song, a spirit of thanksgiving, a spirit of mutual submission to fellow Christians (cf. Ephesians 5:19-21).

However, the terms *baptism* and *filling* or *infilling* are not always synonymous. Believers are baptized only once, but they are filled or refilled many times; Peter was filled in Acts 2:4 and again in 4:31 (cf. also Acts 4:8). Because the believer's relationship with the Spirit is an experience, it may be expected both to have a beginning, and also to be repeatable. The expression "filled with the Spirit" is used in a technical or formal sense when the believer initially appropriates the "promise of the Father," and on this occasion it is synonymous with "baptism." But the same expression "filled with the Spirit" identifies the later state of the believer who remains submitted and surrendered, or who periodically achieves such a state. The occasion of the Baptism is not meant to be a once-for-all experience, but the beginning of a frequently renewed and increasingly sustained relationship. Out of this understanding, the classical Pentecostal slogan declares: "One baptism, many fillings" (cf. Stephen's experience; Acts 2:4; 4:31; 6:8; 7:55). Ian Macpherson once commented: "The baptism in the Spirit is the first breath a person draws, the subsequent fillings are all the breaths that follow."

Another important distinction between expressions is to be noted. Paul writes: "By one Spirit are we all baptized into one body" (1 Corinthians 12:13). Most scholars hold that the preposition *by* denotes the personal agency of the Spirit. Thus, "baptism by the Spirit" is a different event from "baptism in, with, or of the Spirit." Someone comments: "This is the Pauline way of stating the being born again of John 3:7." R. M. Riggs wrote: "They who are Christ's have the Spirit of Christ. The Holy Spirit baptizes them into the body of Christ, and the Holy Spirit abides in their hearts." Wuest expounds on 1 Corinthians 12:13:

> The personal agent in this case who does the baptizing is the Holy Spirit. He places or introduces the believing sinner into the Body of which the Lord Jesus is the living Head. . . . The baptism by the Spirit . . . brings the believer into vital union with Jesus Christ. This means that the baptism by the Spirit is not for power, for in this baptism there is nothing applied to or given the believer. He, the believer, is placed into the Body of Christ.[4]

Those who disagree with the foregoing argue that "by" denotes the location or sphere in which the action takes place. They thereby conclude that baptism by the Spirit is not distinct from any other kind of Spirit baptism. Since Greek authorities are cited on both sides, the issue does not seem open to settlement by this means. However, parallel Scripture passages and scriptural precedents otherwise become significant. Apart from 1 Corinthians 12:13, it is not reported in Scripture that all have received Spirit baptism in the Pentecostal sense, and other instances of the preposition *by* in Scripture definitely imply personal agency. On these grounds, it appears valid to hold that "baptism by the Spirit" is another name for conversion, but Pentecostal baptism is a distinctive event.

Pentecostal Baptism Distinguished From Conversion

To distinguish "baptism in the Spirit" (or the filling or infilling of the Spirit) from "baptism by the Spirit" is to recognize two distinct Spirit baptisms. At conversion, the convert is taken by the Spirit and placed into the body of Christ. It is "baptism by the Spirit" in the sense that the Spirit is the personal agent who does the baptizing. In the Pentecostal experience, the surrendered believer is taken by Christ and placed into the all-pervading and saturating Holy Spirit; it is indeed, "baptism in the Spirit." The believer's union with Christ at conversion results because the Holy Spirit begins to indwell him so that he is a "new creature in Christ Jesus." All who share the divine life of the Spirit are members of Christ's body, and are baptized into it by the Spirit. Scripture speaks of this uniform experience as "one baptism" (Ephesians 4:5). God provides that these believers may thereupon proceed to the experience of being baptized in the Spirit.

Instances that establish that the baptism in the Spirit is subsequent to conversion include the following:

1. In his address on the Day of Pentecost, Peter exhorted: "Repent, and be baptized every one of you in the name of Jesus Christ for the remission of sins, and ye shall receive the gift of the Holy Ghost" (Acts 2:38). Repentance and the remission of sins were seen as a distinct accomplishment, to be followed later by the gift of the Holy Spirit in the pattern that the 120 had enjoyed.

2. The people of Samaria participated in a stirring revival: "But when they believed Philip preaching . . . they were baptized, both men and women" (Acts 8:12). However, it was upon these people that Peter and John laid hands that they might receive the Holy Spirit. "As yet he was fallen upon none of them: only they were baptized in the name of the Lord Jesus. Then laid they their hands on them, and they received the Holy Ghost" (8:16, 17).

3. Cornelius is described as "a devout man, and one that feared God . . . and prayed to God alway" (Acts 10:2). Clearly, he manifested a warmly genuine spiritual life. However, only after Peter's message did he and his people receive the baptism of the Holy Spirit (cf. Acts 10:44).

4. Saul of Tarsus underwent a soul-stirring, life-changing experience with God. He became submissive and prayerful in the manner of a convert. However, it was not until 3 days later that Ananias prayed for him that he might receive the Holy Spirit (cf. Acts 9:9, 11, 17).

DESIGNATION	TIME	SUBJECT	AGENT	ELEMENT	SCRIPTURE
Baptism by the Spirit	at conver-sion	penitent sinner	Holy Spirit	Body of Christ	1 Cor. 12:13
Water Baptism	after conver-sion	convert	pastor	water	Mt. 28:19
Baptism in the Spirit	after conver-sion	be-lievers	Christ	Holy Spirit	Acts 2:4

Figure 8. A comparison of three baptisms.

5. The Ephesians were gospel converts who had demonstrated their faith by being baptized in the name of the Lord Jesus. Scripture describes them as "disciples," and this term is equivalent to "Christians." Paul accepted this fact and asked: "Have ye received the Holy Ghost since ye believed?" [or literally: "Have you believed and received the Holy Spirit?"] (Acts 19:2). Only when Paul laid hands on them did they receive the Spirit in Pentecostal fashion.

Scripture is thus seen to depict two distinct experiences that are called "Spirit baptism." Jointly, they are the divine provision for the convert to appropriate within his experience the finished work of Christ. *Experience one* identifies with: baptism by the Spirit (1 Corinthians 12:13), being born of the Spirit (John 3:5), receiving the Spirit of life in Christ (Romans 8:2), assuring that the Spirit of God dwells within (Romans 8:9), or being given the earnest of the Spirit in one's heart (2 Corinthians 1:22). *Experience two* identifies with: baptism with the Spirit (Acts 1:5), being filled with the Spirit (2:4), experiencing the Spirit falling upon (10:44) or coming upon the believer (19:6), or simply receiving the Spirit (8:17).

Pentecostals would not agree with James D. G. Dunn who argues that the Greek aorist participle, when combined with the aorist verb, always indicates simultaneous action. Dunn is attempting to establish that to believe is simultaneously to receive the Holy Spirit. While it is often the case as Dunn suggests, he overlooks many scriptural constructions that would deny his theory (cf. Matthew 22:25; Acts 5:10; 13:51; 16:24). Thus, it must be maintained that Paul's words give scope for a two-part event: 1) believing, 2) receiving the Holy Spirit.[5]

The position taken by Thomas Smail (who notes that he is following F. D. Bruner) would likewise be unacceptable to Pentecostals because he too wants to deny a "second blessing" doctrine. He argues that the unity of the gospel is marred and the role of Christ obscured if "God himself is offering us two distinct gifts, first salvation and justification in Christ, and then a receiving of the Holy Spirit which adds what was lacking in the first."[6] Smail seems unable to separate the concept of legal provision and experiential appropriation, or of Jesus the Saviour and Jesus the Baptizer. The gospel can legitimately have more than one phase; Christ can provide for more than one aspect of mankind's needs. The Holy Spirit can both regenerate and baptize, and God's sovereignty just as much allows Him to baptize believers as to save sinners.

Spirit Baptism and Sanctification

One of the fruits of Spirit baptism is access into a new measure of personal holiness. Paul spoke of his ministry "being sanctified by the Holy Ghost" (Romans 15:1), and both he and Peter used the expression "sanctification of the Spirit" (cf. 2 Thessalonians 2:13; 1 Peter 1:2). Following Pentecost, Peter and John were observed by members of the Sanhedrin who "took knowledge of them, that they had been with Jesus" (Acts 4:13). The office work of the Holy Spirit is to be the personal channel to convey the mind and attitudes of Jesus Christ into the heart and life of the believer. His essential nature is emphasized by His usual title "Holy Spirit." His work would appear to be concerned with practical rather than positional sanctification—how the believer behaves rather than what Christ legally and officially declares him to be.

Most Pentecostals emphasize that the practice of personal surrender and commitment to Biblical standards are a vital aspect of the practical sanctification entailed in true Christian living. Alice Shevkenek writes: "Being filled with the Holy Spirit is no guarantee that you will bear more fruit, for the Holy Spirit is given us for power to serve, and to bear fruit you must abide in Christ, and be purged and cleansed by Him through the Word."[7] George and Harriet Gillies write: "You are no 'holier' after receiving the Baptism than you were before. But you now have the power of Jesus, the potential power, within you to overcome evil and be a witness for Christ."[8] Donald Gee took a similar stand:

The scriptural truth is that following the Baptism of the Spirit there may be a great amount of personal sanctification still needed in the believer, and this will proceed as the child of God now goes on to "walk in the Spirit." Gal. 3:2, 3, and 5:16-25. It is vain to think that any "crisis" or "blessing" or "experience" can take the place of a continual "walking" in the Spirit—however helpful such a crisis often undoubtedly be.[9]

The Holy Spirit's sanctifying operations in the believer are seen as progressive rather than instantaneous. Spiritual maturity and the overall achievement of experiential sanctification (i.e., sanctification achieved in one's experience) take time, and there is no shortcut to them. The baptism in the Spirit is the filling of the vessel rather than its cleansing. The Spirit's power to produce holiness is in proportion to the believer's measure of submission to Him in everyday life. Forgiveness of sin at conversion, and the banishment of sin in everyday living, are two distinct achievements. The Spirit's fullness does not in itself require the believer to have progressed through the various stages of spiritual growth, but it does constitute a gateway to these stages. Spirit baptism is a spiritual penetration of one's life. Holiness ought to be the expression of that life in character. Primarily, what is being established is a relationship to a Person.

Historically, at least since the time of John Wesley in the 18th century, there have been Christians who have taken an opposite view to the foregoing, and they therefore have sought a once-for-all sanctifying experience. In some cases, this pursuit of entire sanctification has been linked with the pursuit of the baptism in the Holy Spirit. Congregational "perfectionists" Charles G. Finney (1792-1875) and Asa Mahon (1799-1889) of Oberlin College urged a dynamic spiritual experience that they alternately referred to as "the baptism of the Holy Ghost" or "Christian Perfection." In today's generation, a representative of the Church of the Nazarene notes: "We believe that the baptism with the Holy Spirit and entire sanctification are one and the same experience."[10] By and large, it is agreed that the Topeka Bible School and Azusa Mission Pentecostals almost surely saw the experience of Spirit baptism either as the achieving of sanctification, or as the outcome of this achievement.

Some Pentecostal denominations, such as the Holiness and most of the Church of God groups, have not changed from the original 20th-century position identifying Spirit baptism and sanctification. However, as already noted, the majority of Pentecostals see sanctification as a progressive fruit-bearing that is related to the life of Jesus Christ. Spirit baptism is concerned with power for service. These doctrines, which have won wide acceptance among Pentecostals, are credited for their development and original dissemination to Rev. W. H. Durham who ministered in the Los Angeles and Chicago areas following the Azusa revival. Durham did not so much deny the role of sanctification or holiness, but he taught that Spirit baptism resulted in spiritual power to be used both for service and for holy living. His crusade came to be described as establishing a commitment to "the finished work of Calvary," and for a time discussion concerning it constituted a divisive issue among Pentecostals. A later controversy concerning the Godhead thus was known as the "New Issue."

The Spirit and Baptism by Fire

John the Baptist predicted of Jesus Christ: "He shall baptize you with the Holy Ghost and with fire" (Matthew 3:11; cf. Luke 3:16). Holiness preachers of the 19th century commonly expounded this promise to teach a special once-for-all experience whereby spiritual fire would consume utterly the dross of sin. Believers were urged to pursue a "fire baptism sanctification" or a "baptism of burning love" or simply a "baptism of fire." Some saw fire baptism as an experience separate from Spirit baptism; others saw it as a particular aspect of Spirit baptism. Today's scholars, at least for the most part, no longer maintain these distinctions. It is often suggested that John's words could be simplified to declare: "He shall baptize you with the fiery Holy Ghost," or, "He shall baptize you with the fire of the Holy Ghost."

The Holy Spirit relates to fire in various ways: 1) The "cloven tongues like as of fire" on the Day of Pentecost spoke of the impartation of holy zeal to assure that the disciples were "on fire for God," 2) Since the two references to fire in the context in Matthew 3 (vv. 11, 12) denote the fire of judgment, the Spirit's ministry to judge and, as it were, consume sin is in view, 3)

Henry H. Ness commented: "What fire does in the natural, the Holy Spirit does in the spiritual realm." Light, warmth, purification, and power are each the result both of natural fire and the fiery Holy Spirit, 4) Elder Cumming suggests that the baptism by fire is the inevitable fiery tests "which God appoints to His people." 5) Frank M. Boyd embraces various views when he writes:

> Baptism in the Holy Ghost is not one thing and baptism with fire another, but the former is the reality of which the latter is the symbol. . . . The Holy Ghost would be in the heart a Spirit of fire—fire for death or life, to purify or destroy. God's presence in man's heart is His greatest gift. It may truly be called a fire. It separates good from evil. It purifies. It tests.[11]

Walvoord declares that the intention of the Scriptures is to contrast the ministry of Christ in beginning the Church Age, with His ministry in beginning the millennial age. The bestowal of the Holy Spirit at Pentecost began the Church Age; the millennial age will begin with the outpouring of consuming fire upon the armies of Antichrist in the battle of Armageddon. Thus: "The Lord Jesus shall be revealed from heaven . . . in flaming fire taking vengeance" (1 Thessalonians 1:7, 8). As it were, John saw both the Spirit baptism of the Church and the fire baptism of Armageddon in a single panoramic vision.

Spirit Baptism and Day-by-day Fullness

Although Pentecostalism places great emphasis on the initial infilling of the Holy Spirit, the need for a constant fullness of the Spirit is also generally emphasized. The slogan: "One baptism, many fillings," has already been noted, together with the present continuous implications of: "Be filled with the Spirit" (Ephesians 5:18). Pentecostal pioneer B. F. Laurence wrote in 1916: "It is the purpose of God that this immersion into the Spirit be an abiding thing; that the Spirit become our dwelling place." Decades later, charismatic Stephen Clark wrote: "What God is interested in is not people who once had the experience of being baptized in the Spirit, but He is interested in people who are now living in the Spirit."[12] Pentecost is not just a past event to be remembered, but a present experience constituted in the Spirit's abiding control and anointing on the believer's life.

Scripture sets forth the day-by-day fullness of the Spirit as a fact of the Christian life: "The anointing which ye have received of him abideth in you" (1 John 2:27); "That good thing which was committed unto thee keep by the Holy Ghost which dwelleth in us" (2 Timothy 1:14); "Quench not the Spirit" (1 Thessalonians 5:19). Following the Day of Pentecost, Peter continued to be increasingly indwelt by the Spirit, and on that basis appeared before the Sanhedrin "filled with the Holy Ghost" (Acts 4:8). Horton says of this Scripture passage:

> The form of the Greek verb clearly indicates that this was indeed a new filling. . . . The idea is not that he had lost anything from the previous filling. God just increased his capacity and poured out the Spirit anew upon him in all His wisdom and power.[13]

Similarly, the seven who were chosen for the work of deacons were qualified in part because they were "full of the Holy Ghost" (Acts 6:3); and Scripture says of Barnabas: "He was a good man, and full of the Holy Ghost" (11:24). The task of maintaining the fullness of the Holy Spirit has been called "the believer's awesome responsibility." Ruth Paxon once wrote: "The fullness of the Holy Spirit is not optional but obligatory."

One Biblical fact in regard to the Spirit's fullness was personally taught by Jesus. "He that believeth on me, as the Scripture hath said, out of his belly shall flow rivers of living water. (But this spake he of the Spirit . . .)" (John 7:38, 39). The term *rivers* implies a fullness and a plentitude far exceeding any single small deposit. The condition, set forth in the preceding verse, is simply that one must thirst. To the degree that one thirsts, he is invited to drink without restriction, even to the point of being filled so as to become an overflowing river. Eager desire that assures continual submission and yieldedness is the believer's channel that he might maintain the continued inflow and outflow of the Holy Spirit. Though the baptism in the Spirit, which is an entrance into a new realm, may not be repeatable, the continuing filling of the Spirit is the believer's privilege throughout his earthly lifetime.

10

The Gifts of the Holy Spirit
(Part 1)

A commitment to belief in the gifts of the Spirit, or the *charismata,* is a commitment to a belief in miracles. For this reason, the acceptance of the gifts of the Spirit as God's provision for contemporary church life is a matter of controversy among evangelicals. It is, of course, characteristic of Pentecostals to hold that spiritual gifts are meant to operate in this age. The exercise of such gifts gives a distinctive character to Christian life and service, for if God ministers miraculously, the results are conspicuously different from the outcome when only human intellect and talent operate.

The Doctrine of Spiritual Gifts in History

The student notes with interest the account of manifestations of spiritual gifts following the close of the New Testament era. A number of sources can be cited:

Justin Martyr (c. 108-168) wrote to Trypho, a Jewish leader: "The Church is speaking in tongues, prophesying, and praying for the sick by the power of the Holy Spirit."

Irenaeus (c. 130-202) in his work *Against Heresies* is thought by many to have been describing known practices of his day: "We also hear many brethren in the church who possess prophetic gifts, and who through the Spirit speak all kinds of languages ... whom also the apostle [i.e., Paul] terms 'spiritual.'"

Tertullian (c. 160-222) in *Against Marcion* declares that his subject would prove himself orthodox if he could produce "prophets [who] have foretold things to come, and also made manifest the secrets of the heart"; or if he could "produce some psalm, some vision, some prayer in the spirit of ecstasy, which means apart from the exercise of mind, to which is added also an interpretation of tongue."

Hippolytus (c. 170-235) of Rome, wrote in *The Apostolic Tradition:* "If anyone among the laity appear to have received a gift of healing by a revelation, hands shall not be laid upon him, because the matter is manifest."

Novatian (c. 200-258) describes the work of the Holy Spirit in *De Trinitate:* "This is he who appoints prophets in the church, instructs teachers, directs tongues, brings into being powers and conditions of health, carries on extraordinary works, furnishes discernment of spirits, incorporates administrations in the church, establishes plans, brings together and arranges all other gifts there are of the charismata" (trans. by Dr. Ron Kydd).

Cyprian (d. 258), Bishop of Carthage, in his *Epistles,* speaks of God's imparting special revelations, and he comments: "I know that to some men dreams are seen to be ridiculous and visions silly, but certainly more so to those who choose to think badly of the priests than to those who are favorable to them."

Origen (c. 184-254) in *Against Celsus* defends Christianity against its apostate critics: "They no longer have any prophets or wonders, though traces of these are to be found to a considerable extent among Christians. Indeed, some works are even greater; and if our word may be trusted, we also have seen them."

Dionysius the Great of Alexandria (c. 190-265) in *Eusebius* testified: "A God-sent vision came to me and strengthened me, and a word which came to me commanded me."

From approximately the midpoint of the third century, surviving references to the gifts of the Spirit become less frequent, or less forthright, but the thread is not lost.

Eusebius of Caesarea (260-340), the eminent church historian, spoke of "the splendor of the gifts of the Spirit . . . which flash forth and shine upon His Church." He declared that "those who aim at that which is better prepare themselves for the reception of these gifts."

Pachomius (292-348), an Egyptian monk, left a testimony that is questioned by many, but which has value in revealing interests and anticipations of that time. According to the record, when Pachomius found he needed to know both Greek and Latin, neither of which he knew, he prayed, and God imparted them to him as gifts. He reported that the gift of Latin required 3 hours of prayer.

Athanasius (296-373) of Alexandria wrote: "We know bishops who work miracles . . ."; and, "It is good and needful for us to pray that we may receive the gift of discernment."

Macarius (300-390) of Egypt, author of *Spiritual Homilies*, commented at length on Paul's enumeration of the gifts of the Spirit in Corinthians. He clearly implies that he expects that these gifts be manifested in the lives of his readers.

Cyril of Jerusalem (315-386) in his catechetical lectures (equivalent to classroom notes in a theological college) gives evidence of being familiar with the operation of spiritual gifts. He spoke of the gifts of the word of wisdom, prophecy, and casting out demons (exorcism), and of receiving the Heavenly Gift.

Didymus the Blind (313-398) of Alexandria wrote of the spiritual gifts, and cited Paul's instructions to the Corinthians. He described God's provision of: "one or two or three charismata. . . . But when someone will become perfect he has no longer the earnest of Spirit, but the Spirit himself becomes all in every one." Didymus held that the believer received the charismata in proportion as he or she obeyed God.

Basil the Great (329-379) of Cappadocia is reputed to have been endued with several spiritual gifts. In *On Faith*, he wrote of "the Paraclete . . . who divideth and worketh the gifts that come of God." In *Shorter Rules* he explains that one can pray without understanding when he prays in tongues. In general, his works cite scriptural passages teaching the operation of spiritual gifts, and he applies them to the congregations of his day.

Gregory Nazianzen (330-390), Bishop of Cappadocia, in his sermon "On Pentecost" cites and applies verses from Corinthians that promise spiritual gifts—1 Corinthians 14:27, 29. Elsewhere, Gregory wrote of popular confusion on the subject of the Holy Spirit, and he showed concern that people be rightly taught in these matters.

Gregory Nyssa (335-395), the third member of the Cappadocian school, wrote of spiritual gifts, including tongues, as customary in the churches that he knew. He taught that spiritual gifts must be balanced by the fruit of the Spirit, and he emphasized the universal bestowment of spiritual gifts. His *Life of St. Macrina* reports numerous instances of the operation of the charismata.

Epiphanius of Salamis (315-403) in his *Firmly Anchored Man* cites the scriptural promises of the gifts of the Spirit, and plainly relates them to his personal experience and expectation.

Chrysostom (347-407), who from 398 was bishop of Constantinople, left numerous written sermons and Biblical expositions. He repeatedly mentioned the continued operation of the charismata. At the same time, he lamented the prevailing unworthy life-styles of his day that discouraged spiritual phenomena. His overall contribution is to establish that the charismata were less common in his day than they had been at an earlier time.

Palladius of Helenopolis (367-430) in his *Lausiac History*, reported many examples of spiritual gifts, but he did not develop the subject theologically.

The Venerable Bede (673-735) records many miraculous healings, and he tells of the spiritual gifts of utterance upon the monk Caedmon. Through a special anointing, Caedmon was able to transpose Scripture freely into English poetry.

Symeon (or Simeon) the New Theologian (940-1022) of Constantinople promoted the pursuit of spiritual gifts and deeper godliness in the lives of his monastic associates. He wrote: "It is impossible for a man who seeks with all his soul not to find Him and be enriched by His gifts."

Hildegard of Bingen (1098-1178) enjoyed a ministry of "singing in tongues" that equipped her to present "concerts in the Spirit." She testified to a special divine anointing that gave her the words, but later she prepared a dictionary to facilitate their translation.

Gregory Palamas (1296-1359), the bishop of Thessalonica from 1347, wrote of life among monks in the monastery of Mount Athos. He reported: "Most of the charismata of the Spirit . . . are given to the worthy [monks] in time of prayer." Gregory discussed the gifts of the Spirit on the basis of New Testament teachings, and he seemed quite familiar with their operation.

Other traditional figures and saints of the church reputed to have manifested spiritual gifts, including tongues, miracles, and healings, were: St. Dominic of Spain (d. 1221), St. Anthony of Padua (d. 1231), St. Clare of Montefalco (d. 1275), Angelus Clarenus (d. 1337), and Vincent Ferrer (d. 1419).

An interesting suggestion by Eddie Ensley, that is enthusiastically endorsed by J. Rodman Williams, is that the traditional Catholic practice called "jubilation" (Latin: *Jubilatio)* is merely another way of identifying the exercise of spiritual gifts. The practice of jubilation in worship is described by numerous writers, beginning with Augustine (354-430) and extending to the early modern era (14th century). Ensley reports, in varying degrees of depth, jubilation experiences in the lives of at least 23 church leaders or their movements during this era. Out of this background, jubilation identifies worship consisting of a flow of sounds apart from known words that accompanies intense spiritual experience, or sometimes a spontaneous singing apart from the use of known words. Miracles of healing and other miraculous events often accompanied exercises of jubilation.

It is clear that both within, and possibly outside of, conventional terminology some manifestations of the charismata were retained during the early Christian era and through the Middle Ages. However, it was not the case that the manifestation and understanding of charismata enjoyed priority in the mainline church. A particular weakness was the failure to develop a thoughtful, scholarly, Biblical doctrine of miraculous spiritual gifts. In spite of the insights and attainments of the Church of the early and medieval eras, there was little to transmit to the modern era. Ruthven comments: "By the time of the Reformation, the doctrine of miracles in the Church had degenerated into virtually animistic superstition."[1] The Reformers, therefore, rejected almost all visible miraculous elements and tended to conclude that the age of miracles was past. Out of this background, Protestantism for many centuries was committed to the denial of the miraculous. Any systematic effort to study the gifts of the Spirit has traditionally been discouraged.

The Nature and Identity of the Gifts of the Spirit

The Greek New Testament identifies the gifts of the Spirit primarily by two terms: *charismata* (e.g., Romans 11:29; 1 Corinthians 12:4), and *pneumatika* (e.g., 1 Corinthians 12:1). *Charismata* occurs 17 times, and it is widely used in speaking of spiritual gifts. Derived forms are: *charisma* which is singular (*charismata* is plural), *charisms,* and the adjective *charismatic.* Charismata denotes that which is bestowed out of grace, favor, or special kindness, and the word derives from the same root as "charity." Someone has defined charismata as: "gifts given us in spite of the fact that we do not deserve them," or, "the concrete realization of divine grace." It depicts complete independence between the recipient's worth and skills, and that which he receives from God. The term *pneumatika* is an adjectival form of the Greek word for spirit, and it connotes whatever is of or from the Spirit. In three instances the King James translators render this term *spiritual gifts,* although, precisely, it is "spirituals."

The gifts of (or given by) the Spirit are distinguished from the gift of the Spirit himself. The one Holy Spirit is the Gift (Gk., *doran);* each of the charismatic bestowments is a gift (Gk., *charisma).* "Then Peter said unto them, Repent, and be baptized . . . and ye shall receive the gift of the Holy Ghost" (Acts 2:38); "On the Gentiles also was poured out the gift of the Holy Ghost" (Acts 10:45). All Christians are granted the gift of the Holy Spirit; only some Christians prove to be recipients of any given individual gift of the Spirit. He in sovereign wisdom proceeds by "dividing to every man severally as he will" (1 Corinthians 12:11). The gift of the Spirit is a personal bestowment for the benefit of the recipient; the gifts of the Spirit, though manifested through individuals, are for the good of all (cf. 1 Corinthians 12:7).

In the four New Testament lists of God's gifts to His church, 22 different items are named: word of wisdom, word of knowledge, faith, gifts of healings, miracles, prophecy, discerning of spirits, tongues, interpretation of tongues, practical service or ministry, teaching, stirring faith in others or encouraging, liberally contributing (to others' needs), leadership or ruling, showing mercy or compassion, apostles, prophets, evangelists, pastor-teachers, teachers, assistants or helpers, and administrators (cf. 1 Corinthians 12:8-10; Romans 12:4-8; Ephesians 4:8-11; 1 Corinthians 12:28). Obviously, this unselected list combines elements of different types. The Catholic catechism, with seven gifts of the Spirit, proceeds with a similar unselected listing: wisdom, understanding, knowledge, counsel, piety, fortitude, and fear of the Lord.

It is significant that all four lists are from the epistles of Paul. The variety of forms indicates that he wished to impress that spiritual gifts are more than spectacular miracles. While the gifts do involve miracles, it is also the case that the gracious ministry of born-again believers are His gifts as well. Redeemed humans serving mankind may constitute a true spiritual gift to those who are served. The whole of Christian life and service is intended to be the arena of the Spirit's activity. Concerning the four lists, Horton comments: "It seems better to take all of these lists as merely giving samplings of the gifts and callings of the Spirit, samplings taken from an infinite supply."[2]

But in spite of the preceding, there is definite warrant for the special study of the nine gifts of 1 Corinthians 12. This portion of Scripture particularly uses the word *gift* to denote a divine charisma; other uses of "gift" concern the provision of a person who is to be a minister or worker (or that which enables one to be such a person), or the provision of a quality or attribute that will refine character. Spiritual gifts constituted as ministers in the Church are ordinarily discussed in studies in ecclesiology; spiritual gifts as matters of character and attitude involve devotional, instructional, and practical aspects of enlightened Christian living. Only Paul's list in Corinthians sets forth a systematic enumeration of the divine charismata in the first of the three senses of "spiritual gifts."

The charismata are God's divine provision to assist and expand the work of the Church in fulfilling its tasks on earth. They have been described as providing that "there shall be no fundamental difference between the ministry of Christ and the ministry of the Church." Jepson writes: "The genuine gifts of the Spirit are God in action through Christ by the power of the Holy Spirit in the Church."[3] Since Jesus' promise was that Spirit baptism would result in power (Acts 1:8), His method of implementing and outworking that power is particularly through the gifts of the Spirit. In a miraculous way, God provides His supernatural gifts through ordinary humans, so the manifestation of a gift is both divine and human. God's channels are truly "workers together with him" (2 Corinthians 6:1).

Among the purposes of the charismata or spiritual gifts are: 1) To convince the unbeliever: "And thus are the secrets of his heart made manifest; and so falling down on his face he will worship God" (1 Corinthians 14:24); 2) To gain attention and win interest on behalf of the gospel message: "They were all amazed and marveled" (Acts 2:7); 3) To inform and guide God's people: "A certain prophet named Agabus . . . said, Thus saith the Holy Ghost . . ." (Acts 21:11); 4) To glorify God: "All men glorified God for that which was done" (4:21); 5) To minister the power of God: "Then Peter said . . . In the name of Jesus Christ of Nazareth rise up and walk" (3:6).

The Nine Gifts of First Corinthians

Tertullian suggested one of the earliest known classifications of the gifts of the Spirit: Power, Sympathy, Administration, and Utterance. However, the classification that is commonly used today has three categories: Revelation (or information)— the word of wisdom, the word of knowledge, discerning of spirits; Power (or action)—healings, miracles, faith; Utterance (or vocal)—tongues, interpretation of tongues, prophecy. These classifications will be used only to guide in chapter divisions, since the gifts each seem to stand on its own merits.

The Gift of the Word of Wisdom

The expression "word of wisdom" connotes a statement or pronouncement that is prudent, shrewd, and clever. It consists of a capacity at the appropriate time, and on behalf of a particular issue, to exercise superior good judgment. The outcome has the appearance of great skill, wide experience, or even judicious cunning. One who exercises this gift enjoys a specific insight into the mind and purpose of God that can be translated into ordinary problems and issues of life. Horton says:

> The Word of Wisdom is therefore the supernatural revelation, by the Spirit, of Divine Purpose; the supernatural unfolding of His plans and purposes concerning things, places, people, individuals, communities, nations.[4]

In some situations, the gift of the word of wisdom is equivalent to God-given tact or unusual spiritual understanding. It has been called "holy quick-wittedness."

The fact that it is "word of" or "utterance of" implies that the imparted wisdom is neither exhaustive nor universal, but that which is directed to a particular time and place. As it were, the word of wisdom operates as a "flash of inspiration." Riggs comments: "Neither is there a transfer of great reservoirs of wisdom and knowledge, but a 'word'—a revelation, an expression sufficient for the occasion—of the wisdom and knowledge of God."[5] The believer does not receive wisdom in the abstract, but a particular portion of wisdom, or a wise insight, that he is able to apply to a specific situation. The process may be compared to an attorney's provision of legal advice to his client to enable him to resolve a particularly difficult issue. The word of wisdom would appear quite properly to apply to whatever realms concern the believer—spiritual, ethical, intellectual, or practical.

The word of wisdom may be directed toward the right application of knowledge. The facts made available by knowledge, are thus interpreted or applied to implement the possibility that is most satisfactory. Wisdom is often needed to determine the correct application of the truths of Scripture and the most effective manner of applying them to this generation. Myer

Pearlman once wrote concerning the application of the word of wisdom:

> It may include (a) skill in managing affairs—"Wherefore brethren, look ye out among you seven men full . . . of wisdom" (Acts 6:3); (b) prudence in dealing with persons outside the Church—"Walk in wisdom toward them that are without" (Colossians 4:5); (c) skill and discretion in imparting Christian truth—"Whom we preach, warning every man, and teaching every man in all wisdom" (Colossians 1:28).

One of the classic illustrations of divinely given wisdom is Solomon's handling of the case of the disputed infant (cf. 1 Kings 3:16-28). Two notable instances in Jesus' life are His word to the accusers of the woman taken in adultery, and His reply to the question concerning tribute: "He that is without sin among you, let him first cast a stone at her" (John 8:7); "Render therefore unto Caesar the things that are Caesar's; and unto God the things that are God's" (Matthew 22:21). At the first general conference of the Church at Jerusalem, there was "much disputing" until James offered his simple formula. Harmony and oneness of spirit resulted: "Then pleased it the apostles and elders with the whole church" (Acts 15:22). Possible instances of this gift in Paul's ministry might be: his shrewd vindication of himself before the magistrates of Philippi (16:35-39), his use of the altar to the unknown God as a theme in preaching in Athens (17:22-32), and his mention of the resurrection as a means of dividing his enemies in the Sanhedrin (23:6-10). Concerning Stephen, Scripture says his opponents "were not able to resist the wisdom and the spirit by which he spake" (6:10).

Scripture exalts wisdom, particularly divine wisdom: "Wisdom is better than rubies; and all things that may be desired are not to be compared to it" (Proverbs 8:11); "O the depth of the riches both of the wisdom and knowledge of God" (Romans 11:33). In Old Testament times, God shared His wisdom with a select few; resulting in Bezaleel's craftsmanship (Exodus 31:3), Joshua's leadership (Deuteronomy 34:9), and Solomon's kingly rule (1 Kings 3:11-28). An interesting New Testament promise concerns Christian believers "brought before kings and rulers" for His name's sake. Jesus instructed them "not to meditate before what ye shall answer: For I will give you a mouth and wisdom, which all your adversaries shall not be able to gainsay nor resist" (cf. Luke 21:12-15). To all Christians, the promise is extended: "If any of you lack wisdom, let him ask of God, that giveth to all men liberally, and upbraideth not; and it shall be given him" (James 1:5).

The Gift of the Word of Knowledge

The gift of the word of knowledge is concerned with the immediate awareness of facts without the aid of the senses. It constitutes a sharing of a fragment of God's omniscience, so that God makes known to humans something He knows but they do not. Horton writes: "The Word of Knowledge is the supernatural revelation by the Holy Spirit of certain facts in the mind of God."[6] Carter explains the gift as "a supernatural revelation of the existence, or nature, of a person or thing, of the knowledge of some event, given to us by the Holy Spirit for a specific purpose."[7] It is knowledge in the sense of information, or through possession of the power to recognize. Montgomery's version renders the name of this gift "a word of insight." Many suggest that, on occasion, the "word of knowledge" may constitute foreknowledge, and thus it may be concerned with future events.

Biblical examples of divinely imparted knowledge that either parallel this gift or directly illustrate its use include: David's insight into his possible future at Keilah (1 Samuel 23:12); Elisha's knowledge of Gehazi's duplicity (2 Kings 5:26); Elisha's awareness of the strategy of the Syrian army (2 Kings 6:9-12); Simeon's identification of Mary's babe (Luke 2:26); Jesus' prior vision of Nathanael (John 1:48); Jesus' knowledge of the marital status of the woman at the well (John 4:17, 18, 29); Peter's awareness of Ananias' deception (Acts 5:1-6); and Paul's perception of the faith of the cripple at Lystra (14:8-10), or his knowledge of the shipwreck that was about to occur (27:10). Interestingly, in some cases, the word of knowledge was given through a vision or a special divine messenger (cf. Acts 9:10-16; 27:23). This gift parallels the word of wisdom in being specifically a "word," and in applying to realms other than the spiritual.

In at least some cases, there appears to be a close relationship between the gift of the word of knowledge and the ministry of a prophet. When Jesus disclosed that He knew the inner thoughts of the woman at the well, she responded: "Sir, I perceive that thou art a prophet" (John 4:19). Moses, who enjoyed an extensive unfolding of divine knowledge in being granted the story of Creation and its aftermaths, was numbered among the prophets: "There arose not a prophet since in Israel like unto Moses, whom the Lord knew face to face" (Deuteronomy 34:10). An alternate early Old Testament name for a prophet was "seer" (cf. 1 Samuel 9:9), which meant simply "one who sees," in the sense of one who knows or has insight. Paul's concept of the "mystery of Christ" (Ephesians 3:4) appears to relate to his own remarkable experience in being granted divine insight. He mentions an occasion when "he was caught up into paradise, and heard unspeakable words, which it is not lawful for a man to utter" (2 Corinthians 12:4); the "mystery," he says, "is now revealed unto his holy apostles and prophets by the Spirit" (Ephesians 3:5).

It is of interest to note that the Eastern Orthodox churches recognize an order of ministers based on the gift of the word of knowledge, plus both wisdom and prophecy. Such a minister is known as a *starets* (or *staretz*). In most cases, a *starets* is a monk, but lay people of both sexes also qualify. A *starets* is thought to enjoy the gifts and graces of Jesus Christ, so that he can counsel the perplexed and declare God's prescription for each individual case.

The gift of the word of knowledge may extend from awareness of elemental matters to comprehensive facts that only Deity could make known. In some cases, its exercise could remain virtually unrecognized; in others, it would impressively point to God. In all cases, however, it concerns divine knowledge communicated by direct impression and not by any experience of the physical human senses. Holder describes the functioning of this gift:

By this means, secret sin has been exposed; causes of sickness sometimes revealed, and when matters are put right, healing has been given. Deliverances in times of danger have come through fervent prayer, when the presence of danger has been revealed to a person sometimes many thousands of miles away.[8]

Although God has equipped man with normal facilities for acquiring facts, there are occasions when His work and workers call for more insights than they have access to acquire. For this purpose, the gift of the word of knowledge has been given.

The Gift of Discerning of Spirits

The Holy Spirit manifests the gift of discerning of spirits to enable the believer to form judgments and recognize identities in the realm of spirits. The term *discerning* (lit., discernings) in the original connotes a judgment made possible by an insight that sees through externals and perceives basic underlying reality. Donald Gee describes the operation of this gift as "a piercing of all that is merely outward, and seeing right through; then forming a judgment based on that insight."[9] By means of this gift, human natural senses are supplemented by appropriate divine powers, so that humans are able to relate in understanding in the spirit world. The gift of discerning of spirits does not enable one to discern people; it is not "discernment" in the abstract, but simply what it purports to be: the discerning or analytic classification and judgment of spirits.

Spirits that may operate in the believer's sphere include divine, satanic, and merely human. The latter is illustrated by Peter and John who desired to consume the Samaritans by fire. Jesus "rebuked them, and said, Ye know not what manner of spirit ye are of" (Luke 9:55). Similarly, when Peter objected to his Master's plans, Jesus said: "Thou art an offense unto me: for thou savorest not the things that be of God, but those that be of men" (Matthew 16:23). The gift of discerning of spirits equips the believer to judge the type of spirit that is functioning, and it links with the admonition to "try the spirits" (1 John 4:1). Various Biblical standards are given to apply to this task (cf. Matthew 7:15-23; 1 Corinthians 12:3; 1 John 4:1-6). However, the gift would function by direct divine impression, and it would override any procedure of gathering factual data by the process of trying (i.e., testing) the spirits.

A variety of spirits, both good and bad, are constantly at work among mankind. The occult is a real realm of spirit beings whose goal is to deceive and destroy mankind. Hagin writes:

> The Old Testament has frequent references to what is called in older versions "familiar spirits," or in modern versions "mediums, fortune tellers, wizards, sorcerers, or witches." Other Biblical designations include: demonic spirits, spirits of devils [or demons], spirit of error, seducing spirits, or lying spirits. Natural human insight is certainly incapable of judging in this realm. In some cases the evil spirit may counterfeit or supplant the Holy Spirit. In today's scene there are accounts of Christian workers being granted the gift of discerning of spirits to identify a preacher-deceiver whose specialty was telling people "something about themselves . . . their name and address . . . how much money they had in their purses . . . what they had in their pockets.[10]

Some evil spirits are particularly deceiving because they appear so innocently harmless: "For Satan himself is transformed into an angel of light" (2 Corinthians 11:14).

Paul appears to have exercised the gift of discerning of spirits when he recognized the source of information and the motivating power of the soothsaying maiden at Philippi. Thus, he proceeded to cast out the unclean spirit (cf. Acts 16:16-18). It may also have been through the manifestation of this gift that Peter was certain of the underlying nature of the spirit of Simon the sorcerer (8:23), and Paul certain of the identity of Elymas the sorcerer (13:8-11). In each case, a divine judgment was pronounced in view of the apostolic insight into the true spirit of those concerned.

It does not necessarily follow that the power to cast out demons and evil spirits (exorcism) is granted simultaneously with the gift of discerning of spirits. The power of exorcism is ordinarily thought of as one aspect of the gift of the gifts of healings. Nevertheless, the typical Biblical pattern saw the recognized evil spirit either cast out or in some way restricted or judged. Jesus said: "I cast out devils [demons] by the Spirit of God" (Matthew 12:28). Of Jesus' ministry it was declared: "[Jesus of Nazareth] went about doing good, and healing all that were oppressed of the devil" (Acts 10:38). An interesting incident in Jesus' ministry involved the man who lacked the power of speech: "And when the devil [demon] was cast out, the dumb spake: and the multitudes marveled" (Matthew 9:33). Thus, a physical healing was achieved through exorcism.

The gift of discerning of spirits should be distinguished from the word of knowledge. This latter gift relates to insights into facts of every sort such as: moral, material, personal, spiritual, or historical. The one insight involved in discerning of spirits concerns the existence and operation of spirit beings. It is not human shrewdness, nor is it mere human suspicion, but it is the provision of eyesight and hearing (and to carry through the figure: taste, touch, and smell) in the realm of spirits. A parallel Old Testament event would be that involving Elisha's servant when the Syrian army besieged Dothan:

And Elisha prayed, and said, Lord, I pray thee, open his eyes, that he may see. And the Lord opened the eyes of the young man; and he saw: and, behold the mountain was full of horses and chariots of fire round about Elisha (2 Kings 6:17).

The Gifts of
the Holy Spirit
(Part 2)

In following the conventional division of the gifts of the Spirit into three groups of threes, the final six gifts constitute the gifts of power and gifts of utterance. Each gift may be individually discussed.

The Gift of the Gifts of Healing

This gift manifestation of the Holy Spirit is defined by Harold Horton: "These gifts . . . are the miraculous manifestation of the Spirit for the banishment of all human ills whether organic, functional or nervous; acute or chronic."[1] The power of God, as embodied in the resurrection life of Jesus Christ, is made available for the exercise of all possible facets of the healing arts in the human body and mind. In the three Biblical references to the gift (1 Corinthians 12:9, 20, 28), in the original, both terms are plural. If the construction of 1 Corinthians 12 is maintained in parallel form, since verse 4 declares that what is to follow is a list of gifts, it is technically accurate to refer to "the gift of the gifts of healings." The implication is that he to whom the manifestation of the Spirit is given, is, in turn, given an assortment of individual healing portions to convey to those who need them. In the words of Purkiser: "These are specific gifts for specific instances of healing."[2] Or as Corsie comments: "Every healing is a special gift. There are no healers."[3]

In the case of this manifestation of the Holy Spirit, not only does the human channel receive a gift, but also that which the Spirit gives the channel to perform is itself the giving of a gift.

The relationship might be paraphrased: "The human channel receives a package of healing remedies to be shared as gifts with others." The whole procedure is an instance of divine charismata, and therefore neither the personal merit of the one ministering the gift, nor that of the one receiving the healing portion, is the basis of bestowment. At both levels, it is, as it were, divine charity rather than human merit or even human faith. The sovereignty of the Spirit is particularly in evidence here, and the ultimate recipient of healing administered through the channel of this gift may be either a believer or an unbeliever as the Spirit wills.

The gift of the gifts of healings shares with tongues and miracles the special status of being given on a twofold basis: to the individual (1 Corinthians 12:7) and to the church (12:28). These gifts serve particularly as wonder-causing signs that attract attention and gain a hearing: "And fear came upon every soul: and many wonders and signs were done by the apostles" (Acts 2:43). Gifts of healings are wonders in the literal sense that they cause the observer to wonder, and they are signs in the sense that they constitute a token or evidence of divine intervention. That which Scripture identifies as a miracle is a deed or act of power. As a gift of the Spirit, God provides healings to equip the Church and its workers with the credentials needed to fulfill the Great Commission.

Donald Gee wrote of the gift of healing:

> It appears to be a spiritual gift especially connected with the ministry of the evangelist, and granted to those called to fill that office. . . . It often gave the apostles an open door in their evangelistic work; as, for instance, the healing of the father of Publius by Paul (Acts 28:8-10).[4]

A similar scriptural case, under the ministry of Peter, concerns the healing of Aeneas. This man who had been bedfast with paralysis for 8 years was instantly healed: "And all that dwelt at Lydda and Sharon saw him, and turned to the Lord" (Acts 9:35). Such an event validated Peter's divine commission, attested to the truth of the gospel message, and affirmed the reality of the resurrection of Jesus Christ.

Other examples of the bestowment of the gifts of healings in the era of the Early Church would include: the healing of the lame man at the temple gate by Peter (Acts 3:6); the healing of the sick on beds and couches in the street by Peter (5:15); the resuscitation of Tabitha by Peter (9:40); the healing of the lame man at Lystra by Paul (14:10); the resuscitation of Eutychus by Paul (20:12); and Paul's freedom from symptoms after the viper's bite (28:6).

Since the gift of the gifts of healings is primarily a sign gift, its function is distinct from the general provision of divine healing for the Church. God prescribes: "Is any sick among you? let him call for the leaders of the church. . . . And the prayer of faith shall save the sick, and the Lord shall raise him up" (James 5:14, 15). Healing for believers involves a specific promise and Biblical procedure; the gifts of healings are given within the sovereignty of the Holy Spirit if and when He sees the need to confirm the ministry of His servant. There is nothing to prevent a gift of healing from becoming effective for a believer, but if this occurs, it is an instance of divine sovereignty, and it is primarily for the benefit of the minister rather than the one who was healed.

It would ordinarily be necessary for a gift of healing to be visibly miraculous if it is to serve as a wonder-inducing sign. However, it is customary to distinguish healings from miracles (a separate gift) by noting that it is not an inherent requirement in healing that the event appear miraculous. A healing is accomplished when the cause of infirmity is rendered no longer active and, as it were the normal health forces of the body are granted the ascendancy. The full recovery of physical well-being may require an extended period of time. A physician would consider he heals by removing a malignant growth, and yet obviously the restoration of tissue surfaces and physical functions might require several months after the "healing."

In providing gifts of healings, God in no sense undermines His program otherwise. The ordinary price of healing is faith, and even Jesus was subject to this principle: "And he did not many mighty works there because of their unbelief" (Matthew 13:8). When the gifts of healings function, the faith is manifested by the one who ministers rather than by the one who is healed. The minister has trusted God to the degree that the

Holy Spirit confirms his faith and ministry by signs following. The gifts of healings are most surely not intended to detract from the work of the church by providing an alternate healing procedure for those who do not care to obey the instructions in the Book of James (cf. James 5:14, 15). Rather, the gifts of healings serve to advance the work of the church by providing occasion for God's servant to enjoy a divine validation so that he conspicuously qualifies for his task.

The Gift of Faith

Faith that constitutes a gift of the Spirit is called by Weymouth "special faith," and by today's writers it is often referred to as "charismatic faith." This is the faith that Scripture defines: "Now faith is the substance of things hoped for, the evidence of things not seen" (Hebrews 11:1). Harold Horton writes: "The gift of faith is a supernatural endowment by the Spirit whereby that which is uttered or desired by man, or spoken by God, shall eventually come to pass."[5] This spiritual gift is concerned with making it possible for the believer, in a very special manner, to validate the promises of God and to make them personally operative. Literal Scripture also hints that this gift is given on a uniquely selective basis. The phrase "to another" is literally, "to a man of another kind," and only in the case of "diverse kinds of tongues" is this construction repeated. Faith, as a gift of the Spirit, is distinctive from "ordinary" saving faith which is a gift to every Christian: "For by grace are ye saved through faith; and that not of yourselves: it is the gift of God" (Ephesians 2:8).

In contrast with saving faith, the Holy Spirit ministers the special gift of faith to constitute the believer's working faith; thus, "charismatic faith," as noted, "the faith for miracles," or "faith for the miraculous." Grossman speaks of "mountain-moving faith," and he links it with Jesus' promise: "If ye have faith as a grain of mustard seed, ye shall say unto this mountain, Remove hence to yonder place; and it shall remove; and nothing shall be impossible unto you" (Matthew 17:20). This gift constitutes the faith that dares, and the faith that expects great things from God. It is not capricious faith in faith itself, but responsible faith in God. When the lame man at the Gate Beautiful was healed, Peter testified: "The faith which is by him [i.e., God] hath given him perfect soundness in the presence of you all" (Acts 3:16).

Although the person through whom this spiritual gift is manifested may be expected to exercise faith in a special and unusual manner, immediate visible evidence is not demanded. Even charismatic faith remains contrary to sight, for faith and sight are always opposites. Augustine noted: "Faith is to believe what we do not see, and the reward of this faith is to see what we believe." Sooner or later, faith will erupt into action, but this gift is primarily concerned with preparing for that divine eruption. It has been rightly said: "Such faith is never mere reliance on a promise, but always reliance on the Promiser."

The practical outworking of the gift of faith is twofold. In some, the manifestation of the gift assures the maintenance of unswerving belief and trust in God in spite of the most adverse circumstances. Peter, imprisoned just after the execution of James and with every reason to expect the same sentence, was nevertheless able to maintain total personal peace of mind: "And when Herod would have brought him forth, the same night Peter was sleeping between two soldiers . . ." (Acts 12:6). Paul gave evidence of this gift when he stood before his fellow passengers on the ship in the storm and declared: "Be of good cheer:for I believe God, that it shall be even as it was told me" (27:25). The faith of Paul was vindicated, for it was indeed the case that no lives were lost, although the ship was broken up.

In the second type of outworking of the gift of faith there is the accomplishment of mighty works of divine power. The writer to the Hebrews enumerates many of the Old Testament heroes, and he declares that these were men "who through faith subdued kingdoms, wrought righteousness, obtained promises, stopped the mouths of lions, quenched the violence of fire, escaped the edge of the sword, out of weakness were made strong, waxed valiant in fight, turned to flight the armies of the aliens" (Hebrews 11:33, 34). It was surely "the faith of miracles" or "charismatic faith" that enabled Abram to believe for the child that was naturally impossible, David to meet

Goliath, or Elijah to confront the prophets of Baal and not only believe for heavenly fire, but also three times pour water on the firewood. As Clark notes: "The charismatic gift of faith . . . is a gift of praying with a God-given confidence, and it produces extraordinary results."[6]

In certain New Testament events, it is likely that more than one spiritual gift operated at the same time. The cripple at Lystra manifested charismatic faith: "Paul . . . steadfastly beholding and perceiving that he had faith to be healed . . ." (Acts 14:9). Paul, in turn, gave evidence of divinely given faith when he "said with a loud voice, Stand upright on thy feet" (v. 10). The man was healed, and therefore could be said to have received a gift of healing; he experienced an immediate miracle, and therefore the gift of the working of miracles was operative. It is evident that God is not restricted in His ways of working, but no doubt charismatic faith is a factor in many miraculous events.

Other Biblical examples of the gift of faith might be: Jesus' healing of the centurion's servant (cf. Matthew 8:10, "I have not found so great faith, no, not in Israel"); Jesus' destruction of the fruitless fig tree (cf. Matthew 21:21, "If ye have faith, and doubt not, ye shall not only do this which is done to the fig tree, but also if ye shall say unto this mountain, Be thou removed, and be thou cast into the sea; it shall be done"); Jesus' healing the demon-possessed son (cf. Matthew 17:19, 20, "Then came the disciples to Jesus apart, and said, Why could not we cast him out? And Jesus said unto them, Because of your unbelief").

The Gift of the Working of Miracles

Literally, this gift is designated "workings of miracles" and a very rich diversity of operation is implied. The word *miracles* translates the Greek *dunamis* (cf. dynamite), and it describes works of supernatural power or deeds of might, rather than marvels or signs. Nevertheless, a miracle often is a sign, for it is an instance when God's working becomes conspicuously recognizable. Men judge an event to be a miracle when it transcends their understanding of the operations of nature. Horton writes: "A miracle . . . is a supernatural intervention in the ordinary course of the system of nature as we know it."[7] The God who upholds "all things by the word of his power" (Hebrews 1:3) is well able to modify His expression of that power. Such events are normal to God, but to humans they are miracles. The Christian through whom the gift of the working of miracles operates is the channel of miraculous power that projects him into a new dimension of the divine realm.

In the ministry of the church, the gift of the working of miracles serves two purposes: 1) to provide for special needs, and 2) to confirm the gospel witness. In the spirit of the latter, Thomas Aquinas called the gift of miracles "the winged sandals and the staff of the messengers." Such miracles are ordinarily dramatic, outwardly visible events. They are linked in some measure to an act of faith, but they stand apart as distinct events. A helpful distinction is suggested by Hagin: "The difference between the gift of faith and the working of miracles is that the gift of faith receives a miracle and the working of miracles works a miracle."[8]

New Testament miracles that provided for a special need include: multiplying the loaves and fishes to feed the 5,000 (Matthew 14:15-21), turning the water into wine at the wedding of Cana (John 2:1-11), the miraculous transportation of Philip (Acts 8:39, 40), and the raising of Eutychus (Acts 20:9-12). Miracles that confirmed the gospel witness include: the healing of the beggar at the temple gate (3:1-16), the earthquake at Philippi and the subsequent conversion of the jailer and the release of Paul and Silas (16:25-40), Paul's deliverance from ill effects after being bitten by the viper (28:3-6), and the healing of the father of Publius on the island of Melita (28:8-10). A prior miracle, Jesus' walking on the water (Matthew 14:25), certainly served to confirm the deity of Christ to His disciples.

While miracles can be counterfeited (cf. the magicians of Egypt, Exodus 7:11, 12, 22; 8:7, 18), Jesus taught an important principle: "There is no man which shall do a miracle in my name, that can lightly speak evil of me" (Mark 9:29). Interestingly, the unknown disciple referred to by Jesus as doing miracles was actually casting out demons in Jesus' name. While exorcism is a type of healing, it might also be considered one manifestation of the gift of the working of miracles. The kind of divine working that is described as a miracle is clearly what is needed to free the possessed human from a demonic spirit. In Biblical usage, the word *workings* usually identifies either divine or satanic activity, and workings of miracles are therefore one mode of God's warfare against demonic powers. J. Rodman Williams comments: "The only force capable of dealing with the demonic spirit is the Holy Spirit."[9] The term *deliverance* is sometimes used to describe the breaking free from or casting forth of forces that dominate. In some cases, the expression "ministry of deliverance" has been used to describe the gift of the working of miracles.

In the New Testament, one form in which the gift of the working of miracles operated was in bestowing judgment. Paul used this gift to bring blindness upon Elymas the sorcerer who sought to turn Sergius Paulus from the faith (Acts 13:7-11). The casting out of the demon from the soothsaying damsel of Philippi was probably both a judgment (because the maiden had harassed them), and a healing exorcism. Judgment was certainly involved in the death of Ananias and Sapphira (Acts 5:1-11), but it is not clear that Peter ministered a miracle on this occasion. Peter manifested the gift of the word of knowledge, but the judgment seems to have come directly from God without a human channel being involved. Actually, most instances of the working of miracles in the New Testament appear to have been positive works of blessing. Thus, the pattern in the life of Paul:

> God wrought special miracles by the hands of Paul: So that from his body were brought unto the sick handkerchiefs or aprons, and the diseases departed from them, and the evil spirits went out of them (Acts 19:11, 12).

The Gift of Tongues

The gift of the Spirit named in 1 Corinthians 12:10 is literally "varieties of languages." *The Living Bible* renders the two-word phrase of the original: "able to speak in languages [a person] never learned." The better known combination of words that transliterates into the English word *glossolalia* does not occur until the end of the chapter (12:30), but it is repeated frequently in chapter 14. Most scholars hold that divers kinds of tongues, varieties of languages, glossolalia, or strange languages one has not learned, are all equivalent and synonymous expressions. The gift of tongues is typically defined: "The supernaturally given manifestation of speech in languages with which the speaker is not familiar."

There are said to be upwards of 30 allusions to speaking in tongues in the New Testament. Identifying expressions found in the Authorized Version include: speak with other tongues (Acts 2:4); speak with tongues (Acts 10:46; 1 Corinthians 12:3); speak in an unknown tongue (1 Corinthians 14:2, 4); kinds of tongues (1 Corinthians 12:10); and speak with new tongues (Mark 16:17). The Pentecostal would emphasize that tongues are languages, and therefore he would object to a contemporary version that uses the expression "ecstatic utterances" to identify tongues. Speaking in tongues does not have to be any more ecstatic than speaking in English or another known language.

The realm in which the gift of tongues operates is not the human mind, but the human organs of speech. The mind is primarily a spectator to the events, and it neither frames the utterances, nor does it premeditate or prearrange them. The Old Testament story of Balaam illustrates this procedure: "Balaam said unto Balak, Lo, I am come unto thee: have I now any power at all to say anything? The word that God putteth in my mouth, that shall I speak" (Numbers 22:38). Although Balaam was describing the operation of the gift of prophecy, the procedure and relationships he set forth also characterize the gift of tongues. When one is to utter anointed speech, he is mute until God gives him the message.

While the Bible makes a difference between tongues as a sign of Spirit baptism and tongues as a gift of the Spirit, this difference is one of function and not one of kind. It could be said: "Tongues are tongues, whatever their particular function or role." If one chooses to use the term *glossolalia*, then he rightly can apply it either to the tongues on the Day of Pentecost (Acts 2:4), or to the gift of tongues that Paul presents to the Corinthians with instructions for use (cf. 1 Corinthians 12:10, 30; 14:2, 4, 5, 6, 13, 18 ff.). Whether tongues function as a sign or gift, there is one basic phenomenon: the organs of speech of a believing and yielded human are controlled by the Holy Spirit.

God's purposes in giving tongues begin with their role as evidence of the baptism in the Spirit. However, in the lives of most Pentecostal believers, tongues functioning as a gift of the Spirit enlarge their purposes to include the following three specific practical outcomes:

1. *Tongues are a medium of prayer and worship.* Paul wrote: "He that speaketh in an unknown tongue speaketh not unto men, but unto God" (1 Corinthians 14:2); and, "If I pray in an unknown tongue, my spirit prayeth" (14:14). Tongues relate the worshiper directly to God, and transcend the ordinary limitations of human speech. One speaking in tongues has been described as engaging in a "spiritual soliloquy," and Scripture specifically contrasts prayer in the Spirit involving tongues, with prayer framed by human understanding (cf. 1 Corinthians 14:14, 15). Karl Barth referred to tongues as "an attempt to express the inexpressible." Through tongues, prayer and worship are raised to their highest level and elevated far above superficial lip service. Through the Spirit, humans are enabled to worship in spirit and in truth. On occasion, the gift of tongues constitutes a divinely given articulated speech that communicates directly with God. Such tongues may not be intelligible to humans, but they are certainly more than gibberish or a natural ecstatic outburst. In discussing prayer in tongues, Mjorud writes: "Tongues speaking is a new way of praying. . . . It is prayer that is nontaxing, freewheeling, flowing [and] restful."[10]

It is generally held that when the gift of tongues functions as a medium of worship and prayer, even though it is in a public gathering, what is said does not have to be interpreted. This function of the gift contrasts with the gift of tongues as a medium to speak to a congregation—in this latter case it should be interpreted, for it is the congregation rather than God who is being addressed. However, as Paul points out, for the sake of the impression upon the "unlearned" who may be present, the use of the gift of tongues in the public assembly, for whatever purpose, should be suitably controlled.

2. *Tongues are a sign.* Paul wrote: "Wherefore tongues are for a sign, not to them that believe, but to them that believe not" (1 Corinthians 14:22). In general, a manifestation of tongues establishes that God is real and at work through His Holy Spirit. By their existence, tongues proclaim that God has spoken, and that He is to be believed and obeyed. A visible or audible sign becomes necessary wherever there are those who are unable to be convinced by faith alone.

Paul's quotation from Isaiah (Isaiah 28:9-13) relates to a historical prophecy. The prophet had declared that if God's people would not believe and repent, they would suffer conquest by a foreign invader. The unintelligible tongues of the conquerors were to be a sign of divine judgment upon them. Paul was not claiming that the sound of tongues was a sign proclaiming that professed believers were not truly believers, or that they were herewith the subjects of God's judgment. But Paul did see a parallel between his days and those of Isaiah. When it comes to possessing enlightened faith concerning the presence or working of God, or His use of certain human instruments, many Christians experience temporary uncertainty. Under such circumstances, they are among those who "believe not," and tongues are the reassuring sign that they need. However, although a Christian who is not able to commit himself in faith to an aspect of divine truth may be said to "believe not," that certainly does not make him an "unbeliever" in the sense of being an agnostic or atheist.

3. *Tongues are a medium of edification.* Paul declares: "He that speaketh in an unknown tongue edifieth himself" (1 Corinthians 14:4). The manifestation of the gift of tongues calls for the believer's yieldedness, and the establishment of a new sense of communion with God. The relationship is not intellectual, but spiritual; it elevates humans to a dimension and height that far transcends the natural. Such an uplift is truly spiritually edifying. The word *edification* denotes "a process of building up," and in the spiritual realm, this is exactly what tongues accomplish in the believer. Paul saw great value in tongues, and recognizing that only this gift resulted in personal edification, he exhorted: "I would that ye all spake with tongues" (1

Corinthians 14:5). In turn, he gave thanks: "I thank my God, I speak with tongues more than ye all" (14:18).

Most Pentecostals consider that glossolalia is given primarily as a witness to the preaching of the gospel, and not as the medium for that preaching. On the Day of Pentecost, when the various nationals heard in their own tongue "the wonderful works of God" (Acts 2.11), when Peter preached the gospel, he spoke in the one conventional vernacular of that day. In the realm of preaching, the miracle of Pentecost was not so much the empowering of men to speak a foreign tongue, but the empowering of men to speak their own language persuasively on behalf of the gospel. Glossolalia does not ordinarily communicate in preaching, but in conveying God's special message to humans, and sometimes man's special message to God (e.g., through prayer in the Spirit). Primarily, Biblical accounts of tongues depict God's people worshiping and praying rather than preaching.

The gift of tongues or glossolalia ministers in a threefold realm: 1) to the individual believer (one edifies himself, 1 Corinthians 14:4), 2) to the unbeliever (tongues are a sign to those who believe not, 14:22), 3) to the Church or Christian community (this gift takes its place among others, 14:26). Many instances of glossolalia, of course, involve all three realms. However, some matters pertaining to the gift of tongues are set forth as problems, because of a failure to distinguish the primary realm in which the gift is operating.

When tongues minister to the church, they become the most regulated of all gifts. Scripture teaches: no more than three messages in tongues in a given service, tongues are valid in a public service only if an interpreter is present, and the speakers must speak one at a time (cf. 1 Corinthians 14:27, 28). Someone has remarked: "The regulations impose no real bondage, and casting them away provides no real liberty." Although tongues are one of the most common of the gifts of the Spirit, regulations are necessary because some believers lack the discernment to distinguish between instances intended for private communion and those intended for public communication. The gift of tongues is one of nine coequal spiritual gifts; where it is excessively emphasized, it must be restrained; where it is neglected, it must be encouraged.

The Gift of Interpretation of Tongues

This gift provides the ability to know directly and intuitively that which God is seeking to communicate through the gift of tongues. Both the sense and the import of one language is made intelligible in another. The word *interpretation* connotes "to explain thoroughly," and it includes the concepts of exposition and application. Daniel's ministry illustrates this gift (cf. Daniel 5:25-28). Four words were written on the wall: "Numeration, Numeration, Weighing, Division." Daniel's interpretation extended to three sentences that explained the words, and showed who was weighed in the balances and what was numbered and divided. Interpretation is distinguished from translation which basically operates on a word-to-word basis, and requires the understanding of the one who speaks.

It is on the basis of an exposition of the Greek text that Albert Hoy concludes: "An interpretation is perfectly scriptural if it not only explains the utterance in tongues, but also applies its meaning to those who hear."[11] It must follow, of course, that the exercise of this gift must maintain its status as a message from God. It must invoke neither that which is derogatory nor misleading, nor that which seeks personal recognition and respect of persons. Dalton writes:

Interpretation of tongues is the supernatural showing forth by the Spirit of the meaning of an utterance in other languages. This interpretation is not an operation of the mind of the interpreter but the mind of the Spirit of God. . . . The interpretation is just as much a miracle as the original utterance in tongues. Both are utterances equally direct from the mind of the Spirit of God.[12]

The function of the gift of the interpretation of tongues is not a mental performance but a spiritual process. It is not so much that one deliberately and consciously analyzes what he has heard, but rather that he submits to the Holy Spirit to allow Him to communicate as He sees fit. The gift assures that the mind of God is opened to His people. The combination of tongues plus interpretation may have a result equivalent to prophecy, but obviously, two gifts cannot be said to be the same as one. The possibility of the Spirit's speaking through a believer in the first person is not ruled out (cf. Acts 13:2). Although the words spoken are in the known language, the gift of interpretation is a supernatural act of God, and the whole process is a miracle.

But the gift of interpretation entails human participation also. The Holy Spirit does not ordinarily overrule or suppress the human channel that He uses. Richard Dresselhaus has written:

> The Holy Spirit conveys the message, but He uses human instruments as the vehicle. . . . If the individual being moved upon to interpret is timid, poorly educated, or has a speech defect, the utterance will reflect this, but it in no wise obscures the force of what the Spirit has to say.[13]

It is one of the paradoxes of God's use of human instruments that He accepts and functions within the limitations of His chosen ones, while at the same time, He achieves whatever divine work He intended.

The Gift of Prophecy

The believer who ministers the gift of prophecy tells forth the mind of God; through this gift, God declares himself to His people. Stephen Clark writes:

> Prophecy . . . is God making use of someone to tell men what he thinks about the present situation or what his intention is for the future, or what he thinks they should know or be needful of right now.[14]

Prophecy has been called the "poetry of the spirit" because the thoughts expressed and the language used often rise above the abilities of the human subject. Prophecy is ordinarily a vocal utterance, but with proper caution and evaluation in terms of Scripture, written prophecies or symbolic acts would not be excluded from instances of the functioning of this gift (cf. Agabus bound himself with Paul's girdle to convey a prophetic message, Acts 21:10, 11). In all instances of the functioning of the gift of prophecy, God acts through His chosen one to deliver His message to others. A prophecy constitutes some aspect of a revelation of God, although not in the same sense or with the same authority as the Biblical revelation.

The gift of prophecy provides a message from God through a human channel. In many instances, prophecy has much in common with anointed preaching, and in their effect upon an audience, the two procedures could be indistinguishable. However, prophecy does not involve specific preparation by study and research, evaluation of what should be said, or the preparation of outline notes. The basis of prophecy is a personal revelation of the mind and will of God by direct impression. The basis of preaching and teaching is an intelligible exposition of the written revelation of Scripture. In some instances, prophecy probably merges with preaching and teaching ministries, and the presence of the gift is not recognized by the audience, and possibly not even by the one who is speaking. Peter declared that the gift of prophecy fulfilled God's promises: "I will pour out of my Spirit upon all flesh: and your sons and your daughters shall prophesy" (Acts 2:17). At Ephesus, when Paul laid hands on the 12 believers, "they spoke with tongues, and prophesied" (Acts 19:6).

Scripture depicts the gift of prophecy as ministering in a variety of ways:

1) It edifies, builds up faith, or promotes growth in the Lord. "He that prophesieth speaketh unto men to edification" (1 Corinthians 14:3). It has been said: "Prophetic speech is good building material." Prophecy is not for breaking down, but for building up.

2) It serves to exhort believers (cf. 1 Corinthians 14:3). Exhortation ought to motivate believers to greater godliness and encourage them in spiritual matters. Exhortation is not intended to be a "telling off," but a "calling onward." In some contexts, the Biblical word *exhortation* is equivalent to today's term *personal counseling*.

3) It conveys comfort (cf. 1 Corinthians 14:3). Prophecy may become a reassuring consolation regarding all that is spiritually available from God. Prophecy may be constituted of words of

tenderness and personal concern. Such prophecy leads to composure and personal peace.

4) It convicts the unbeliever of sin. "But if all prophesy, and there come in one that believeth not . . . he is convinced of all, he is judged of all" (1 Corinthians 14:24). This passage has been paraphrased: "The unbeliever is convicted of his sin by every speaker; he feels himself judged by all."

5) It communicates facts and ideas. "For ye may all prophesy one by one, that all may learn" (1 Corinthians 14:31). Since the gift of prophecy involves the sharing of the mind of God, its pronouncements necessarily involve an opportunity for God's people to learn. They are enabled to see through the eyes of God.

6) It may predict the future. "A certain prophet, named Agabus . . . said, Thus saith the Holy Ghost, So shall the Jews at Jerusalem bind the man that owneth this girdle" (Acts 21:10). When the gift of prophecy predicts the future, it is likely that it also fulfills one of the other functions already described.

According to Paul, all believers are eligible to prophesy, and the gift is especially to be coveted (cf. 1 Corinthians 14:31: "Ye may all prophesy one by one"; and 14:39: "Covet to prophesy"). However, the New Testament portrayal indicates a careful selectivity in the divine bestowment of the gift. Paul no doubt was impressed to stress prophecy because he was dealing with communal church worship rather than individual. At Caesarea, Paul and his company lodged in the house of Philip the evangelist who "had four daughters, virgins, who did prophesy" (Acts 21:9). Nevertheless, the message that God had for Paul was communicated by a specially sent prophet: "There came down from Judea a certain prophet named Agabus" (Acts 21:10). Not just anyone who has been used to manifest the gift of prophecy apparently is suitable for certain specific tasks.

The gift of prophecy, just as the gift of tongues, is to be regulated in its expression in a public meeting. Prophetic messages are to be presented one by one in succession and not simultaneously (cf. 1 Corinthians 14:31). When a speaker has had his opportunity, he must be willing to yield the floor to another. "If any thing be revealed to another that sitteth by, let the first hold his peace" (1 Corinthians 14:30). There should be a definite limit on the number of prophetic utterances in a given service: "Let the prophets speak two or three, and let the other [lit., others] judge" (14:29). This verse also notes that each prophetic utterance should be subject to judgment or evaluation by the other believers who are present. "Judge" is literally "discern," and it is the same verb that is used in the expression "discerning of spirits." Because the gift of prophecy operates through imperfect human vessels, it is fallible and limited, and must always be subject to evaluation from outside of itself. It is this characteristic of understandable prophecy that may encourage some believers to cultivate tongues which tend to transcend evaluation!

God's order in the Church Age is that the authority of the written Scripture must stand above any other revelations, including the gift of prophecy. A modern prophetic utterance can legitimately neither contradict nor add to the Word of God. Unlike Old Testament prophecies, those of this era can bring no new revelation of abiding authoritative significance. In the history of the church, when prophecy has been exalted above Scripture, the results have been disastrous. For the most part, Pentecostal leaders discourage written transcriptions of prophetic messages on the grounds that such writings could become competitive with the Bible. Notwithstanding, it is commonly claimed that Pitman's Shorthand was invented by the Irvingites (Catholic Apostolic Church) as a technique for recording prophetic messages. Sooner or later, human frailties would almost surely lead to errors in such documents, and it is possible that some of the problems of later Irvingism may be accounted for on these grounds.

Primarily, prophecy is a gift to sharpen, illumine, and energize the already revealed truths of Scripture for their forceful presentation. The operation of the gift of prophecy places the believer into the role of a chosen instrument who shares the divine message with others. Paul exhorted: "Despise not prophesyings" (1 Thessalonians 5:20), perhaps because he recognized the unique ministry of the gift in empowering men to speak out against sin. However, Paul also wrote: "It pleased God by the foolishness of preaching to save them that believe" (1 Corinthians 1:21). Prophecy is not meant to be a substitute for the preached word, any more than it is meant to be a substitute for the written Word.

To some measure, the manifestation of the gift of prophecy provides that the human channel fulfills the ministry of a prophet. However, the New Testament suggests that to be a prophet one must possess other gifts of revelation (cf. 1 Corinthians 14:29-32). Also, the New Testament prophet should be distinguished from his Old Testament counterpart. In Old Testament times, a prophet was often a quasi-political and national leader who was deeply involved with affairs of state. In the New Testament era, when God relates to mankind on a spiritual rather than a national basis, the prophet's ministry is restricted to the realm of the spiritual. The New Testament Church has seen no particular advantage of bestowing titles upon prophets; a sincere recognition of the message of God's spokespersons is all that is necessary. One who is not an administrator, but simply a messenger communicating God's Word, does not ordinarily require designation of an official status.

The ministry of the gift of prophecy is particularly essential during crisis times in the Church. In addition to the ministry of Agabus relating to Paul's future, Scripture also reports:

> And in those days came prophets from Jerusalem unto Antioch. And there stood up one of them named Agabus, and signified by the Spirit that there should be a great dearth throughout all the world: which came to pass in the days of Claudius Caesar (Acts 11:27, 28).

Prophecy, in its role of telling the future, enabled the Church to prepare for the coming famine. On another occasion, the gift of prophecy operated to communicate to the Gentiles their role in the Christian Church: "And Judas and Silas, being prophets also themselves, exhorted the brethren with many words, and confirmed them" (Acts 15:32). It was by this means that the Gentile converts at Antioch learned of their acceptance, and their minimal legal responsibilities within the Church.

The Bestowment and Use of Spiritual Gifts

The administration and operation of the gifts of the Spirit combine the sovereignty of God with various aspects of human involvement. Even though God acts in sovereign freedom, He does not act capriciously. His actions are always purposeful. Those whom He blesses with spiritual gifts are committed to assume appropriate responsibilities. Those who would be His channels must learn to function within the laws under which He operates.

The Bestowment of Spiritual Gifts

Humans are invariably fascinated by the miraculous, and there is widespread desire for the gifts of the Spirit. Thus, there is interest concerning what can be said of the principles applying in regard to the bestowment of spiritual gifts, even if no simple set of firm rules can be formulated.

1. *Divine sovereignty governs the distribution of the gifts.* The sovereign choice of Deity in the bestowment of the gifts of the Spirit may be taken as a basic principle: "All these worketh that one and the selfsame Spirit, dividing to every man severally [individually] as he will" (1 Corinthians 12:11); "God also bearing them witness, both with signs and wonders, and with divers miracles, and gifts [lit., distributions or divided portions] of the Holy Ghost, according to his own will" (Hebrews 2:4). There are no generally recognized promises specifically pertaining to the gifts that the believer is entitled to claim. Spiritual gifts are not depicted as that which is to be appropri-

ated by faith. Particular actions or attitudes may complement the Spirit's bestowment of a gift, but ultimately, the gift that is given is the Spirit's decision. Scripture may hint that all believers receive at least one gift of the Spirit (cf., 1 Corinthians 7:7), but which gift and under what circumstances appear to be the Spirit's choice alone.

2. *The human recipient must will to receive.* Scripture sets forth the believer's part: "Covet earnestly the best gifts" (1 Corinthians 12:31), and "desire spiritual gifts" (14:1). In the case of one who publicly speaks in tongues, he is advised to "pray that he may interpret" (14:13). Earnest desire to the point of covetousness with heartfelt prayer are thus set forth as important aspects of the believer's involvement. No particular merit, otherwise, on the believer's part is specified, because gifts, by their very nature, must be bestowed apart from merit. The attitude of an open, responsive, submissive heart always is meaningful to God. Not every Christian who wants a gift may receive one, but it is certain that those who do receive a gift earnestly want to receive. A gift can be given only when there is a willing recipient. Spiritual gifts are, as it were, living possessions that involve the recipient in a vital personal manner. The desire for spiritual gifts is an enthusiastic commitment to involve oneself in a supernatural ministry for God.

3. *The human and divine roles blend together.* Neither divine sovereignty nor human responsibility operates independently of the other. The traditional Pentecostal adage counsels: "Seek the Giver and not the gift." Thus, the desire for a gift is actually expressed in terms of a desire to give a greater place to Deity in one's life. Paul wrote to the Corinthians: "Even as the testimony of Christ was confirmed in you: so that ye come behind in no gift" (1 Corinthians 1:6, 7). The Holy Spirit's free exercise of sovereign will in the bestowment of a gift is certainly not in direct defiance of the condition and response of the recipient. Palma comments: "A Christian must place himself in a position to be used by the Holy Spirit and to receive spiritual gifts, but the actual bestowal of the gifts is the prerogative of the Spirit."[1] In a later summary he says: "The desire is our responsibility; the distribution, the Spirit's."[2] The atmosphere in

which the gifts flourish may include: the practice of wholehearted worship, unity and mutual love among brethren, and an enthusiastic commitment to fulfill the Great Commission. The actual exercise of a gift, particularly a gift of utterance, is a matter of human commitment and involvement that can be compared to participation by choice and intention in a testimony meeting. However, the human is able to choose to be involved only because simultaneously the Holy Spirit is ministering His divine empowering.

4. *The gifts are given on a strictly personal basis.* The experience of one in this realm is not necessarily the pattern for another: "So we, being many, are one body in Christ, and every one members one of another. Having then gifts differing according to the grace that is given to us" (Romans 12:5, 6); "Are all apostles? are all prophets? are all teachers? are all workers of miracles? Have all the gifts of healing? do all speak with tongues? do all interpret?" (1 Corinthians 12:29, 30). Diversity of individual experience goes hand in hand with the sovereignty of the Spirit in manifesting spiritual gifts. Paul wrote: "Each has his own special gift from God, one of this kind and one of another" (1 Corinthians 7:7, *The Amplified Bible*). It would appear that God the Holy Spirit deliberately avoids all that savors of stereotypes. If men are to respect His sovereignty, then they cannot ascribe undue authority to a fellow human, a memorized formula, a pattern of behavior, or any other humanly devised phenomenon.

5. *The Spirit avoids all force and compulsion.* In the bestowment of the gifts, just as in all His operations, the Holy Spirit's methods are gentle and tender. Servants and slaves may be driven, but sons ordinarily are directed by being led: "For as many as are led by the Spirit of God, they are the sons of God" (Romans 8:14). It is not the Spirit's pattern to seize someone against his will. Dr. David Lim once wrote: "The exercise of the gift depends upon our willingness and readiness, not upon an overwhelming, uncontrollable force." "The spirits of the prophets are subject to the prophets" (1 Corinthians 14:32). Those who desire spiritual gifts should recognize these characteristics of the Spirit.

6. *Gifts typically are given to fill specific needs.* Gifts are not for the personal pleasure and advantage of the recipient, but according to the need of God's people in the overall accomplishment of the work of God on earth and the advance of His church. Paul admonished: "Even so ye, forasmuch as ye are zealous of spiritual gifts, seek that ye may excel to the edifying of the church" (1 Corinthians 14:12). Since spiritual gifts are meant to take their place in achieving the program of God on earth, to some degree their presence or absence depends on that program. Where there are believers committed to spiritual worship and service out of genuine love to God, the gifts of the Spirit most certainly belong, and their manifestation can be expected.

7. *Gifts that have been given are retained by being used.* The example of Timothy establishes this principle. Paul twice exhorted Timothy: "Neglect not the gift that is in thee" (1 Timothy 4:14); and, "Wherefore I put thee in remembrance that thou stir up the gift of God, which is in thee" (2 Timothy 1:6). The conventional image of Timothy is of a somewhat shy young man who may have found it difficult to assert himself even in the realm of spiritual gifts. Paul recognized that the issue was more than merely overcoming a trait of character; Timothy's future in charismatic ministry lay in his stirring up the gift that he had been given. Peter wrote: "As every man hath received the gift [GK., *charisma*], even so minister the same one to another" (1 Peter 4:10). It would appear that many believers who express regret because they have been given no spiritual gift, are actually failing to recognize and manifest the gift they have been given. When one faithfully uses his spiritual gift, or gifts, he not only is a blessing, but also is blessed himself.

8. *Christian leaders may encourage others to receive gifts.* It is specifically noted that the laying on of hands was associated with Timothy's spiritual gift. Paul reported both "the laying on of the hands of the presbytery" (1 Timothy 4:14), and "the putting on of my hands [i.e., Paul's own]" (2 Timothy 1:6). To the Romans, Paul wrote: "I long to see you, that I may impart unto you some spiritual gift" (Romans 1:1). Whether the refer-

ence is to a charismatic gift, and whether Paul would have laid hands on Roman Christians is not reported, but these are plausible assumptions. It is frequently visualized that believers in Biblical times enjoyed the ministry of their leaders in prayer and the laying on of hands, and the outcome was the impartation of spiritual gifts.

But a balanced understanding must be maintained. The sovereignty of the Spirit is an essential aspect. The source of the gifts is God the Holy Spirit, rather than any human leader. The part of humans is to encourage, to instruct, to exemplify, and sometimes to serve as channels for that which God intends to perform. In God's economy, no one human enjoys special grace above another so that he is especially equipped as a repository of spiritual gifts to be given to others. Men can most certainly influence one another, but the actual accomplishments of spiritual works are exclusively wrought by Deity. When a leader lays hands on a candidate for a spiritual gift, the leader does not ordinarily become a channel of divine power, but he does significantly identify with the candidate before both God and humans. The leader's identification endorses the life and ministry of the candidate, and his prayers become the basis of God's action.

God's Use of Spiritual Gifts

Just as it is possible to glean principles implied in Scripture concerning the bestowment of spiritual gifts, it is also possible to discover principles that give insight into God's manner of using the gifts of the Spirit in accomplishing His work on earth.

1. *Spiritual gifts are one mode among others that God uses.* Spiritual gifts always entail the supernatural intervention of God, and therefore they contrast with a mode of working that is limited to the known natural laws of God. The accomplishment of God's objectives may or may not require the supernatural. When God chooses to involve the miraculous to achieve His work, and at the same time involve human workers in the project, His ordinary procedure is to use spiritual gifts. Sometimes He chooses not to involve the miraculous, and sometimes even though there is a miracle, humans are not directly in-

volved as channels. And sometimes, God is miraculously involved through His people, but He chooses not to manifest that which can be specifically identified as a spiritual gift. (e.g., The word of wisdom is a gift of the Spirit, but God also offers divine wisdom to all who lack and ask for it; cf. James 1:5.) The uniqueness of the gifts of the Spirit is not necessarily in what they provide, but in how they provide it.

Scripture depicts interesting contrasts in God's procedures in accomplishing His work on earth. He refrained from intervening when Herod launched his persecution and "killed James the brother of John with the sword" (Acts 12:2). But God ministered miracles to deliver Peter from the Jerusalem prison (12:5-10), and Paul and Silas from prison in Philippi (16:23-34). The Spirit manifested a gift of healing through Paul at Lystra so that the man who was a cripple from birth "leaped and walked" (14:8-11). Nevertheless, Paul found it necessary to report: "Trophimus have I left at Miletus sick" (2 Timothy 4:20). The gift of prophecy functioned to warn Paul of his fate at Jerusalem (Acts 21:10-14), but he seems to have been limited to his own wisdom to decide what he should do with the information.

2. *God gives gifts to serve the Church rather than individuals.* The pattern is that the gifts are not primarily given to the individual, but through the individual to the Church. The presence of one or more gifted individuals in a given situation may be exactly what is needed for the sake of the group as a whole and the achievement of their corporate ministry. Paul's extended analogy of the Church as a body with various members (1 Corinthians 12:21-27) sets forth the value of the gifts to relate their functioning within and on behalf of the Body. The interlude emphasizing love (13:1-13), the stress on the necessity of the intelligibility of what is spoken (14:19), and the commendation of prophecy (15:5), all similarly speak of the divine concern that the gifts are to serve the entire Body. The gifts must be used with love because they are related to and directed toward a body of people, and not merely for the sake of the one who ministers.

3. *The gifts reside in God and remain under His direction.* Scripture depicts spiritual gifts as "manifested" rather than

conferred or bestowed: "But the manifestation of the Spirit is given . . ." (1 Corinthians 12:7). It has been pointed out that spiritual gifts are not "things," but the functioning of a Person—the divine Holy Spirit. Thus, one has a spiritual gift to the degree that the Holy Spirit has him. A gift of the Spirit is a relationship with the divine; in effect, humans are permitted to become stewards of the miraculous ministry of the Holy Spirit in the task of accomplishing the work of God on earth. That which Michael Harper says of prophecy is true of all the gifts: "It is not an ability given to someone to prophesy at will. It is a special anointing given at a selected moment by the Spirit for a distinct purpose."[3] The nature and design of the gifts of the Spirit permit their manifestation only if there is contact with the divine Giver.

The procedures of God in bestowing spiritual gifts are illustrated by Samson's experiences with the anointing of the Spirit. Samson was able to kill the lion: "And the Spirit of the Lord came mightily upon him, and he rent [the lion] as he would have rent a kid" (Judges 14:6). He was able to slay the Philistines at Ashkelon: "And the Spirit of the Lord came upon him, and he went down to Ashkelon, and slew thirty men of them" (14:19). He could break his fetters: "The Spirit of the Lord came mightily upon him, and the cords that were upon his arms became as flax that was burnt with fire, and his bands loosed from off his hands" (15:14). Samson's powerlessness, and subsequent capture by the Philistines, took place because the Spirit of the Lord no longer came upon Samson: "He wist not that the Lord was departed from him" (16:20). When the Spirit of the Lord rested on Samson he performed great feats of power; when there was no anointing Spirit he had little advantage over other men.

4. *The Spirit selects particular humans as His channels.* In spite of the foregoing, it is also to be recognized that God, through His gifts, commits himself to human channels. The gifts of the Spirit entail God the Holy Spirit at work through human individuals. It is typical of the Spirit to be consistent in His choice of vessels. Scripture twice mentions Agabus with his gift of prophecy:

And in these days came prophets from Jerusalem unto Antioch. And there stood up one of them named Agabus, and signified by the Spirit that there should be a great dearth throughout all the world. . . . There came down from Judea a certain prophet named Agabus . . ." (Acts 11:27, 28; 21:10).

There is evidence that 10 or more years intervened between these two references. Thus, the enduring nature of Agabus' gift is clearly indicated. It can be said that the believer "has" a gift as long as he remains under the control of the Holy Spirit in whom the gift resides.

Some have suggested that Paul's words to the Romans apply to spiritual gifts: "For the gifts and calling of God are without repentance" (Romans 11:29). Modern translations encourage this view: "God does not change his mind about those to whom he gives his gifts [the original is charismata] or sends his calling" (literal translation). However, this issue was clarified for many Pentecostals a generation ago by Charles S. Price who wrote: "This scripture has nothing to do with the gifts of the Spirit—it deals only with the promise God made to His people relative to their national salvation."[4] Today, scholars would probably prefer to speak of a primary and secondary application of the text, and it would be agreed that only in a secondary sense could Paul's words be applied to the gifts of 1 Corinthians 12. The consistency and dependability of God is sufficient to enable His child to serve in confident trust, but not in excess to enable him to presume.

The Regulation of Spiritual Gifts

It was to correct abuses in the exercise of spiritual gifts that Paul wrote major sections of the Corinthian epistles. He set forth his concluding principle: "Let all things be done decently and in order" (1 Corinthians 14:40). The need for this exhortation, and factors in the manifestation of the gifts that make possible their misuse, include the following:

1. *God's method of working is cooperative and not arbitrary.* God always permits the believer to share in decisions concerning each mutual project. "We then as workers together

with him . . ." (2 Corinthians 6:1). God considers each believer to be a policy-making partner and, as such, He grants appropriate respect and freedom. "Wherefore thou art no more a servant, but a son" (Galatians 4:7). God permits His spiritual adult partners a rather wide range of behavior, and He simply asks that what is done should always be intended to honor and glorify Him. In commenting on the restrictions on tongues and prophecy in 1 Corinthians 14, Horton writes:

> The Holy Spirit respects our integrity and will not force us to obey the instructions given here. For example, if there are more than three messages in tongues this does not mean the fourth was not of the Spirit. He puts the responsibility on us. If all we will respond to is tongues, He will keep giving us nothing but tongues—and let us stay spiritual babies if we want to.[5]

It has been pointed out that God accepts the principle that the vessel that is filled is entitled to give its own shape to that which it contains. Rufus Moseley taught: "A narrow-minded man receives a narrow-minded revelation, but a genuine revelation nevertheless." Inevitably, the overall personality and perspective of the human subject affect the operation of the Spirit through him.

The believer works together with God even in the manifestation of supernatural spiritual phenomena. God neither dominates the believer nor deprives him of self-control. The one through whom the Spirit is manifested remains responsible to behave reasonably and in a wise and proper manner. Ervin writes:

> The Spirit-filled Christian is permeated with, not invaded by, the Divine Spirit. The charismatic manifestations of the Spirit are voluntary responses, not involuntary reactions, to the Holy Spirit's initiative. Confusion in the expression of the Spirit's gift results from lack of discipline, not loss of consciousness.[6]

The Christian is responsible to become duly informed and adequately disciplined and reasonable in his behavior. By this means he complements the divine working, and he avoids possible pitfalls in the manifestation of spiritual gifts.

2. *Lack of knowledge may result in temporary misuse.* Not

every believer understands all he ought to know, and it is possible for an earnest and sincere believer to commit an honest blunder. Paul wrote: "Now concerning spiritual gifts . . . I would not have you ignorant" (1 Corinthians 12:1). His concern at that time was for people who were freely manifesting spiritual gifts, but out of ignorance were misusing and abusing that which they ministered. These people must either accept Paul's instructions and mend their ways, or reject instruction and sooner or later cease to be anointed by God. Albert Hoy, discussing unscriptural practices in manifesting gifts, sets forth a second rule: "A faithful church member who engages in the practice [of misusing a gift] should not be rebuked but instructed."

Since human channels are involved, limitations and peculiarities of human nature are always important factors. Donald Gee wrote:

There may be a stage, first of all, where the believer is like a child to learn the right exercise of spiritual gifts by implicit obedience to government. . . . But if there is a true spiritual growth this should quickly become unnecessary.[7]

Godly leaders should not hesitate to give counsel, but always in a spirit of Christian love and understanding. Harold Horton wrote:

When a man, giving forth a message in a meeting, says he couldn't help it, and the Spirit compelled him, he is deceiving himself. God does not break His own Word. Such a man should be lovingly and firmly corrected.[8]

3. *Spiritual gifts can be counterfeited.* Some who profess to manifest spiritual gifts may actually be acting only in their own spirit so that the outcome is all of self and not of God. Jesus said:

Many will say to me in that day, Lord, Lord, have we not prophesied in thy name? and in thy name cast out devils? and in thy name done many wonderful works? And then will I profess unto them, I never knew you: depart from me, ye that work iniquity (Matthew 7:23).

A much more deceptive type of counterfeit is that by satanic spirits. Scripture warns: "Beloved, believe not every spirit, but try the spirits whether they are of God: because many prophets are gone out into the world" (1 John 4:1). Satan is an impressive miracle worker: "Even him, whose coming is after the working of Satan with all power and signs and lying wonders" (2 Thessalonians 2:9).

The blood-washed believer is never a victim of satanic spirits; those who operate in this realm do so by deliberate choice. Counterfeit gifts are the outcome of a counterfeit life. However, this is not to say that satanic spirits are always associated with outward vileness or immorality. Satan achieves his objectives when he induces men to defy the known will of God. John provided a useful criterion to evaluate spirits: "Every spirit which confesses that Jesus Christ has come in the flesh is of God, and every spirit which does not confess Jesus is not of God" (1 John 4:2, 3, *RSV*). While the committed Christian, cleansed by the blood of Jesus Christ, need have no fear of being personally possessed by a demonic or satanic spirit, he must be on guard against others who have permitted such a possession. Signs and miracles, if they are not accompanied by a godly life and sound Biblical doctrine, are no evidence of spiritual genuineness.

4. *Believers are obligated to exercise the gifts responsibly.* God does not demand perfection in all areas before the believer can begin to work in any. It would appear possible for an earnest Christian to be so concerned for the manifestation of a spiritual gift that he neglects responsible concern for the impression he makes on others. Paul described the impression made on unlearned or unbelieving visitors to the Corinthian church where the gift of tongues was so freely manifested: "Will they not say that ye are mad?" (1 Corinthians 14:23). Anthony Palma once commented: "Liberty in the Spirit must be governed by responsibility to the body." The believer's zeal must be responsibly restrained by what is wise and best for the whole. Chadwick writes:

Spiritual gifts are no proof of spirituality. . . . The Scriptures make it plain that in a Church that "came behind in no gift, waiting for the coming of the Lord," there were carnalities that would have disgraced a decent pagan assembly. Gifts are not substitutes for Grace.[9]

Not all Christians achieve the ideal of the wise and responsible Christ-life simultaneously with their achievement of a response to the Spirit's manifestation of gifts. Although Paul and Barnabas cooperated in a charismatic ministry during the first missionary journey (Acts 13:4 to 14:28), they somehow lacked the grace to agree on whether to take John Mark on their second journey (15:36-39). Even these stalwarts of the New Testament evidently fell short of total Christian character maturity. Though lives certainly cannot be totally unworthy and motives irresponsible, it is clear that God permits His channels a wide range of freedom. Some who manifest spiritual gifts still have much to learn.

The Fruit of the Holy Spirit

The expression "fruit of the Spirit" is strictly Biblical even though it is the language of allegory. In a picturesque manner, it identifies the work of the Holy Spirit in reproducing His gracious virtues in the life of the believer. The fruit of the Spirit pertain to the believer's character, while the gifts of the Spirit pertain to the believer's service.

The Identity and Necessity of Spiritual Fruit

The fruit of the Spirit is the harvest that results when a life is lived in abiding submission to the Spirit. In the basic passage, Paul wrote: "The fruit of the Spirit is love, joy, peace, long-suffering, gentleness, goodness, faith, meekness, temperance" (Galatians 5:22, 23). Elsewhere, he commented: "For the fruit of the Spirit is in all goodness and righteousness and truth" (Ephesians 5:9). Peter exhorted:

Add to your faith virtue; and . . . knowledge; and . . . temperance; and . . . patience; and . . . godliness; and . . . brotherly kindness; and . . . charity. For if these things be in you, and abound, they make you that ye shall neither be barren nor unfruitful (2 Peter 1:5-8).

In the Upper Room discourse, Jesus spoke at length on the believer's responsibility to bear fruit (cf. John 15:1-16). The analogy depicts an orchard, with fruit the principal product of the trees. Fruit justifies the existence of a particular tree; its absence eventually leads to the tree's removal. The productive tree not only grows conspicuously above ground, but also has adequate unseen roots. Fruit is not a matter of effort and struggle, but it is the simple expression of the inner life of the tree. In almost all instances, Scripture uses the term *fruit* in the singular. In the analogy of the orchard, just as a basket of apples could be called the fruit of a particular tree, so the individual character traits are each the expression of a single nature. Since to be a Christian is to be born of the Spirit, all believers should bear His fruit.

On occasion, Scripture uses the expression *fruit* to denote souls won or works achieved by the Christian: "I purposed to come unto you . . . that I might have some fruit among you also, even as among other Gentiles" (Romans 1:13). "Not because I desire a gift: but I desire fruit that may abound to your account" (Philippians 4:17). However, this usage is secondary to the use of the term *fruit* to identify virtuous traits of Christian character. The graces or virtues constituting the Spirit's fruit are the blanket expression of one life.

Significant spiritual attainments call for the gifts and the fruit to flourish together. Paul taught that the absence of love, the first of the Spirit's fruit, will annul the gifts (cf. 1 Corinthians 13:1, 2, 8). Paul wrote to the Corinthians: "Ye come behind in no gift" (1 Corinthians 1:7), but he spent the bulk of two epistles instructing them in a worthy Christian walk. To possess gifts without corresponding fruit was an abnormal situation. Jesus taught the means by which religionists would be evaluated: "Ye shall know them by their fruits" (Matthew 7:16). Jesus probably referred both to personal character virtue and to accomplishments in His service.

Just as human powers and abilities do not constitute spiritual gifts, so human resolve and strength of character are not the basis of the virtues that the Spirit intends as His fruit. Though in the manifestation of character virtues, the Holy Spirit may work cooperatively with committed human dedication, the final outcome will be more than the effort of natural man. Ness, speaking of the virtues named by Paul in Galatians, wrote: "These nine spiritual graces cannot be produced by self-endeavor, but only as the Spirit of God himself is allowed to produce them in and through the believer."[1] Donald Gee wrote: "The fruit of the Spirit will . . . be seen as the manifestation and outcome of the divine life put within the believer at regeneration."[2]

Cultivating the Fruit of the Spirit

The contrast in Galatians and other New Testament references is between life in the natural spirit or flesh and life under the impulse of the Holy Spirit. Paul testified: "I know that in me (that is, in my flesh,) dwelleth no good thing" (Romans 7:18). But he encouraged the Roman Christians: "Ye are not in the flesh, but in the Spirit, if so be that the Spirit of God dwell in you" (8:9). God's pattern is that believers "walk not after the flesh, but after the Spirit" (8:4). The unconverted, and even the Christian, receives no help from his natural spirit: "Let us cleanse ourselves from all filthiness of the flesh and spirit, perfecting holiness in the fear of God" (2 Corinthians 7:1). In context, Paul sets forth the pursuit of the fruit of the Spirit as an alternate to the natural life: "Walk in the Spirit, and ye shall not fulfill the lust of the flesh" (Galatians 5:16).

There is a close relationship between the cultivation of the fruit of the Spirit and the pursuit of personal experiential sanctification. (Personal sanctification is sometimes called "progressive sanctification," or in older works "experimental sanctification.") Each is concerned with the modification of character and the achievement of personal holiness. Another way to identify the same goal is to speak of the pursuit of Christlikeness. The enumeration of the nine spiritual fruit has been called "a perfect portrait of Jesus Christ." God's technique for achieving Christlikeness in the believer is by means of the ministry of the indwelling Holy Spirit expressing himself in the fruit of the Spirit. The divine Spirit provides not the mere "imitation of Christ," but the "duplication of Christ" in the life of the believer.

The means of the practical achievement of the fruit of the Spirit is the practice of the life of yieldedness to God the Holy Spirit. The usual means of grace, including reading the Bible, praying, and meditating, certainly apply. There is need for the deliberate denial of the carnal or natural being:

For we know that our old self was crucified with him so that the body of sin might be rendered powerless, that we should no longer be slaves to sin—because anyone who has died has been freed from sin (Romans 6:6, 7, *NIV*).

The fruit of the Spirit will be manifested as the believer remains submitted to the Spirit, as his thoughts and attitudes are dominated by the written Word, and as he resists the expression of his carnal self. Such achievements are likely to grow in intensity, along with other aspects of Christian growth. But the deliberate desire and cooperation of the believer are fundamentally essential.

The Spiritual Fruit of Love

That love which constitutes the fruit of the Spirit is described by Zenas Bicket as "decisive action, in impulsive intoxication." The original word *agape* connotes that which is appropriate to the divine, and in fact the word is uniquely characteristic of Christianity. Since "God is love" (1 John 4:8), this fruit embodies the very essence and nature of God. In Him, love is not merely a sentiment, but a powerful motivation that accounts even for the cross of Calvary (cf. John 3:16). In Father O'Conner's words: "This love is unambiguously Christian, not a merely humanitarian affection." Jesus Christ described, and later exemplified, this love: "Greater love hath no man than this, that a man lay down his life for his friends" (John 15:13).

Love is a motivation or spring of action that finds its chief pleasure in the pleasure of another. Jesus instructed: "Thou shalt love the Lord thy God with all thy heart, and with all thy soul, and with all thy mind. . . . And . . . thou shalt love thy neighbor as thyself" (Matthew 22:37, 39). He declared: "By this shall all men know that ye are my disciples, if ye have love one for another" (John 13:35). Paul emphasized the crucial role of the fruit of love when he broke off his discussion of the gifts of the Spirit to interject what we know as 1 Corinthians 13. He introduced the discussion on love by noting: "Yet show I unto you a more excellent way" (1 Corinthians 12:31). James called "love" the Christian's "royal law." "If ye fulfill the royal law according to the Scripture, Thou shalt love thy neighbor as thyself, ye do well" (James 2:8).

God provides that: "The love of God is shed abroad in our hearts by the Holy Ghost which is given unto us" (Romans 5:5). This divine love is meant to color all the outlooks and conduct of the believer. Paul instructed: "Walk in love, as Christ also hath loved us, and hath given himself for us an offering and a sacrifice to God" (Ephesians 5:1, 2). The church of Biblical times is described by Ervin: "Without love, the apostles are dictators, the elders and deacons are merely busybodies, and the teachers pedants."[3] The point of the account of the post-Resurrection appearance of Jesus to Peter and the query: "Lovest thou me?" was that Peter would never confess to divine (i.e., *agape*) love. As Jesus asked: "Do you love me with divine love?" Peter twice answered: "I love you with human love." The third time Jesus asked: "Do you love me with human love?" and Peter still answered: "I love you with human love." As difficult as it may be for a human to concede possession of divine love, only love of this caliber satisfies God and constitutes the fruit of the Spirit.

The spiritual fruit of love is the antidote to hostility between Christians:

Brethren . . . by love serve one another. For all the law is fulfilled in one word, even in this; Thou shalt love thy neighbor as thyself. But if ye bite and devour one another, take heed that ye be not consumed one of another (Galatians 5:13-15).

Love should direct the believer in his concern for the well-being even of the erring brother: "Ye ought rather to forgive him. . . . Wherefore I beseech you that ye would confirm your love toward him" (2 Corinthians 2:7, 8). Love is a means to unity: "That their hearts might be comforted, being knit together in love" (Colossians 2:2). Love is a means to the enlargement of spiritual vision:

That Christ may dwell in your hearts by faith: that ye, being rooted and grounded in love, may be able to comprehend with all saints what is the breadth, and length, and depth, and height . . . (Ephesians 3:17, 18).

When love, the fruit of the Spirit, rightly functions, it enables the believer to cope with life's demanding circumstances. Divinely implanted love remains unmoved even in the face of chastening and discipline, and it extends not only to one's friends, but also to his enemies. This love motivates the believer as a Christian witness to attempt to bring the God who loves to all men, and to bring all men to God's love. Paul's discourse on love (1 Corinthians 13) enumerates a total of 15 attributes of love: 7 positive and 8 negative. In this passage, several other fruit of the Spirit (e.g., long-suffering, goodness, faith, meekness) are named as expressions of love. It is thus emphasized that love is the basis of other spiritual graces, and absolutely essential in the life of every Christian. Clearly, it is by God's design that love is named first in enumerating the fruit of the Spirit.

The Spiritual Fruit of Joy

Spirit-imparted joy is an inner gladness or sense of delight. However, such joy is not so much an emotional stir, but what has been described as a rational (or perhaps a volitional) feeling arising out of a sense of God's favor. In response to the Spirit's ministration of this fruit, the believer manifests joy in all his outlooks and attitudes. Such basic joy is uniquely Christian, and it has been said that joy as an attribute of character constitutes one of the most obvious signs of a true experience with God. Scripture gives a major place to joy, and the Authorized Version of the English Bible uses the word or its immediate derivatives a total of 200 times. The bulk of these references identify joy as a spiritual event. As C. S. Lewis once wrote: "Joy is the serious business of heaven."

It is suggested that the Greek word for joy, *chara,* may be the source of the English word *hurrah.* However, the joy that is the Spirit's fruit is not at all an exuberant reaction to circumstances, but an attribute of character. This joy is wholly distinct from what Sigmund Freud calls the "pleasure principle." It is not merriment, laughter, or reveling. Though material and earthly joy may sometimes make humans worse, spiritual joy always makes them better. Such spiritual joy can exist simultaneously with sorrow, and in the face of tragedy and adversity. It may thrive even though the believer suffers persecution, imprisonment, and the hostility of wicked men.

In operating in the believer, the spiritual fruit of joy becomes a positive principle relating to hope, confidence, and optimism. It is not a feeling, but an attitude or perspective; it is a way of seeing and understanding. It has been said: "Joy is not a matter of position, but of disposition." This Spirit-imparted joy is sufficient to counteract natural human reactions of discouragement, depression, morbid sorrow, and self-pity. The emphasis by some on the power of positive thinking appears to be an adaptation of the Biblical provision of the fruit of spiritual joy. Scripture calls for joy even where it doesn't seem to belong: "My brethren, count it all joy when ye fall into divers temptations; knowing this, that the trying of your faith worketh patience" (James 1:2, 3).

The joyful outlook is a New Testament keynote. "The disciples were filled with joy, and with the Holy Ghost" (Acts 13:52). "They caused great joy unto all the brethren" (15:3). "The God of hope fill you with all joy and peace in believing . . . through the power of the Holy Ghost" (Romans 15:13). "These things write we unto you, that your joy may be full" (1 John 1:4). "Neither count I my life dear unto myself, so that I might finish my course with joy" (Acts 20:24). "Unto him that is able to keep you from falling, and to present you faultless before the presence of his glory with exceeding joy" (Jude 24). As the ministry of the Spirit in the lives of individuals and the Church increased in the New Testament, so joy also increased.

The believer's achievement of spiritual joy links with his growth in Christlikeness. Although Jesus was "the man of sorrows," His life and ministry were founded on and motivated by joy. As the 70 disciples returned and He proceeded to instruct them: "In that hour Jesus rejoiced in Spirit" (Luke 10:21). Even on the eve of His crucifixion, Jesus reassured His disciples: "These things have I spoken unto you, that my joy might remain in you" (John 15:11). In the Old Testament, Jesus is depicted as prophetically declaring: "I delight to do thy will, O my God" (Psalm 40:8). And the writer to the Hebrews sees joy as Jesus' motivation for Calvary: "[Jesus] for the joy . . . set before him endured the cross" (Hebrews 12:2).

When the Holy Spirit enters the human, He ministers joy: "Ye became followers . . . having received the word in much affliction, with joy of the Holy Ghost" (1 Thessalonians 1:6). Joy is a criterion of eligibility for citizenship in the Kingdom: "For the kingdom of God is . . . righteousness, and peace, and joy in the Holy Ghost" (Romans 14:17). Peter knew something of this Spirit-imparted joy, and he wrote of "joy unspeakable [i.e., too great for words] and full of glory" (1 Peter 1:8). The Holy Spirit will see the full consummation of His ministry of bestowing joy in the era that is yet future: "The ransomed of the Lord shall return, and come to Zion with songs and everlasting joy upon their heads: they shall obtain joy and gladness, and sorrow and sighing shall flee away" (Isaiah 35:10). It has been said: "The Christian has joy in review, joy in possession, and still greater joy in prospect." How appropriate that the Spirit minister joy as a fruit in each believer's life!

The Spiritual Fruit of Peace

Spirit-imparted peace (Gk., *eirene*) denotes a sense of calmness, harmony, a complete lack of hostility, or a beneficent serenity. Such peace begins as an aspect of salvation, and the consciousness of a right relationship with God. "Therefore being justified by faith, we have peace with God through our Lord Jesus Christ" (Romans 5:1). The Christian gospel is "the gospel of peace" (Ephesians 5:15), and the believer serves the "God of peace" (Romans 15:33). Jesus Christ is rightly called "The Prince of Peace." Paul knew something of this spiritual fruit, for he wrote: "And the peace of God which passeth all understanding [lit., surpasses all our powers of thought] shall keep [lit., garrison, guard, set a watch upon] your hearts and minds through Christ Jesus" (Philippians 4:7). Paul saw this peace providing the believer with an impenetrable defense against destructive worry, care, and unbelief.

The manifestation of peace as a fruit of the Spirit is rooted in the acts of the Spirit and not the events of the believer's life. Spiritual peace can reign in the midst of difficult, conflicting, hostile circumstances. God's way primarily involves a change in the believer's heart and mind: "Thou wilt keep him in perfect peace, whose mind is stayed on thee" (Isaiah 26:3). This peace is in the realm of the Spirit, not in the realm of material things: "For the kingdom of God is not meat and drink; but righteousness, and peace . . . in the Holy Ghost" (Romans 14:17); "To be carnally minded is death; but to be spiritually minded is life and peace" (Romans 8:6).

Peace given by the Holy Spirit is not frozen tranquility. It is peace illustrated by the busy harvest scene when all the energies of men and machines are devoted to cooperative productivity. It is a way of life whereby the believer concentrates with committed and unhampered heart to the task at hand. It is a Christian walk under God's leadership in response to the exhortation: "Let the peace of God rule in your hearts" (Colossians 3:15). It is the practical implementation of divine wisdom: "The wisdom that is from above is first pure, then peaceable. . . . And the fruit of righteousness is sown in peace of them that make peace" (James 3:17, 18).

A particular application of the spiritual fruit of peace is to see it as God's answer to mental and physical tension. Humans who suffer from tension experience a tautness of their nervous and muscular systems, often because their body is working against itself. God's peace subdues and relaxes, and it constitutes an exact prescription to relieve self-destroying tension. One of the greatest triumphs of divine peace is in the arena of the human heart, which someone has called "the world's greatest battlefield."

The reign of peace does not disqualify the believer from "[fighting] the good fight of faith" (1 Timothy 6:12). But even while the believer battles for his Lord, within there is inner peace and total absence of destructive conflict. It is not that the believer is "too nice to fight," but rather that he is divinely empowered to resist fighting himself, or fighting those people and values that God desires perpetuated. As the fruit of peace develops, God's child manifests that trait of character that exempts him from tension, hostility, and conflict. He becomes the poised, integrated person, wholly free from tearing and confusing motivations.

There is a close relationship between appropriating peace as a fruit of the Spirit, and truly knowing Jesus Christ. Paul said of Christ: "He is our peace" (Ephesians 2:14). Jesus promised His followers: "Peace I leave with you, my peace I give unto you: not as the world giveth, give I unto you. Let not your heart be troubled, neither let it be afraid" (John 14:27). Later, in His Upper Room discourse He declared: "These things I have spoken unto you, that in me ye might have peace" (16:33). It is certainly not surprising that Christ's followers included the wish for peace in the traditional apostolic salutation: "Grace be unto you, and peace . . ." (Revelation 1:4; cf. 2 John 3; 1 Peter 1:2). The fruit of inner peace must characterize the life of every victorious Christian.

The Spiritual Fruit of Long-suffering

The concept of long-suffering (Gk., *makrothumia)* literally entails keeping the borderline of passion at a distance (cf. *makros,* afar or distant; *thumos,* the animating spirit or passion). In the modern idiom, it would be the opposite of possessing a short temper fuse. The believer manifests long-suffering when he maintains self-restraint in the face of annoying provocation. It is a case of being patient and without hostility in the face of both intentional and unintentional follies and provocations of others, including one's fellow Christians. The believer willingly suppresses his own desires in favor of the needs and desires of others. The word *patience* is a suitable synonym for this fruit of the Spirit.

Scripture repeatedly exhorts to patience and long-suffering: "Walk worthy of the vocation wherewith ye are called, with all lowliness and meekness, with long-suffering, forbearing one another in love" (Ephesians 4:1, 2); "Now we exhort you brethren . . . be patient toward all men" (1 Thessalonians 5:15); "Reprove, rebuke, exhort with all long-suffering and doctrine" (2 Timothy 4:2); "Strengthened with all might, according to his glorious power, unto all patience and long-suffering with joyfulness" (Colossians 1:11). God earnestly desires the quality of patience or long-suffering that His people might rightly relate to their fellow Christians. Downer says of long-suffering: "It avoids quarrels; it heals injuries; it promotes forgiveness and good will. It gives the soft answer that turneth away wrath."[4] Someone describes this quality as: "Love on the anvil, bearing the blows of suffering."

True spiritual long-suffering embodies a strength and a sense of positive victory. It is not mere resignation, unusual personal fortitude, blasé apathy, or careless insensibility. When this fruit of the Spirit is manifested, the believer bears up in poise and equanimity in spite of stress, hardship, and testing. He maintains an unwearied perseverance in doing good; he accepts the actions of others with forbearance; and he totally refrains from attempting to avenge wrong to himself. James wrote: "We count them happy which endure. Ye have heard of the patience of Job, and have seen the end of the Lord [i.e., the conclusion God brought about]" (James 5:11). The manifestation of the spiritual fruit of long-suffering leads one not merely to endure suffering, but if necessary for the glory of God, to endure that suffering gladly. This fruit enables the believer to react in a true Christian manner to unjust treatment at the hands of others.

When the Spirit communicates long-suffering as a spiritual fruit, He communicates one of the basic attributes of God: "The Lord God, merciful and gracious, long-suffering, and abundant in goodness and truth" (Exodus 34:6). Every convert should be grateful that God is "long-suffering to us-ward, not willing that any should perish" (2 Peter 3:9). Whereas the typical human response to provocation is hostile reaction, this spiritual fruit assures that the yielded believer is enabled to partake of divine patience. God shares His attributes because He asks the believer to share His work. Virtually all worthy accomplishments in Christian service require prolonged patience, for even the good seed will only "bring forth fruit with patience" (Luke 8:15). James admonished: "Let patience have her perfect work, that ye may be perfect and entire" (James 1:4). In effect, James is saying that one who lacks patience is incomplete as a Christian.

The Spiritual Fruit of Gentleness

The word *gentleness* (Gk., *chrestotes*) is particularly equivalent to kindness or graciousness, and on occasion equivalent to goodness, generosity, or honesty. As a character trait, gentleness denotes a spirit and will that are exercised to assure the utmost consideration of others. The believer manifesting the spiritual fruit of gentleness is truly a gentleman or gentlewoman. He is good-natured, fair, sweet-tempered, usefully helpful, and tender of feeling. He always seeks to put others in the best possible light. Gentleness is power over one's power. It is the exercise of civility and good manners even in the face of rudeness and ignorance. Hopkins describes this fruit: "It is the very opposite of rudeness, boisterousness, and coarseness. Real gentleness is the right use and proper government of strong feelings."[5] There is a close connection between the Spirit's role in communicating gentleness as a spiritual fruit and the scriptural figure of the Spirit as a dove.

Secular writings from the era of the New Testament use the word *gentleness* to identify favorable traits such as: a good citizen, a friendly god [pagan gods are in view], or a brave soldier. In an interesting aside, Moody notes: "In Greek the noun for 'Christ' *(Christos)* and the adjective for 'kind' *(chrestos)* were often mixed. The fruit of the Spirit mixes them even more."[6] As a spiritual fruit in the believer, gentleness assures a mellow kindness and Christlikeness that results in genuine usefulness to one's fellows. That usefulness could include showing material kindness to someone in need. But more particularly, the greatest kindness any believer can render to his fellow humans is to share the message and person of Jesus Christ. In manifesting gentleness, the believer treats his fellows the same way God has treated him. He fulfills the Biblical admonition: "Be ye kind one to another, tenderhearted, forgiving one another even as God for Christ's sake hath forgiven you" (Ephesians 4:32).

The true Christian gentle person will never, either intentionally or unintentionally cause pain to others. It is to be noted that true gentleness to others may call for a certain quality of toughness with oneself. Such gentleness or kindness is never wasted, even if it has no effect on the recipient, it most certainly will benefit the bestower. Gentle people can nevertheless be effective leaders, but they enforce with a smile instead of with a sword. Actually, gentleness can accomplish many things that violence will fail to do. In poignant and meaningful words, King David addressed his testimony to God: "Thy gentleness hath made me great" (Psalm 18:35). David's survival and later exaltation were strictly dependent on the fact that God is gentle.

Paul commendably exemplified the spiritual fruit of gentleness. He reported of his ministry to the Thessalonians that he had been "gentle among you, even as a nurse cherisheth her children" (1 Thessalonians 2:7). He instructed: "The servant of the Lord must not strive; but be gentle unto all men" (2 Timothy 2:24). In an extended figure, Paul portrayed the believer as selecting this attribute of character much as he selects his clothing: "Put on therefore, as the elect of God, holy and beloved, bowels of mercies [i.e., tenderness of heart], kindness [or gentleness] . . ." (Colossians 3:12). The Christian's means to gentleness is the specific appropriation of this divine quality through submitting to the ministry of the gentle Holy Spirit.

The Spiritual Fruit of Goodness

Goodness (Gk., *agathosune*) as a fruit of the Spirit, includes both a character that is virtuous and a character that is kind. It is a special way of living for others and expecting no other recompense than the privilege of enlarging one's soul. It is constituted in practical beneficence and a zeal for good. It is a deliberate effort to help put the world right. Hopkins has written: "Goodness is love in action, love with its hands to the plow, love with the burdens on its back, love serving God and humanity, love following in His steps who 'went about doing good.' "[7] A primary synonym for "goodness" is *generosity*. The one manifesting goodness is generous with himself toward others, and generously submissive in his will toward God. He gives himself in service to his fellows, and in obedience to the moral standards of God. Stanley Horton comments concerning the fruit of goodness: "This is what makes us God's noblemen. The best way to describe it is being like Jesus."[8]

One aspect of goodness relates to a practical interest in the temporal well-being of others. Although the Bible does not call the Samaritan "good," all history knows him as the "Good

Samaritan." In caring for the physical needs of the injured traveler, he exemplified the behavior pattern of one manifesting the spiritual fruit of goodness. True goodness or generosity is a process of giving from the heart. Even though material goods are shared, it is the case: "Nothing the heart gives away is gone; it is kept in the hearts of others." This fruit of the Spirit enables God's people to transform material goods from millstones to angels' wings.

But an even more significant function of goodness is in the realm of the spiritual. Scripture describes Barnabas as "a good man, and full of the Holy Ghost and of faith" (Acts 11:24). Barnabas' goodness qualified him to minister in the revival in Antioch (11:26), and to be chosen as Paul's companion for the first missionary journey (13:1-3). That Christian, in whom the spiritual fruit of goodness is manifested, has been said to double the length of his existence. To share spiritual truth and blessing with others is a surpassing satisfaction and delight. Not surprisingly, the character trait of goodness is identified only in Biblical writings, and it seems to have been unknown in secular Greek.

Jesus taught that goodness is divine in its origin: "There is none good but one, that is God" (Matthew 19:17). St. Thomas Aquinas repeated this thought when he wrote: "Of all things there is one goodness, and yet many goodnesses." Thomas was saying that human goodness is merely a reflection of the divine. The impartation of God's goodness makes possible the fulfillment of Paul's desire: "That ye might walk worthy of the Lord unto all pleasing, being fruitful in every good work [literally, fruitful in every goodness]" (Colossians 1:10). The outworking of this fruit was evidently what Paul had in mind for the believers of Galatia: "As we have therefore opportunity, let us do good unto all men, especially unto them who are of the household of faith" (Galatians 6:10).

The Spiritual Fruit of Faith

Since the other eight fruit of the Spirit concern character, we may consider this to be true for faith also. Although the Greek original uses the same word for faith the fruit and faith the gift, it is warranted in this context to consider that faith is a matter of fruit expressed in character. Implied are such qualities as: the fulfillment of duty, faithfulness, trustworthiness, dependability, loyalty, constancy, steadfastness, conscientiousness, punctuality, and veracity. He in whom the fruit of faith thrives enjoys an implicit, obedient, adventurous confidence in God. His wholehearted commitment assures that he faithfully discharges entrusted duties, for he is unwavering in his relation to God, to himself, and to his calling. The term *faithfulness* particularly describes the manifestation of faith in character, although it should be noted that there is no particular grammatical or etymological reason establishing this equivalency.

Translators use a number of variant expressions to replace "the fruit of faith." Weymouth calls it "good faith," while J. B. Phillips chooses "fidelity." Conybeare and Howson speak of "truthfulness," and in an accompanying footnote they explain: "The word seems to have this meaning here; for faith (in the larger sense) could not be classed as one among a number of the constituent parts of love."[9] There is wide agreement that the Bible intends to apply faith to personal character. Moody refers to it as "this dependable quality"; Carter calls it "an aspect of the sanctified life." Both Donald Gee and Harold Horton contrast faith the fruit as the provision for character with faith the gift as a provision for power.

One of the emphases of Scripture is that those who are classed as God's servants are expected to manifest the fruit of faith so as to constitute faithfulness of service:

Who then is a faithful and wise servant, whom his lord hath made ruler over his household, to give them meat in due season? Blessed is that servant, whom his lord when he cometh shall find so doing. . . . Well, done, thou good and faithful servant (Matthew 24:45, 46; 25:21).

Not only the servant, but also the manager or steward is to be faithful: "Moreover it is required in stewards, that a man be found faithful" (1 Corinthians 4:2).

The unswerving constancy of Paul in the later years of his ministry impressively illustrates the expression of the fruit of faith in human character. Paul responded to the prophetic disclosure of future bonds and afflictions: "None of these things move me, neither count I my life dear unto myself" (Acts 20:24). What was promised to the church in Smyrna no doubt applies to all believers: "Be thou faithful unto death, and I will give thee a crown of life" (Revelation 2:10). God desires faithful, established believers "rooted and built up in him, and stablished in the faith" (Colossians 2:7). The fruit of faith leads the believer out of mere sentimental emotionalism into an unswerving decision to rest steadfastly in His hands.

The Spiritual Fruit of Meekness

Meekness is an inward grace that extends both toward God and to one's fellow humans. The original term *(prautes)* rendered "meekness," is equivalent also to "mildness" or "gentleness." The word is from roots meaning to soothe, to cause passion to abate, to make soft, to tame, or to calm down. On occasion, a form of this word was used to describe an animal that had been domesticated and had become responsive to his master's command. Donald Gee wrote: "Meekness is that willing acceptance of a greater will than our own, that brings us into harmony with the universe as God plans it."[10] For some, meekness simply means a surrender to the will of God. Elder Douglas Head described the spiritual fruit of meekness as a "lowly estimate of ourselves; gentleness, mildness . . . not flabbiness, but power under control, power that is channeled. . . . There is nothing negative about meekness."[11]

In the Biblical pattern, meekness belongs to one who serves; it has been called "the clothing of a servant." The meek man volunteers to serve, not because he personally possesses power, but because he is willing to become God's instrument for great achievements. As Z. J. Bicket once observed: "Meekness does not grow out of self-abasement but out of awareness that the mighty hand of God rests over all of life." The meek man sees God as his defense, so he does not need to strive to defend himself; he sees God as his guide, so he does not have to seek to chart his own course. Meekness qualifies any believer to become mighty in God's eternal plan and purpose. There is a sense of surrender in meekness, a willingness to commit one's resources to God and His purposes, a readiness to place one's total self in His hands for His pleasure.

God is delighted when the Holy Spirit is permitted to express the fruit of meekness in the life of the believer. Indeed, He uniquely favors meek people: "The meek shall he guide in judgment: and the meek will he teach his way" (Psalm 25:9); "The meek shall inherit the earth" (Matthew 5:5). Paul exhorted: "For I say . . . to every man that is among you, not to think of himself more highly than he ought to think" (Romans 12:3). In his own ministry, Paul found meekness a powerful lever to move God's people to action: "I Paul myself beseech you by the meekness and gentleness of Christ" (2 Corinthians 10:1). Peter exhorted Christian wives to manifest "the ornament of a meek and quiet spirit" (1 Peter 3:4). James sets forth a principle of God's dealing with humans: "Humble yourself in the sight of the Lord and he shall lift you up" (James 4:10).

In many earthly situations, pressures that beset the believer seem to call for attitudes and behavior that are otherwise than meek. Nevertheless, the Biblical pattern endorses meekness. In his efforts to lead the Israelites to the Promised Land, Moses was continually thwarted and provoked by his difficult followers. In the face of biting personal criticism, "the man Moses was very meek, above all the men which were upon the face of the earth" (Numbers 12:3). God saw to it that the leadership of Moses, the man of meekness, was sustained and vindicated. Meekness belongs in the character of the great servant of God in every age, even though Christians are likely to desire this virtue the least, and ancient Greeks and Romans considered it a quality to be despised. Jesus Christ, who mightily conquered death and hell and the grave, rightly said of himself: "I am meek and lowly in heart" (Matthew 11:29).

The Spiritual Fruit of Temperance

The capacity for personal self-government to assure full control of one's appetites and instincts is the outcome of the spiritual fruit of temperance. The original word *(egkrateia)* denotes "holding in with a firm hand," and it speaks of freedom from extremes. The believer, in whom the Spirit achieves temperance, controls and restrains all of his drives and motivations, so that all are kept in balance and none attains destructive mastery. The expression *self-control* is a suitable synonym for temperance. The temperate believer exercises self-control of all appetites, tempers, and passions—physical, mental, and spiritual. To submit to the Holy Spirit is the first step in denying one's own spirit, and it becomes the basis of total self-control.

The Spirit's fruit of temperance assures that each legitimate activity and interest occupies its rightful position and proportion in life. The believer's energies are directed so that he or she achieves the greatest potential. Paul compared the Christian life with that of an athlete in training when every element must be properly controlled:

Every man that striveth for mastery is temperate in all things. . . . I therefore . . . keep under my body, and bring it into subjection: lest that by any means, when I have preached to others, I myself should be a castaway (1 Corinthians 9:24-27).

While some instances of self-control lead to careful moderation (e.g., eating), others lead to total abstinence (e.g., illicit sex). In his day, Paul could observe self-control to the extent that he agreed totally to abstain from meat for the sake of the spiritually unenlightened: "If meat make my brother to offend, I will eat no flesh while the world standeth" (1 Corinthians 8:13).

Temperance is an essential quality for the serving Christian, and for every mature believer: "A bishop must be . . . temperate" (Titus 1:8), and "the aged men be sober, grave, temperate" (Titus 2:3). Solomon wrote: "He that ruleth his spirit [is better] than he that taketh a city" (Proverbs 16:32); "He that hath no rule over his own spirit is like a city that is broken down, and without walls" (25:28). In Peter's enumeration of the seven virtues to be added to faith, he notably included temperance in the fourth place on the list. This virtue must appear in the believer's life if he is to be neither "barren nor unfruitful in the knowledge of our Lord Jesus Christ" (2 Peter 1:8). By being temperate, the believer can "abstain from fleshly lusts, which war against the soul" (1 Peter 2:11). It has been said: "Self-control through Spirit-control precedes the full manifestation of the power of God."

Just as the other fruit of the Spirit transcend self, temperance too is divine. It is not the control of self by self, but control of self by yielding to the control of the Spirit. Paul described his struggles with his carnal self: "The good that I would, I do not; but the evil which I would not, that I do" (Romans 7:19). Only when the divine element entered in, did he achieve victorious control. He describes this later stage of victory for those "who walk not after the flesh, but after the Spirit" (Romans 8:4). Temperance was one of the three subjects discoursed upon by Paul before Felix. The Roman governor apparently recognized that it was a divine virtue to which he was challenged, for "Felix trembled" (Acts 24:25). James notes that "the tongue can no man tame" (James 3:8). Only when man's resources are enlarged by that which is "from above," does man attain the basic ideal God has planned.

Other Relationships of the Holy Spirit

Inasmuch as the Holy Spirit is God in His personal outgoing and ministry to mankind, every attitude of resistance and rejection against God is actually immediately directed against the Holy Spirit. The offender's basic contact is with God the Holy Spirit, and thus Scripture identifies several possible offenses.

The Offense of Blaspheming the Spirit

The offense of blasphemy is the most discussed and emphasized of all offenses against the Holy Spirit. Jesus said: "Blasphemy against the Holy Ghost shall not be forgiven unto men" (Matthew 12:31; cf. Mark 3:29; Luke 12:10). In the context in Matthew, Jesus spoke these words to the scribes when they credited Jesus' miracles to Satan (cf. also Mark 3). The issue involved the malicious and deliberate denial of the visible evidence. It was not merely an honest mistake, but an evaluatively derived conclusion that constituted a judgment. While the word *blasphemy* means basically "injurious talk," it is also approximately synonymous with speaking impious words or committing unworthy acts against God, or exercising contempt and indignity against God.

Since the Bible describes blasphemy against the Spirit as not being forgiven, such blasphemy is commonly referred to as the "unpardonable sin." More accurate usage prefers the expression "unpardoned sin." That person is unpardoned who continues his willful way, contemptuously unresponsive to the tender wooing and constraint of the Holy Spirit. As it were, he

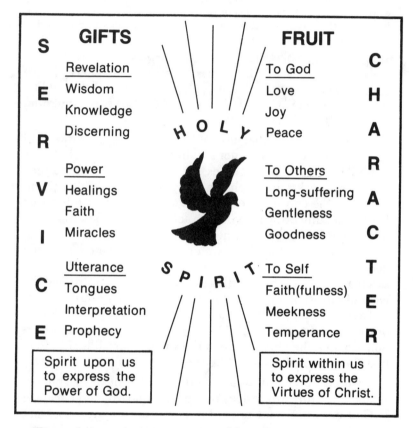

Figure 9. A comparison-summary of the gifts and fruit of the Holy Spirit.

spurns the Holy Spirit and denies His personality and His authoritative role as Deity. Writes Kuyper:

He who desecrates, despises, and slanders the Spirit, . . . as tho He were the Spirit of Satan, is lost in eternal darkness. This is a willful sin, intentionally malicious. It betrays a systematic opposition to God.[1]

That man has blasphemed the Holy Spirit when he deliberately turns his back on the light in preference to darkness. He chooses to refuse to be forgiven. Such a state is illustrated by the case of King Saul: "But the Spirit of the Lord departed from Saul" (1 Samuel 16:14).

It is popularly said that it is not an act of life, but an attitude of heart that results in a sinner's dying unpardoned. While this statement is not false, it does not totally represent matters. There is a sense in which the blasphemer, at a given point, arrives at the conscious experience of deliberately relegating Deity to an unworthy place. By an act of will, one determines to deny the knowledge that he possesses. Blasphemy does involve a decision, but the maintenance of the outcome of the decision becomes an attitude. Other things being equal, as long as a man lives, it is his privilege to submit to the Spirit that the work of salvation might begin within him. Paul described himself as one "who was before a blasphemer, and a persecutor . . . but I obtained mercy" (1 Timothy 1:13). Sin remains unpardoned when the very nature of the sin, because it is the sin of blasphemy, involves rejecting the channel of pardon.

It would be clearly understood that the sin of blasphemy against the Holy Spirit does not remain unpardoned because: 1) God does not want to pardon it, 2) God's mercy does not reach to such a level, or 3) Christ's provision is inadequate. Calvary provides for every sin, no matter how vicious or vile, and it even makes provision for blasphemy against the Saviour. However, the one condition applying to Calvary's provision is that it must be accepted and appropriated. Since it is through the Holy Spirit that the new birth and all of Calvary's benefits are conveyed, if that Spirit is rejected, God has no other means to convey His gifts of grace to mankind. The new life in Jesus Christ is implemented in the believer exclusively by the Holy

Spirit, and without Him spiritual death and condemnation must remain.

Many years ago, John Owen wrote:

> For as God has not another Son to offer another sacrifice for sin . . . neither has He another Spirit to make that sacrifice effectual for us, if the Holy Ghost in His work be despised and rejected.

It is evident that blasphemy against the Holy Spirit is not a sin of ignorance or innocence. It involves the offender, clearly knowing better, deliberately and willfully rejecting the divine wooing. Augsburger writes:

> The sin of blasphemy against the Spirit . . . is the final result of a person's persistent rejection of and disrespect for the call of the Spirit. The nature of this sin is that of being closed to the revelation and redemption of Christ being testified by the Spirit. One blasphemes the Spirit when he repudiates the Spirit's call to Christ as the one way of salvation.[2]

The Offense of Resisting the Spirit

To resist is to oppose, to stand contrary to, or to withstand. The Spirit is resisted whenever man gives expression to his rebellious heart. Stephen addressed the council: "Ye stiffnecked and uncircumcised in heart and ears, ye do always resist the Holy Ghost" (Acts 7:51). Although these men observed outward religious form, probably with meticulous care, they resisted the Spirit, not sometimes, but always. They acted out of wrong motives and while continuing to reject the truth the Spirit sought to convey. To resist the Spirit is the New Testament equivalent of the Old Testament state of being "stiffnecked" (cf. Exodus 32:9; Deuteronomy 9:6; 2 Chronicles 30:8). God declared: "He that being often reproved hardeneth his neck, shall suddenly be destroyed, and that without remedy" (Proverbs 29:1). Even in the days before the Flood, humans resisted God, and therefore He responded: "My Spirit shall not always strive with man" (Genesis 6:3).

Paul reports that the unbeliever typically excuses himself by denying that he resists. Such a person feigns ignorance and asks: "Who hath resisted his [God's] will?" (Romans 9:19).

There is a close relationship between resisting the Spirit and not believing God. Torrance comments: "What else is unbelief but resistance to the Holy Spirit?" Primarily, it is the sinner who resists the Holy Spirit, although on a temporary basis a professed believer probably might do so also. Resisting the Spirit includes all human attitudes that accept a degree of obedience that is less than complete surrender to God. It may be noted that humans who live in a state of deliberate resistance to the Holy Spirit forfeit their own happiness and personal adjustment. To resist Him is to invite human misery.

The Offense of Insulting the Spirit

Scripture speaks of the one "who . . . hath done despite unto the Spirit of grace" (Hebrews 10:29). The word *despite* connotes to insult, to despise, to injure the personal status of another, to outrage, or to treat contemptuously. Thus, to do despite is to commit willful sin performed as an open revolt. It is possible that Simon the sorcerer, who sought to buy a gift of the Spirit with money, and then failed properly to repent, was guilty of insulting the Holy Spirit. The one who insults the Holy Spirit, as it were, makes a deliberate choice to do so, and he makes no later effort to achieve a reconciliation. It is suggested that the willful human decision to use one's own abilities to achieve salvation rather than to depend on the Spirit's provision is an insult to the Spirit. The sinner who thus insults the Spirit, and the sinner who blasphemes the Spirit, would each be lost. Thus, in at least some cases, the offenses of insulting and blaspheming merge into one.

The Offense of Grieving the Spirit

The root meaning of the word *grieve* is "to make sorrowful" or "to cause sorrow to," and possible synonyms are: to hurt, to offend, and to distress. Sanders writes: "Grieve is a love word. One can anger an enemy, but not grieve him. . . . Only one who loves can be grieved."[3] Thus the grieving of the Spirit is primarily the act of a believer, for it is toward believers that the Spirit assumes a tender and affectionate attitude. The believer grieves the Spirit when he is directed by carnal motives and thereby manifests such attitudes as: worldliness, unbelief, ingratitude, lack of prayer, falsehood, uncontrolled anger, dishonesty, bitterness, or idle and evil speech. Not only would a believer grieve the Spirit by disobeying Him, but also by ignoring His presence. Primarily, the grieving of the Spirit takes place at the level of inner motives, for He searches the heart and knows what is within, even before it is translated into action.

An Old Testament text that speaks of this offense against the Spirit is rendered "they rebelled and vexed his Holy Spirit" (Isaiah 53:10) in the Authorized Version, but "vexed" becomes "grieved" in the Revised Standard Version. In New Testament times, Paul wrote to the Ephesians: "And grieve not the Holy Spirit of God, whereby ye are sealed unto the day of redemption" (Ephesians 4:30). It has been noted that although the Ephesian church had a remarkable beginning (Acts 19), within a decade distractions had arisen (cf. Ephesians 5:18). A generation later, John wrote: "Remember therefore from whence thou art fallen, and repent, and do the first works" (Revelation 2:5). A church that is guilty of grieving the Spirit is clearly in a state of spiritual decline.

The response of the Spirit in the event that He is grieved by the believer is to convict. He ceases to relate in warm fellowship, and instead ministers condemnation and conviction. Joy, power, and communion that normally characterize the believer's life are severed when the Spirit is grieved. It is not so much that the grieving of the Spirit terminates divine life, but it does interrupt fellowship with the divine, and thereby forfeits usefulness. Though the Spirit does not depart, He abides with a new relationship: that of conviction, in place of the comfort that He normally bestows. He who should be our best friend becomes a virtual enemy. The obvious response for the believer who finds himself in such circumstances is to confess and forsake sin, and thus depart from that which grieves the Spirit.

The Offense of Quenching the Spirit

The term *quench* or its equivalents, such as "stifle" and "extinguish," convey the analogy of putting out a fire or flame.

Once again, this offense against the Spirit is committed by believers, for it was to the Thessalonian church that Paul wrote: "Quench not the Spirit" (1 Thessalonians 5:19). These words have been paraphrased: "Do not suppress or subdue expressions of the Spirit in your fellowship"; or more simply: "Do not extinguish the Spirit's fire." When one quenches the Spirit, he deliberately hinders the Spirit's promptings, he stands opposed to His will, and he refuses to obey His call. Sanders writes: "When worldly methods are substituted for spiritual, when the praise of men is preferred to the praise of God, when service is self-originated rather than God-directed, the Spirit may be quenched."[4]

While it is not always the case, it has been suggested that the believer grieves the Spirit by saying "yes" to Satan, and quenches the Spirit by saying "no" to God. Certainly the Spirit is quenched when self takes control, and the carnal and natural governs the life. Whatever denies the ministry of the Spirit quenches the Spirit. He is quenched when human opinions are substituted for His direction, when His plan is rejected by human will, His gifts ignored, His work resisted, or when the commitment to the work of God is merely halfhearted. When someone figuratively "pours cold water on" any aspect of the Spirit's ministry, he is quenching the Spirit. The suppressing of His "fire operations"—His ministry to transmit divine holiness—constitutes a quenching. The unhindered flame of the Spirit is meant to consume dross and produce the sanctified life. On occasion, ceasing to provide fuel (our submission) could constitute a means of quenching the Spirit's fire.

Other Offenses Against the Spirit

The Spirit may be lied to. Ananias was guilty of this offense. Peter asked: "Why hath Satan filled thine heart to lie to the Holy Ghost?" (Acts 5:3). In his action, Ananias was seeking the esteem and reward of men in the name of brotherly love, and he therefore deliberately defended what for him was a sin. He professed to be devoutly serving God, but he was actually living for himself. To lie to the Spirit is to thwart His purposes on earth, and to undo and destroy those virtues that He represents. It was not surprising that God found such deception and falsehood to be so offensive that He visited destruction upon Ananias.

The Spirit may be tempted. This offense was committed not only by Ananias, but also by his wife Sapphira. In his further query, Peter asked: "How is it that ye have agreed together to tempt the Spirit of the Lord?" (Acts 5:9). One tempts the Spirit when he disbelieves the Spirit and, as it were, forces Him to prove himself—the outcome is that the Spirit is provoked. That which underrates or devalues the Spirit provokingly tests or tempts Him, so He must prove He means what He says. The attempt to coax the Spirit to accept and endorse behavior that falls short of His standards or that denies His values is likewise tempting the Spirit.

The Spirit may be ignored. This offense is not named in Scripture, but it is amply illustrated. The disciples at Ephesus responded: "We have not so much as heard whether there be any Holy Ghost" (Acts 19:2). Paul wrote to the Christians of Galatia: "Having begun in the Spirit, are ye now made perfect by the flesh?" (Galatians 3:3). Christians who fail to maintain an awareness and response to the Holy Spirit are guilty of the offense of ignoring Him. He is vitally interested in the believer and his welfare, and if the provisions of God are to be exemplified in the convert, the Spirit must be given a large place.

The Holy Spirit in the Future

Just as it is the case that in Old Testament times the ministry of the Spirit to mankind was somewhat different in nature from that enjoyed in the Church Age, so His ministry in the future will be modified. Limited scriptural reports give information concerning the role of the Spirit in various future events and eras.

The Spirit at the Rapture of the Church

The occasion known as the rapture of the Church, when Jesus Christ catches up believers to be with himself, will involve a very special manifestation of the Holy Spirit. The in-

stant metamorphosis that will transmit the fullness of divine
life into living and dead mortal bodies will be the Spirit's
unique work: "But if the Spirit of him that raised up Jesus from
the dead dwell in you, he that raised up Christ from the dead
shall also quicken your mortal bodies by his Spirit that dwelleth in you" (Romans 8:11; cf. Romans 8:22, 23). "He that
soweth to the Spirit shall of the Spirit reap life everlasting"
(Galatians 6:8). In this transformation of natural human bodies
into glorified bodies, the Spirit will act "in the twinkling of an
eye." The glorified body will be forever free from sin, sickness,
and death.

It seems valid to conclude that the predicted cessation of
spiritual gifts will occur at the Rapture: "Whether there be
prophecies, they shall fail; whether there be tongues, they shall
cease; whether there be knowledge, it shall vanish away" (1
Corinthians 13:8). The Church on earth in this era is the host
and channel of the Holy Spirit's operation, and when the
Church is gone, present relationships on earth will no longer
continue. The section that follows explains the Spirit's departure with the Church. However, the cessation of earthly
spiritual gifts will not be a loss for the Church, for it will be in
the presence of Jesus Christ. Horton comments: "Gifts only
cease in the sense that they are swallowed up in the Whole of
which they are a part."

The Spirit During the Tribulation

The present ministry of the Holy Spirit to abide on earth and
restrain the most glaring instances of evil will cease at the onset
of the Tribulation period: "For the mystery of lawlessness . . . is
already at work in the world, [but it is] restrained only until he
who restrains is taken out of the way" (2 Thessalonians 2:7,
The Amplified Bible). When the Church is translated, the Spirit
will cease in His ministry of permanently abiding on earth as
He now does in the Church Age. It will not be the privilege of
Tribulation converts to be indwelt by the Holy Spirit in order to
become "new creatures in Christ Jesus" in the manner of today's Christians. Those who repent and come to God during the
Tribulation will enjoy a status paralleling that of Old Testa-

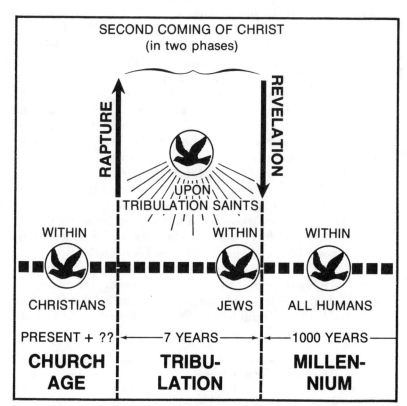

Figure 10. Time line of the Spirit and His relationships.

ment believers: "Abraham believed God, and it was counted unto him for righteousness" (Romans 4:3). Tribulation saints, as Abraham, will know God's justification, but not the Spirit's regeneration or His inner abiding.

Notwithstanding, the Holy Spirit will certainly continue His ministry in the realm of mankind during the Tribulation period. Under the symbol of "seven spirits," which apparently denotes plentitude, the Spirit is depicted during the time of the Tribulation as being "sent forth into all the earth" (Revelation 5:6). Apparently, the Spirit will have some part in ripening to judgment the forces of Antichrist, for in every era, He provides the occasion when men either submit and decide for God, or resist and become increasingly convinced in their resistive stand. As a further ministry in that era, the Spirit will anoint, empower, and sustain both the Jewish and Gentile remnants, and thus lay the foundation for the conversion of the Jewish nation and the perseverance of believers, even to the point of martyrdom.

It would be evident that those who are to seal their testimony by their own blood will be vitally dependent on the Holy Spirit for all that they achieve spiritually. Even though the Spirit will not make them regenerate, He will provide the necessary spiritual impetus to enable them to believe God that it may be counted to them for righteousness. John describes the Tribulation saints in two categories:

> I saw under the altar the souls of them that were slain for the word of God, and for the testimony which they held. . . . And white robes were given unto every one of them. . . . After this I beheld, and, lo, a great multitude, which no man could number, of all nations, and kindreds, and people, and tongues, stood before the throne, and before the Lamb, clothed with white robes, and palms in their hands (Revelation 6:9-11; 7:9).

The Spirit at the Revelation of Christ

At the revelation of Jesus Christ, the divine Son of David, long rejected by His people, will at last assume His place as King of kings. The Holy Spirit will suitably anoint and empower Him for His new role: "There shall come forth a rod out of the stem of Jesse. . . . And the Spirit of the Lord shall rest upon him, the spirit of wisdom and understanding, the spirit of counsel and might, the spirit of knowledge and of the fear of the Lord" (Isaiah 11:1, 2). It may be said that the governing skill of the divine Christ will be exercised in and through the Holy Spirit.

The very fact that Christ shall reveal himself and return as the mighty Conqueror to overthrow Antichrist and his armies is an outcome of the work of the Spirit. The Jews will turn to Him and receive Him as their own because of the Spirit's outpouring upon them: "I will pour water upon him that is thirsty, and floods upon the dry ground: I will pour my Spirit upon thy seed, and my blessing upon thine offspring" (Isaiah 44:3). "And shall put my Spirit in you, and ye shall live, and I shall place you in your own land" (Ezekiel 37:14). "And I will pour upon the house of David, and upon the inhabitants of Jerusalem, the spirit of grace and of supplications: and they shall look upon me whom they have pierced, and they shall mourn for him" (Zechariah 12:10). The outpouring of the Spirit at the close of the Tribulation leads to the revelation of Christ because the outpoured Spirit engenders in the hearts of the Jews that repentance and acceptance of their Messiah that they previously have refused.

The Holy Spirit During the Millennium

One of the vital aspects of the Millennium is the fact of a general outpouring of the Holy Spirit. Once more all believers will be indwelt by the Spirit, just as in the Church Age. "And I will put my Spirit within you, and cause you to walk in my statutes" (Ezekiel 36:27). Thus, once more the knowledge of God will be made to constitute specifically a spiritual experience. Walvoord writes:

The filling of the Holy Spirit will be common in the millennium, in contrast to the infrequency of it in other ages, and it will be manifested in worship and praise of the Lord and in willing obedience to Him as well as in spiritual power and inner transformation.[5]

In conjunction with the Spirit's outpouring during the millennial period, the long-blinded heart and mind of the Jew will at last turn to the Lord, and Joel 2:28-32 will be fulfilled in entirety: "And it shall come to pass afterward, that I will pour out my spirit upon all flesh." The many Old Testament promises of an abundant outpouring upon national Israel will at that time come to pass. God will cleanse the hearts of His people, put His Spirit within them, and write His law on their inward parts (Ezekiel 36:25-29; Jeremiah 31:31-34). Ridout describes the Millennium as a time when the Holy Spirit "presides over all this blessed work of national resurrection, remission, restoration, and regeneration." Thus, this glorious Third Person of the Godhead will indeed at last come into His rightful place in relation to all mankind. He will be present on earth to witness the fruit of His own gracious working throughout all the centuries of human existence.

Appendices

Some North American Pentecostal Denominations

	Approx. no. homeland churches in 1970s
Apostolic Church of Pentecost	140
Apostolic Faith (Baxter Springs, Kansas)	60
Apostolic Faith (Portland, Oregon)	45
Apostolic Overcoming Holy Church of God*	300
Assemblies of God	9,208
Associated Brotherhood of Christians*	40
Bible Way Church of Our Lord Jesus Christ World Wide*	350
California Evangelistic Association	50
Calvary Pentecostal Church	22
Christian Church of North America	111
Church of God (Cleveland, Tennessee)	4,905
Church of God (Huntsville, Alabama)	2,035
Church of God Founded by Jesus Christ	37
Church of God in Christ	4,676
Church of God in Christ, International	1,041
Church of God Mountain Assembly	100
Church of God of Prophecy	1,791
Church of God World Headquarters	2,025
Church of Our Lord Jesus Christ of the Apostolic Faith*	155
Congregational Holiness Church	151
Elim Fellowship	20

*Denominations primarily holding to the "oneness" or "Jesus Only" concept of the Godhead.

Emmanuel Holiness Church	56
Fire Baptized Holiness Church of God of the Americas	300
Free-Will Baptist Church of Pentecostal Faith	135
Glad Tidings Missionary Society	14
House of David	66
Independent Assemblies of God International	136
International Church of the Foursquare Gospel	741
International Pentecostal Church of Christ	91
Italian Pentecostal Church of Canada	16
National David Spiritual Temple of Christ Church Union	66
New Apostolic Church of North America	327
Open Bible Standard Churches	275
Original Church of God, Inc.	70
Pentecostal Assemblies of Canada	851
Pentecostal Assemblies of the World*	700
Pentecostal Assemblies of Newfoundland	139
Pentecostal Church of God of America, Inc.	1,250
Pentecostal Church of Zion, Inc.	13
Pentecostal Free Will Baptist Church	176
Pentecostal Holiness Church, Inc.	1,350
United Full Gospel Churches	50
United Fundamental Church	300
United Holy Church of America	470
United Pentecostal Church*	2,900
Zion Evangelistic Fellowship	96

This list has been gathered from directories, and in some cases, direct polls, but recent amalgamations, divisions, or changes in name or doctrine may not be reflected.

Common Objections to Pentecostalism

Objection 1: Tongues and miracles ceased at the end of the Biblical era, and present-day phenomena are an illusion.

There is no Biblical or logical basis for claiming that tongues and similar charismata were withdrawn by God at the close of the New Testament era. God had promised: "It shall come to pass afterward, that I will pour out my Spirit upon all flesh" (Joel 2:28). On the Day of Pentecost, Peter declared this promise was being fulfilled, and the range of its fulfillment extended to "all that are afar off" (Acts 2:39). Inasmuch as the Day of Pentecost is typically characterized as "the birth day of the Church," those who are "afar off" can only be believers who were to be in the Church even in the end of the Church era. From the Day of Pentecost to the present, God has not changed His order of government or administration in regard to His people. Charismata will cease when the Church Age ends (1 Corinthians 13:8-10), for then that which is perfect will have come. Wherever the Church ministers and its ordinances are observed, tongues and charismatic miracles can be expected to belong.

Objection 2: If the Pentecostal experience is normal for all Christians, what about great saints prior to the 20th-century Pentecostal outpouring?

Pentecostals repeatedly go on record as sincere admirers of great Christians of past generations. They share equally with other believers in acclaiming such as: Augustine, Luther, Calvin, Knox, Wesley, Finney, and Moody. They freely include the classical commentaries and Biblical expositions as a treasured part of their spiritual heritage. However, the Pentecostal suggests that at least some, and perhaps many, Christian heroes and heroines actually enjoyed a personal charismatic experience, even though they may not have expounded or confessed it publicly. (See chapter 7.) Great Christians out of the past who knew nothing of a charismatic dimension, nevertheless, walked in dedicated sincerity according to the light they had. In doing that, they became powerful people of God. For a Christian never to learn that God in his generation baptized believers according to Acts 2:4 is not in itself grounds for an inferior status before God. Even the "greatest" saints would almost surely admit they had only begun to enter into the potential of all God offered to provide. But the one sure formula for second class spiritual citizenship is a closed heart and unyielded will to believe and receive that which one in his better inner self knows God really intends for him.

Objection 3: Tongues are not a supernatural sign, but a psychological inducement and a subconscious response to personal emotional feelings.

There was no prior pattern to the first day of Pentecost, but tongues and all the associated phenomena were there in full manifestation. Peter related all of these events to the fulfillment of the promise of Joel: "This is that which was spoken by the prophet Joel" (Acts 2:16). Pentecost was therefore the fulfillment of a long-standing divine plan linked to the promises and purposes of God. Even if it can be shown that tongues have occurred among humans in other contexts than Holy Spirit enduement, there is a genuine Biblical pattern for tongues. God's people experience tongues because they submit to His Spirit and direct worship to His Son. Pentecostalism is concerned with tongues as the outcome of devoted, Bible-based, committed prayer and worship. It is not a matter of emotionalism per se, psychological ecstasy, hypnosis, or mental suggestion. Even those deaf from birth, when they enter into a Pentecostal experience, speak coherent translatable tongues. In no way can tongues that fulfill the Biblical pattern be dismissed as a mere natural psychological reaction.

Objection 4: It is a divisive doctrine to claim tongues is the basis of distinguishing Spirit-filled Christians from those who are not.

The distinctive doctrine of Pentecostalism is no more divisive than that of other denominations. In their day, the doctrines of justification by faith, the Christian's responsibility for personal holiness, the practice of believer's baptism, or seeing the Communion service as a simple memorial were controversial and divisive issues. Today, a large segment of Protestant Christendom freely agrees on these matters or, if need be, agrees to disagree. Divisiveness does not inhere in specific Biblical doctrines, but in human attitudes toward them. Admittedly, it has sometimes been the case that a Pentecostal convert has become offensive to other Christians in his exuberance and enthusiasm to share his new insights. But more frequently, for no other action than acceptance of Pentecostalism, the Pentecostal brother is expelled from his established Christian circle. Pentecostals would hold that the divisiveness is the result of the prejudices of their Christian peers, and not inherent in Pentecostalism itself.

Objection 5: Pentecostalism overemphasizes the doctrine of the Holy Spirit at the expense of rightly worshiping the Lord Jesus Christ.

It is possible that a critic can find an occasional example of misplaced emphasis, but not likely one truly representative of enlightened and responsible Pentecostalism. A fundamental objective of all Pentecostals is that through the Spirit they may enjoy more of the power of God so as to serve and worship Christ more effectively. Commitment to Jesus Christ is foremost in every genuine Christian's life, and Pentecostalism is simply God's unique provision to make better Christians. In general, the greater place one gives to the Spirit in His charismatic bestowments, sooner or later, the greater place he will be impelled by that Spirit to give to the Lord Jesus Christ.

Mormonism and the Holy Spirit

Some who do not accept the Pentecostal position have claimed that Pentecostalism finds its source in the Church of Jesus Christ of Latter-Day Saints (i.e., Mormonism). Thus, Pentecostalism is non-Biblical and perhaps on a par with plural marriages or baptism for the dead. Such an association would justify its rejection by a Bible believer.

There is indeed evidence that, beginning in the 1830s, a tongues phenomenon was associated with Mormonism. By 1861, however, Mormon leaders were attempting to discourage the public manifestation of tongues. At this time, they wrote concerning the practice of tongues: "It has brought ridicule and disrespect from the ungodly." Notwithstanding, tongues remained in evidence. It is reliably reported that when the original tabernacle in Salt Lake City was dedicated in 1867, "hundreds of elders spoke in tongues."

Mormonism teaches that there is "the baptism or birth of water" to be followed by "the baptism or birth of the Spirit." They link this latter with the gifts of the Spirit—the charismata. The "Articles of Faith" of Mormonism state: "We believe in the gift of tongues, prophecy, revelation, visions, healing, interpretation of tongues, etc." However, Mormons tend to adopt the view that tongues constitute a minor gift, and if they do occur, they are likely to be celestial rather than earthly.

The fact that Mormons teach, and have been known to practice, aspects of charismata, neither denies nor confirms the Pentecostal position. Mormons declare that they derive their beliefs in this area from the Bible, and they quote texts to prove it. Whatever objections the evangelical has to Mormonism, he cannot object to the use of Biblical sources. It so happens that the Bible teaches Pentecostalism, and Mormons choose to accept at least some aspect of what is taught. The concerns of Pentecostalism do not at all relate to sources in Mormonism, but to sources in Scripture that they may ever be better understood and more faithfully implemented.

The Holy Spirit and the Latter Rain

In the earlier decades of 20th-century Pentecostalism, much was made of the analogy between the spiritual outpouring and the Biblical latter rain. God's promises were quoted: "I will give you the rain of your land in his due season, the first rain and the latter rain, that thou mayest gather in thy corn and thy wine and thine oil" (Deuteronomy 11:14); "God . . . hath given you the former rain moderately, and he will cause to come down for you the rain, and the latter rain in the first month" (Joel 2:23). The Pentecostal experience was seen as fulfilling predictions by Christian leaders of past generations:

Another great work of the Spirit which is not accomplished is the bringing on of the latter day glory: in a few more years . . . the Holy Spirit will be poured out in a far different style from the present (C. H. Spurgeon).

Another outpouring of the Spirit is yet to come, the latter rain, which will ripen the gospel grain for the world's great harvest or the end of the world (J. Elwin Woodward).

The "Latter Rain Covenant" doctrine was widely accepted in the formative decades of Pentecostalism. It was believed the second phase of Joel's prophecy of the outpouring of the Spirit was to be fulfilled just prior to Christ's return. Thus, the Pentecostal outpouring was the latter rain, and a sure indication of the imminency of Christ's return.

The writings of David Wesley Myland, first published in 1910, based the prediction of Christ's return on rainfall charts of Palestine. Pentecostals freely related natural and spiritual rainfall, and saw all events pointing to the same conclusion. In the 1920s, W. T. Gaston wrote:

As there was an early and latter rain in connection with seed time and harvest, so the gospel dispensation was to have its early and latter rain, beginning with Pentecost, and ending with the final harvest of souls just before the second coming of Christ.[1]

The notable outcomes of these backgrounds in Pentecostalism were twofold:

1) The new movement almost became known as the "Latter Rain Movement." Eventually, "Pentecostal" won out, but "Latter Rain" was popular for many years. 2) The movement was vitally conscious of the possibility of Christ's soon return. Early-day Pentecostals frequently were indifferent to their material and cultural lot (and the lot of their children) because they were wholeheartedly convinced that their spiritual experience was a prophetic indicator of the end of the present world order.

Questions and Projects

Chapter One

1. In a testimony of a page or so tell what dealings and experiences you have had with the Holy Spirit.

2. Find a reference to the Holy Spirit in 24 New Testament Books (one for Matthew, one for Mark, etc.).

3. Briefly report on Jesus' teaching concerning the Holy Spirit. Cite the key verses that quote His teaching.

4. Trace the dealings David had with the Holy Spirit. If you had lived in his day do you think you would have recognized the personality of the Holy Spirit?

5. Prepare a brief report concerning the origin and development of the Apostles' Creed.

6. Briefly report concerning catechetical schools in the Early Church.

7. Report in more detail concerning Basil of Cappadocia and his associates.

8. Report in more detail concerning the division of the Eastern and Western churches.

9. Report in more detail concerning the Wesleyan revivals in England (18th and 19th centuries), the Presbyterian revival in America (late 18th century), or the Welsh revival (1904).

Chapter Two

1. What answer would you give to one who held that the only truly Biblical title is "Holy Ghost"?

2. Why does the designation "Spirit of God" seem to some to detract from the Spirit's personality?

3. Write your own brief essay on the word *Paraclete*.

4. Can one whose doctrine is partly false nevertheless enjoy the blessing of the Holy Spirit who is the Spirit of truth?

5. Set forth your opinion concerning the degree to which holiness of life is essential for a relationship to the Spirit of Burning, whose symbol is fire.

6. Comment on the significance to you personally that the Holy Spirit is revealed to be the Spirit of life and breath.

7. What applications can you make concerning the Spirit's ministry that emerge from the fact that He is depicted under the symbols of: 1) cloud, 2) rain, 3) dew?

8. Describe the use and importance of a seal in Biblical times, and show how these facts apply to the Spirit's work today.

9. Why is a dove so commonly used to represent the Spirit, since there are seven or more other distinct Biblical symbols that also represent Him?

10. Comment on the rightness or wisdom of depicting the Holy Spirit under the symbol of wine.

Chapter Three

1. What do you consider the distinguishing marks or defining characteristics of "personhood" to be?

2. Is it possible to make a distinction between the Holy Spirit and the Spirit of Christ? Explain.

3. Why would it be the case that the Fathers in the era of the Early Church failed to recognize the Spirit's deity?

4. Comment on whether or not you believe the personality of the Spirit is adequately recognized by the average Christian.

5. It has been said the Church in the fourth century and thereafter divorced the person of the Holy Spirit from His work. Comment on this claim.

6. One evidence of the Spirit's personality is His ministry to "strive" with sinners (cf. Genesis 6:3). Investigate this word (Heb., *dun*) and its English connotations.

7. What evidence would you present to a new Christian to convince him the Holy Spirit is a person?

Chapter Four

1. Report in more detail on Augustine and his teachings.

2. What is your opinion concerning the eternal destiny of Ananias and Sapphira?

3. Is there any sense in which the Spirit is subordinate to Father and Son?

4. In your opinion, which of the works of the Holy Spirit best establishes the fact of His deity?

5. Palma writes: "It is perfectly natural for one who believes the Holy Spirit to be God to pray to Him occasionally." Comment on this statement.

6. Comment on the role of the Holy Spirit in producing the Scriptures.

7. In your own words describe what is to be understood by the Spirit's role in "proceeding."

8. Describe what it means to you personally to know the Holy Spirit is God.

Chapter Five

1. If the Holy Spirit is responsible for convicting sinners, what role is left to the gospel worker?

2. Describe the working of the Spirit upon Samson and King Saul in the Old Testament. How much of the experience of these men in relation to the Spirit is repeated in the lives of today's believers?

3. Set forth your personal view and interpretation of the significance of the insufflation.

4. If the Old Testament operations of the Holy Spirit are described as "under the sovereign will of God," how is this different from His operations today?

5. How important do you believe the ministry of the Holy Spirit to be in the Church today?

6. How much of Jesus' experience with the Spirit is a pattern for believers? What is unique to Him?

7. Why are Bible believers usually opposed to the claim that man's spirit is a fragment of the divine?

Chapter Six

1. What is your opinion concerning the first step in the process of regeneration? Does it begin with the sinner or with the Spirit?

2. How would you distinguish between the legitimate assurance of the Spirit and a false sense of security that would permit careless living?

3. If the Holy Spirit is so concerned with practical sanctification, how do you account for some Pentecostals who otherwise give the Spirit a large place, but fail in the practice of personal holiness?

4. Does the strengthening of the Spirit reach to man's physical nature, or is it solely spiritual?

5. In a concise paragraph advise someone who wishes to be guided by the Spirit, but doesn't know how to proceed.

6. In your opinion is "praying in the Holy Ghost" (Jude 20) the same experience as "the Holy Ghost making intercession for us" (Romans 8:26)? Explain.

7. How does the Spirit's ministry to commune and fellowship have bearing on participation by Pentecostal Christians in the ecumenical movement?

8. How do you reconcile the role of a human teacher with that of the Holy Spirit our Teacher? (cf. 1 John 2:27).

Chapter Seven

1. In your opinion, was Joel 2:28-32 entirely fulfilled on the Day of Pentecost? Explain.

2. Why is the experience of the baptism in the Holy Spirit called "the promise of the Father"?

3. Report additional information concerning Montanism.

4. Report on one of the orders that is believed to have adopted charismatic practices: Jansenites, etc.

5. Report additional data concerning the Camisards, the Ranters, the Quakers, or the Shakers.

6. Report additional details concerning Edward Irving and the Catholic Apostolic Church.

7. What do you consider the strengths and weaknesses of the

charismatic movement as compared with classical or denominational Pentecostalism?

8. F. D. Bruner rejected Pentecostalism on the ground that nothing should be added to the gospel of salvation. Simon Tugwell responded: "While we may agree with Bruner that Christianity plus is no longer Christianity, Pentecostalism has come in to protest against Christianity minus." Evaluate Tugwell's response out of history and experience.

9. Walter J. Hollenweger once wrote: "The modern charismatic movement has not broken into the evangelical churches, but into the middle-of-the-road churches and into the Catholic church. That would call for a change of policy among Pentecostals. Their friends are not where they expect them." Comment on this observation.

Chapter Eight

1. Investigate the word *baptize* and report on its various meanings and implications.

2. What is your understanding of what occurs when one receives the baptism in the Spirit?

3. Read the Biblical accounts of the five occasions of Spirit baptism in Acts from one or more modern versions or paraphrases. What new insights, if any, do you glean from these versions?

4. What is your personal view concerning the role of laying on of hands in receiving the baptism in the Spirit?

5. Answer each of the following critics of Pentecostalism:

a. "Tongues-speaking similar to that found among Christians today is also found among pagans and apostates. It cannot . . . be considered to be the sign that the Spirit of God is at work in a man" (C. W. Parnell).

b. "There is not an indication in the New Testament epistles that there is a baptism of the Spirit that believers are without, a baptism that the believers are bidden to seek, a baptism the evidence of which is the speaking in tongues" (L. E. Maxwell).

c. In effect, Frederick Dale Bruner declares that there is one and only one baptism which occurs at conversion. There is no second experience to be described as the baptism in the Spirit.

He concludes: "Simple faith in Christ receives everything God has to give."

d. "We are never told, commanded, or urged to seek the baptism of the Holy Spirit. The idea is alien to the Scriptures" (W. A. Criswell).

6. Why do most Pentecostals insist that tongues are not merely a sign of Spirit baptism, but a necessary sign?

7. Explain Paul's query: "Do all speak with tongues?" in the light of the position of orthodox Pentecostalism.

Chapter Nine

1. What Biblical evidence would support the claim that Spirit baptism equips one to be a better soul winner?

2. Although the text defends the slogan "One baptism, many fillings" some Pentecostals do not agree. Which side do you take? Explain.

3. Expound Romans 6:4: "Therefore we are buried with him by baptism into death." Which baptism is meant?

4. If the doctrine of the baptism in the Spirit is a Biblical truth, why did God apparently allow the Church to neglect it until the 20th century?

5. Discuss the issue of the possibility of a Christian's achieving sanctification instantly through a prayer experience in contrast with sanctification in life's activities.

6. In your opinion, how important is the practice of the fullness of the Spirit in the believer's life?

7. Is it displeasing to God for someone to understand the doctrine of Spirit baptism, but make no effort to receive?

8. Could the Holy Spirit bestow a genuine experience of baptism upon someone who otherwise was significantly in error in regard to the doctrine of the Bible?

9. Can the experience of baptism in the Spirit be lost?

10. Gelpi writes: "The Pentecostal Christian is capable of coming to regard prayer as a panacea or as a replacement for human activity." React to this statement.

Chapter Ten

1. Memorize and write from memory the names of the nine gifts (1 Corinthians 12) and the nine fruit (Galatians 5).

2. Does the operation of a spiritual gift always appear supernatural to those who observe? Explain and illustrate.

3. If the gifts of the Spirit provide wisdom and knowledge, why is study and scholarly application necessary?

4. Investigate the four scriptural lists of gifts of the Spirit. What data beyond that of the textbook do you derive?

5. On the basis of the numerous Bible references to wisdom, write a short essay on the subject.

6. Out of your own personal experience cite examples of the word of wisdom, knowledge, or discerning of spirits.

7. How important do you feel it to be that the ministry of exorcism accompany the gift of discerning of spirits?

8. Discuss how you would recognize the word of wisdom, word of knowledge, or discerning of spirits.

Chapter Eleven

1. Compare and contrast the ministry of divine healing through the gifts of healings or through the implementation of James 5:14, 15.

2. If the Spirit chose to manifest the gift of faith through you would you prefer faith as unswerving trust, or faith for mighty works? Explain.

3. What evidence can you give to disprove the claim that "the age of miracles is past"?

4. Compare tongues the gift in Corinthians with tongues the sign in Acts. What is in common? What is different?

5. Report on your personal experiences or impressions in regard to the gift of interpretation and its place in the life of the church.

6. Michael Harper wrote: "Speaking in tongues is not a sign of Christian maturity." React to this statement.

7. In your opinion, does the gift of prophecy function sufficiently in the average Pentecostal church? If you feel changes are needed, how should they be achieved?

8. Charismatic writer Smail coins the word *omnicompetent*, meaning "capable of doing all things." He writes: "In the New Testament there is no trace of the omnicompetent ministers our churches are always seeking, but there is a promise of an om-

nicompetent congregation." Evaluate this comment in the light of God's promise of spiritual gifts.

Chapter Twelve

1. What evidence do you find in the Book of Acts that gifts of the Spirit were manifested through Peter? Name them.

2. Can a believer manifest a spiritual gift under the control of his own will? Explain.

3. Prepare your own verse-by-verse commentary on 1 Corinthians 14. Include suitable references.

4. Hoekema, in speaking of 1 Corinthians 14 declares: "The main point of the entire chapter [is] the superiority of prophecy to tongues." Do you agree?

5. How would you respond to an evangelist who claimed he had the power to convey spiritual gifts by the laying on of his hands?

6. Is it proper for a human leader to direct spiritual manifestations such as the operation of the gifts in a public meeting?

7. A speaker declared that it was his goal to possess all nine gifts of the Spirit. What is your opinion of this goal?

8. How does one know the Spirit desires to manifest the gift of prophecy or tongues through him or her?

9. What advice would you give someone who sought help to achieve a spiritual gift?

Chapter Thirteen

1. In general, how does one attain the fruit of the Spirit in his or her life?

2. Explain the expression "royal law" (James 2:8).

3. How can you reconcile such traits as joy and peace when it is all too evident that the believer lives in a "vale of tears" and is commissioned to "fight the good fight"?

4. Apart from love, which of the fruit of the Spirit do you feel is most lacking in the average believer's life?

5. Other than Jesus, can you find men and women who were Biblical examples of the spiritual fruit of: a) long-suffering, b) gentleness, c) goodness, d) meekness?

6. In your opinion, is it possible to manifest the fruit of the Spirit while pursuing a business career?

Chapter Fourteen

1. Prepare a further report on the subject of the unpardonable sin and blasphemy against the Holy Spirit. Discuss and explain this matter to your own satisfaction.

2. How would you describe the spirit and behavior of someone guilty of resisting the Holy Spirit?

3. What Biblical examples can you find of those who grieved the Spirit?

4. Pentecostal leaders who attempt to control the behavior of worshipers in a public service are sometimes charged with "quenching the Spirit." Comment on this charge—when might it be valid, and when not?

5. What is there about the Holy Spirit that makes Him susceptible to so many different offenses?

6. Discuss further the matter of salvation during the Tribulation period.

7. What do you understand to be the role of the Spirit in the future conversion of national Israel?

8. Will redeemed Christians be able to see and talk to the Holy Spirit in heaven?

Notes

CHAPTER 1

[1]Harry L. Turner, *The Voice of the Spirit* (Harrisburg: Christian Publications Inc., n.d.), p. 37.

[2]Lloyd Neve, *The Spirit of God in the Old Testament* (Tokyo: Seibunsha, 1972), p. 2.

[3]W. H. Griffith Thomas, *The Holy Spirit of God* (Grand Rapids: Wm. B. Eerdmans Pub. Co., 1955), p. 16.

[4]Neve, *op. cit.*, p. 129.

[5]Two other historical surveys are included in this book: a survey of historical Pentecostalism (glossolalia), and a survey of the history of spiritual gifts (charismata).

[6]John F. Walvoord, *The Holy Spirit* (Wheaton, IL: Van Kampen Press, 1954), p. 15.

[7]See Lycurgus M. Starkey, *The Work of the Holy Spirit* (Nashville: Abingdon Press, 1962), p. 17.

[8]Fredrick Dale Bruner, *A Theology of the Holy Spirit* (Grand Rapids: William B. Eerdmans, 1970), p. 45.

[9]H. B. Copinger's *Bibliography* lists titles of 3,000 works pertaining to the Catholic Apostolic Church.

CHAPTER 2

[1]J. Oswald Sanders, *The Holy Spirit and His Gifts* (Grand Rapids: Zondervan Publishing House, 1970), p. 20.

[2]F. E. Marsh, *Emblems of the Holy Spirit* (Grand Rapids: Kregel Publications, 1963), p. 219.

[3] *Ibid.*, p. 164.

[4] J. W. Jepson, *What You Should Know About the Holy Spirit* (Van Nuys, CA: Bible Voice Books, 1975), p. 30.

CHAPTER 3

[1]Alan Richardson, *An Introduction to the Theology of the New Testament* (New York: Harper & Row, 1958), p. 101.

[2]Mark G. Cambron, *Bible Doctrines* (Grand Rapids: Zondervan Publishing House, 1954), p. 118.

[3]Myer Pearlman, *Knowing the Doctrines of the Bible* (Springfield, MO: Gospel Publishing House, 1937), p. 281.

[4]Arthur C. Downer, *The Mission and Ministration of the Holy Spirit* (Edinburgh: T & T Clark, 1909), p. 144.

[5]J. Oswald Sanders, *The Holy Spirit of Promise* (London: Marshall, Morgan and Scott, 1940), p. 22.

CHAPTER 4

[1]John F. Walvoord, *The Holy Spirit* (Wheaton, IL: Van Kampen Press, 1954), p. 15.

[2]Edward H. Bickersteth, *The Holy Spirit, His Person and Work* (Grand Rapids: Kregel Publications, 1959), p. 69.

CHAPTER 5

[1]Abraham Kuyper, *The Work of the Holy Spirit*, translated by Henri De Vries (Grand Rapids: Wm. B. Eerdmans Publishing, 1956), p. 27.

[2]*Ibid.*, p. 46.

[3]Arthur C. Downer, *The Mission and Ministration of the Holy Spirit* (Edinburgh: T & T Clark, 1909), p. 41.

[4]John F. Walvoord, *The Holy Spirit* (Wheaton, IL: Van Kampen Press, 1954).

[5]John Owen, *The Holy Spirit: His Gifts and Power* (Grand Rapids: Kregel Publications, reprint of 1954), p. 36.

[6]Mark G. Cambron, *Bible Doctrines* (Grand Rapids: Zondervan Publishing House, 1954), p. 124.

[7]Michael Green, *I Believe in the Holy Spirit* (Grand Rapids: Wm. B. Eerdmans Publishing Co., 1975), p. 19.

[8]Kuyper, *op. cit.*, p. 52.

[9]Walvoord, *op. cit.*, p. 92.

[10]Downer, *op. cit.*, pp. 224-5.

[11]Stanley M. Horton, *What the Bible Says About the Holy Spirit* (Springfield, MO: Gospel Publishing House, 1976), pp. 128, 129.

[12]Anthony D. Palma, *The Spirit–God in Action* (Springfield, MO: Gospel Publishing House, 1974), p. 38.

[13]Ralph M. Riggs, *The Spirit Himself* (Springfield, MO: Gospel Publishing House, 1949), p. 44.

[14]William G. MacDonald, *Glossolalia in the New Testament* (Springfield, MO: Gospel Publishing House, n.d.), p. 2.

[15]J. Elder Cumming, *Through the Eternal Spirit* (London: Marshall, Morgan & Scott, 1937), p. 75.

CHAPTER 6

[1]Roy Hession, *Be Filled Now* (Fort Washington: Christian Literature Crusade, n.d.), p. 22.

[2]Kenneth S. Wuest, *Untranslatable Riches From the Greek New Testament* (Grand Rapids: Wm. B. Eerdmans Publishing Co., 1945), p. 111.

[3]George M. Flattery, "How the Holy Spirit Leads," *Paraclete* (Vol. 5, No. 3 [Summer, 1971]), p. 9.

⁴Edmund L. Tedeschi, "The Holy Spirit in Action," *Paraclete* (Vol. 4., No. 2 [Spring, 1970]), p. 13.

⁵P. S. Brewster, *The Spreading Flame of Pentecost* (London: Elim Publishing House, 1970), p. 135.

⁶Fredrik Wisloff, *I Believe in the Holy Spirit* (Minneapolis: Augsburg Publishing House, 1939), p. 135.

⁷Larry W. Hurtado, "What Are 'Spiritual Songs'?" *Paraclete* (Vol. 5, No. 1 [Winter, 1971]), p. 10.

⁸J. Rodman Williams, *The Era of the Spirit* (Plainfield: Logos International, 1971), p. 33.

CHAPTER 7

¹J. Oswald Sanders, *The Holy Spirit and His Gifts* (Grand Rapids: Zondervan Publishing House, 1970), p. 48.

²Frederick Dale Bruner, *A Theology of the Holy Spirit* (Grand Rapids: Wm. B. Eerdmans Co., 1970), p. 37.

³Stephen B. Clark, "Confirmation and the Baptism of the Holy Spirit" (Pecos: Dove Publications, 1969), p. 3.

⁴Morton T. Kelsey, *Tongue Speaking* (Garden City: Doubleday & Company, 1964), pp. 42, 43.

⁵John Stevens Kerr, *The Fire Flares Anew* (Philadelphia: Fortress Press, 1974), p. 38.

⁶Donald W. Dayton, "From 'Christian Perfection' to the 'Baptism in the Holy Ghost,'" *Aspects of Pentecostal-Charismatic Origins*, Vinson Synan, Editor (Plainfield: Logos International, 1975), p. 51.

CHAPTER 8

¹Frank Holder, *The Holy Spirit* (Kisumu [Kenya]: Evangel Publishing House, n.d.), p. 9.

²Louis Talbot, "The Baptism in the Holy Spirit" (privately published pamphlet).

³Mark G. Cambron, *Bible Doctrines* (Grand Rapids: Zondervan Publishing House, 1954), p. 140.

⁴Charles W. Conn, *Pillars of Pentecost* (Cleveland, TN: Pathway Press, 1956), p. 67.

⁵H. C. Hathcoat, *Charismatic Truths* (Tulsa: Light of Life Publishers, 1966), p. 56.

⁶Reuben A. Torrey, *The Holy Spirit* (New York: Fleming H. Revell Co., 1927), p. 141.

⁷Verla A. Mooth, "The Age of the Spirit" (Pecos: Dove Publications, 1972), p. 49.

⁸*Ibid.*, p. 50.

⁹Carl Brumback, *What Meaneth This?* (Springfield, MO: Gospel Publishing House, 1947), p. 235.

CHAPTER 9

¹J. Elder Cumming, *Through the Eternal Spirit* (London: Marshall, Morgan & Scott, 1937), p. 73.

[2]Jasper A. Huffman, *The Holy Spirit* (Winona Lake: The Standard Press, 1944), p. 104.

[3]Anthony A. Hoekema, *What About Tongue-Speaking?* (Grand Rapids: Wm. B. Eerdmans Co., 1966), p. 59.

[4]Kenneth S. Wuest, *Untranslatable Riches From the Greek New Testament* (Grand Rapids: Wm. B. Eerdmans Publishing Co., 1945), p. 85.

[5]For a further discussion see: Stanley M. Horton, *What the Bible Says About the Holy Spirit* (Springfield, MO: Gospel Publishing House, 1976), pp. 159-161.

[6]Thomas A. Smail, *Reflected Glory* (Grand Rapids: Wm. B. Eerdmans Publishing Co., 1975), p. 43.

[7]Alice Shevkenek, "Things the Baptism in the Holy Spirit Will Do for You" (Published by the author, 1972), p. 10.

[8]George and Harriet Gillies, "A Scriptural Outline of the Baptism in the Holy Spirit" (Monroeville: Banner Publishing Co., 1972), p. 11.

[9]Donald Gee, *Pentecost* (Springfield: Gospel Publishing House, 1932), p. 47.

[10]D. Shelby Corlett, *God in the Present Tense* (Kansas City, MO: Beacon Hill Press, 1974), p. 22.

[11]Frank M. Boyd, *The Holy Spirit* (Springfield, MO: Gospel Publishing House, n.d.), p. 41.

[12]Stephen B. Clark, "Baptized in the Spirit" (Pecos: Dove Publications, 1970), p. 18.

[13]Horton, *op. cit.*, p. 150.

CHAPTER 10

[1]Jon Ruthven, "The Cessation of the Charismata," *Paraclete* (Vol. 3, No. 2 [Spring, 1969]), p. 25.

[2]Stanley M. Horton, *What the Bible Says About the Holy Spirit* (Springfield, MO: Gospel Publishing House, 1976), p. 209.

[3]J. W. Jepson, *What You Should Know About the Holy Spirit* (Van Nuys: Bible Voice Books, 1975), p. 113.

[4]Harold Horton, *The Gifts of the Spirit* (Bedfordshire: Redemption Tidings Bookroom, 1946), p. 63.

[5]Ralph M. Riggs, *The Spirit Himself* (Springfield, MO: Gospel Publishing House, 1949), p. 123.

[6]Horton, *op. cit.*, p. 48.

[7]Howard Carter, *The Gifts of the Spirit* (London: Defoe Press, 1946), p. 30.

[8]Frank Holder, *The Holy Spirit* (Kisumu [Kenya]; Evangel Publishing House, n.d.), p. 29.

[9]Donald Gee, *Concerning Spiritual Gifts* (Springfield, MO: Gospel Publishing House, 1937), p. 51.

[10]Kenneth Hagin, *The Holy Spirit and His Gifts* (Tulsa: Published by the author, n.d.), p. 78.

CHAPTER 11

[1]Harold Horton, *The Gifts of the Spirit* (Bedfordshire: Redemption Tidings Bookroom, 1934), p. 106.

[2]W. T. Purkiser, "The Gifts of the Spirit" (Kansas City, MO: Beacon Hill Press, 1975), p. 42.

[3]Eldin R. Corsie, "The Ministry Gifts," *Pentecostal Doctrine*, P. S. Brewster, Editor (London: Elim Pentecostal Churches, n.d.), p. 110.

[4]Donald Gee, *Concerning Spiritual Gifts* (Springfield, MO: Gospel Publishing House, 1937), p. 38.

[5]Horton, *op. cit.*, p. 135.

[6]Stephen B. Clark, "Spiritual Gifts" (Pecos: Dove Publications, 1969), p. 15.

[7]Horton, *op. cit.*, p. 121.

[8]Kenneth Hagin, *The Holy Spirit and His Gifts* (Tulsa: Published by the author, n.d.), p. 92.

[9]J. Rodman Williams, *The Era of the Spirit* (Plainfield: Logos International, 1971), p. 25.

[10]Herbert A. Mjorud, "Glossolalia" (Minneapolis: Mjorud Evangelistic Association, n.d.), p. 8.

[11]Albert L. Hoy, *The Gift of Interpretation* (Battle Creek:Grounds Gospel Publishing, 1948), p. 18.

[12]Robert C. Dalton, *Tongues Like as of Fire* (Springfield, MO: Gospel Publishing House, 1945), p. 105.

[13]Richard Dresselhaus, "The Interpretation of Tongues" *(Paraclete*, Vol. 6, No. 4 [Fall, 1972]), p. 11.

[14]Stephen B. Clark, *Spiritual Gifts* (Pecos: Dove Publications, 1969), p. 18.

CHAPTER 12

[1]Anthony D. Palma, *The Spirit—God in Action* (Springfield: Gospel Publishing House, 1974), p. 50.

[2]*Ibid.*, p. 80.

[3]Michael Harper, "Prophecy, a Gift for the Body of Christ" (London: The Fountain Trust, 1964), p. 19.

[4]Charles S. Price, "The Gifts of the Spirit" in *Golden Grain* (Vol. 11, No. 8), p. 7.

[5]Stanley M. Horton, *What the Bible Says About the Holy Spirit* (Springfield, MO: Gospel Publishing House, 1976), p. 234.

[6]Howard M. Ervin, *"These Are Not Drunken as Ye Suppose"* (Plainfield: Logos International, 1968), p. 158.

[7]Donald Gee, *Concerning Spiritual Gifts* (Springfield, MO: Gospel Publishing House, n.d.), p. 88.

[8] Harold Horton, *The Gifts of the Spirit* (Bedfordshire: Redemption Tidings Bookroom, 1946), p. 157.

[9]Samuel Chadwick, *The Way to Pentecost* (Berne: Light and Hope Publications, 1937), p. 110.

CHAPTER 13

[1]Henry H. Ness, *Dunamis and the Church* (Springfield, MO: Gospel Publishing House, 1968), p. 101.

[2]Donald Gee, *Concerning Spiritual Gifts* (Springfield, MO: Gospel Publishing House, n.d.), p. 65.

[3]Howard M. Ervin, *"These Are Not Drunken as Ye Suppose"* (Plainfield: Logos, 1963), p. 152.

[4]Arthur C. Downer, *The Mission and Ministration of the Holy Spirit* (Edinburgh: T. & T. Clark, 1909), p. 264.

⁵F. W. Hopkins, *The Holy Spirit's Family* (Anderson: published by the author, 1938), p. 33.

⁶Dale Moody, *Spirit of the Living God* (Philadelphia: The Westminster Press, 1968), p. 114.

⁷Hopkins, *op. cit.*, p. 42.

⁸Stanley M. Horton, *What the Bible Says About the Holy Spirit* (Springfield, MO: Gospel Publishing House, 1976), p. 179.

⁹W. J. Conybeare and J. S. Howson, *The Life and Epistles of St. Paul* (London: Longmans, Green & Co, 1870), p. 491, note.

¹⁰Donald Gee, *Fruitful or Barren* (Springfield: Gospel Publishing House, 1969), p. 67.

¹¹Elder Douglas Head, "The Fruits of the Spirit" in *The Holy Spirit's Ministry,* C. Wade Freeman (ed.), (Grand Rapids: Zondervan Publishing House, 1954), p. 62.

CHAPTER 14

¹Abraham Kuyper, *The Work of the Holy Spirit,* Translated by Henri De Vries (Grand Rapids: Wm. B. Eerdmans Publishing Co., 1956), p. 612.

² Myron S. Augsburger, *Quench Not the Spirit* (Scottdale, PA: Herald Press, 1961), p. 91.

³J. Oswald Sanders, *The Holy Spirit and His Gifts* (Grand Rapids: Zondervan Publishing House, 1940), p. 92.

⁴*Ibid.,* p. 98.

⁵John F. Walvoord, *The Holy Spirit* (Findlay: Dunham Publishing Company, 1958), p. 234.

APPENDICES

¹ W. T. Gaston, "The New Birth and the Baptism in the Holy Spirit" (n.d.), p. 28.

Bibliography

Books

Arthur, William. *The Tongue of Fire.* London: The Epworth Press, 1956 (first published in 1856).

Atter, Gordon F. *The Third Force.* Peterborough: The College Press, 1962.

_____. *Rivers of Blessing.* Toronto: Full Gospel Publishing House, 1960.

Augsburger, Myron S. *Quench Not the Spirit.* Scottdale, PA: Herald Press, 1961.

Bales, James D. *Pat Boone and the Gift of Tongues.* Searcy: Published by the author, 1970.

Bennett, Dennis, and Rita. *The Holy Spirit and You.* Plainfield, NJ: Logos International, 1971.

Bickersteth, Edward H. *The Holy Spirit: His Person and Work.* Grand Rapids: Kregel Publications, 1959.

Bittlinger, Arnold. *Gifts and Ministries.* Grand Rapids: William B. Eerdmans Co., 1973.

Bresson, Bernard L. *Studies in Ecstasy.* New York: Vantage Press, 1956.

Brewster, P. S. *Pentecostal Doctrine.* London: Elim Pentecostal Churches, 1976.

_____. *The Spreading Flame of Pentecost.* London: Elim Publishing House, 1970.

Bridge, Donald, and David Phyers. *Spiritual Gifts and the Church.* London: InterVarsity Press, 1973.

It should be noted that not all the works listed in the Bibliography support the Pentecostal position. Some are specifically intended to deny the work of the Holy Spirit in this manner. However, they are included because their questions and objections gave direction to the author in many discussions and explanations.

Brownville, C. Gordon. *Symbols of the Holy Spirit*. New York: Fleming H. Revell Co., 1945.

Brumback, Carl. *What Meaneth This?* Springfield, MO: Gospel Publishing House, 1947.

_____. *Suddenly . . . From Heaven*. Springfield, MO: Gospel Publishing House, 1961.

Bruner, Frederick Dale. *A Theology of the Holy Spirit*. Grand Rapids: William B. Eerdmans, 1970.

Brunk, George R., ed. *Encounter With the Holy Spirit*. Scottdale, PA: Herald Press, 1972.

Bube, Richard H. *A Textbook of Christian Doctrine*. Chicago: Moody Press, 1955.

Buntain, D.N. *The Holy Ghost and Fire*. Edmonton: The Rock Publishing Co., n.d.

Cambron, Mark G. *Bible Doctrines*. Grand Rapids: Zondervan Publishing House, 1954.

Carter, Charles W. *The Person and Ministry of the Holy Spirit*. Grand Rapids: Baker Book House, 1974.

Carter, Howard. *The Gifts of the Spirit*. London: Defoe Press, 1946.

Chadwick, Samuel. *The Way to Pentecost*. Berne: Light and Hope Publications, 1937.

Chafer, Lewis Sperry. *He That Is Spiritual*. Grand Rapids: Dunham Publishing Co., 1964.

Christenson, Larry. *Speaking in Tongues*. Minneapolis: Dimension Books, 1968.

_____. *A Message to the Charismatic Movement*. Minneapolis: Bethany Fellowship, 1972.

Cockin, F. A. *God in Action: A Study in the Holy Spirit*. Edinburgh: Penguin Books, 1961.

Conn, Charles W. *Pillars of Pentecost*. Cleveland, TN: The Pathway Press, 1956.

Conner, Walter T. *The Work of the Holy Spirit*. Nashville: Broadman Press, 1940.

Conybeare, W. J., and J. S. Howson. *The Life and Epistles of St. Paul*. London: Longmans, Green & Co., 1870.

Corlett, D. Shelby. *God in the Present Tense*. Kansas City, MO: Beacon Hill Press, 1974.

Cumming, J. Elder. *Through the Eternal Spirit*. London: Marshall, Morgan & Scott, 1937.

Cutten, George B. *Speaking With Tongues*. New Haven, CT: Yale University Press, 1927.

Dalton, Robert C. *Tongues Like as of Fire*. Springfield, MO: Gospel Publishing House, 1945.

Damboriera, Prudencio. *Tongues as of Fire*. Washington: Corpus Books, 1969.

Davidson, Leslie. *Pathway to Power*. Watchung: Charisma Books, 1972.

Downer, Arthur C. *The Mission and Ministration of the Holy Spirit*. Edinburgh: T. & T. Clark, 1909.

Dunn, James D. G. *Baptism in the Holy Spirit*. London: SCM Press Ltd., 1970.

Durasoff, Steve. *Bright Wind of the Spirit*. Englewood Cliffs, NJ: Prentice-Hall, 1972.

Dyer, Luther B., ed. *Tongues*. Jefferson City: Le Roi Publishers, 1971.

Ensley, Eddie. *Sounds of Wonder*. New York: Paulist Press, 1977.

Ervin, Howard M. *"These Are Not Drunken as Ye Suppose"* Plainfield, NJ: Logos International, 1968.

Evans, Louis H. *Life's Hidden Power*. London: Marshall, Morgan & Scott, 1958.

Fitzwater, P. B. *Christian Theology*. Grand Rapids: Eerdmans Publishing Co., 1948.

Ford, J. Massingberd. *Baptism of the Spirit*. Techny: Divine Word Publications, 1971.

Freeman, C. Wade, ed. *The Holy Spirit's Ministry*. Grand Rapids: Zondervan Publishing House, 1954.

Frost, Robert. *Aglow With the Spirit*. Northridge: Voice Christian Publications, 1965.

Gee, Donald. *Concerning Spiritual Gifts*. Springfield, MO: Gospel Publishing House, n.d.

_____. *Fruitful or Barren*. Springfield, MO: Gospel Publishing House, 1969.

_____. *Pentecost*. Springfield, MO: Gospel Publishing House, 1932.

_____. *The Pentecostal Movement*. London: Elim Publishing Co., 1949.

_____. *Spiritual Gifts in the Work of the Ministry Today*. Los Angeles: LIFE Alumni Association, 1963.

Gelpi, Donald L. *Pentecostalism: A Theological Viewpoint*. New York: Paulist Press, 1971.

Gilquist, Peter E. *Let's Quit Fighting About the Holy Spirit*. Grand Rapids: Zondervan Publishing House, 1974.

Gordon, A. J. *The Ministry of the Spirit*. Philadelphia: The Judson Press, 1894.

Green, Michael. *I Believe in the Holy Spirit*. Grand Rapids: Wm. B. Eerdmans Publishing Co., 1975.

Gromacki, Robert Glenn. *The Modern Tongues Movement*. Philadelphia: Presbyterian and Reformed Publishing Co., 1967.

Grossman, Siegfried. *Charisma, The Gifts of the Spirit.* Wheaton, IL: Key Publishers Inc., 1971.

Gutzke, Manford G. *Plain Talk About the Holy Spirit.* Grand Rapids: Baker Book House, 1970.

Hagin, Kenneth. *The Holy Spirit and His Gifts.* Tulsa: Published by the author, n.d.

Hamilton, Michael P., ed. *The Charismatic Movement.* Grand Rapids: Wm. B. Eerdmans Pub. Co., 1975.

Hardy, C. E. *Pentecost.* Louisville: Pentecostal Publishing Co., 1929.

Harper, Michael. *As at the Beginning.* London: Hodder and Stoughton Ltd., 1965.

Harris, Ralph W. *Spoken by the Spirit.* Springfield, MO: Gospel Publishing House, 1973.

Hathaway, W. G. *A Sound From Heaven.* London: Victory Press, 1947.

Hathcoat, H. C. *Charismatic Truths.* Tulsa: Light and Life Publishers, 1966.

Hendry, George S. *The Holy Spirit in Christian Theology.* Philadelphia: The Westminster Press, 1956.

Hillis, Don W., ed. *Is the Whole Body a Tongue?* Grand Rapids: Baker Book House, 1974.

Hoekema, Anthony A. *What About Tongues Speaking?* Grand Rapids: Wm. B. Eerdmans Publishing Co., 1966.

Holder, Frank, *The Holy Spirit.* Kisumu, Kenya: Evangel Publishing House, n.d.

Hollenweger, W. J. *The Pentecostals.* Minneapolis: Augsburg Publishing House, 1972.

Hopkins, F. W. *The Holy Spirit's Family.* Anderson: Published by the author, 1938.

Horton, Harold. *The Gifts of the Spirit.* Bedfordshire: Redemption Tidings Bookroom, 1946.

Horton, Stanley M. *What the Bible Says About the Holy Spirit.* Springfield, MO: Gospel Publishing House, 1976.

Howard, David M. *By the Power of the Holy Spirit.* Downers Grove, IL: InterVarsity Press, 1973.

Huffer, Alva G. *Systematic Theology.* Oregon: The Restitution Herald, 1960.

Huffman, Jasper A. *The Holy Spirit.* Winona Lake: The Standard Press, 1944.

James, Maynard. *I Believe in the Holy Ghost.* Minneapolis: Bethany Fellowship Inc., 1965.

Jepson, J. W. *What You Should Know About the Holy Spirit.* Van Nuys, CA: Bible Voice Books, 1975.

Jones, James W. *Filled With New Wine.* New York: Harper and Row, 1974.

Jorstad, Erling, ed. *The Holy Spirit in Today's Church.* Nashville: Abingdon Press, 1973.

Kelsey, Morton T. *Tongues Speaking.* New York: Doubleday & Co., 1964.

Kendrick, Klaude. *The Promise Fulfilled: A History of the Modern Pentecostal Movement.* Springfield, MO: Gospel Publishing House, 1961.

Kerr, John Stevens. *The Fire Flares Anew.* Philadelphia: Fortress Press, 1974.

Kirkpatrick, Dow, ed. *The Holy Spirit.* Nashville: Tidings, 1974.

Kuyper, Abraham. *The Work of the Holy Spirit.* Trans. by Henri De Vries. Grand Rapids: Wm. B. Eerdmans Publishing, 1956.

Lindblad, Frank. *The Spirit Which Is From God.* Springfield, MO: Gospel Publishing House, 1928.

MacDonald, A. J. *The Holy Spirit.* London: S.P.C.K., 1950.

MacGorman, Jack W. *The Gifts of the Spirit.* Nashville: Broadman Press, 1974.

Mackintosh, Donald. *Tongues Are for Real.* College Place: Published by the author, 1973.

Macpherson, Ian. *Like a Dove Descending.* Minneapolis: Bethany Fellowship, Inc., 1969.

Marsh, F. E. *Emblems of the Holy Spirit.* Grand Rapids: Kregel Publications, 1963.

Mahan, Asa. *The Baptism of the Holy Ghost,* n.p., n. d.

McConkey, James H. *The Three-Fold Secret of the Holy Spirit.* Pittsburg: Silver Publishing Co., 1867.

McLean, Glen S. *The Baptism in the Holy Spirit.* Eston, Saskatchewan: Full Gospel Bible Institute, n.d.

McPherson, Aimee Semple. *The Foursquare Gospel.* Los Angeles: Foursquare Publications, 1969.

Mills, Watson E., ed. *Speaking in Tongues—Let's Talk About It.* Waco: Word Books, 1973.

Moody, Dale. *Spirit of the Living God.* Philadelphia: The Westminster Press, 1968.

Myland, D. Wesley. *The Latter Rain Pentecost.* Chicago: Evangel Publishing House, 1910.

Nelson, P. C. *Bible Doctrines.* Springfield, MO: Gospel Publishing House, 1948.

Ness, Henry H. *Dunamis and the Church.* Springfield, MO: Gospel Publishing House, 1968.

Neve, Lloyd. *The Spirit of God in the Old Testament.* Tokyo: Seibunsha, 1972.

Nichol, John Thomas. *Pentecostalism.* New York: Harper and Row, 1966.

Ockenga, Harold J. *The Spirit of the Living God*. New York: Fleming H. Revell, 1947.

Oglesby, Stuart R. *You and the Holy Spirit*. Atlanta: John Knox Press, 1952.

Owen, John. *The Holy Spirit: His Gifts and Power*. Grand Rapids: Kregel Publications, 1953 (reprint).

Pache, Rene. *The Person and Work of the Holy Spirit*. Chicago: Moody Press, 1954.

Palma, Anthony D. *The Spirit—God in Action*. Springfield, MO: Gospel Publishing House, 1974.

Palmer, Edwin H. *The Person and Ministry of the Holy Spirit*. Grand Rapids: Baker Book House, 1958.

Parnell, Chris W. *Understanding Tongues-Speaking*. Nashville: Broadman Press, n.d.

Pearlman, Myer. *Knowing the Doctrines of the Bible*. Springfield, MO: Gospel Publishing House, 1937.

Pethrus, Lewi. *The Wind Bloweth Where It Listeth*. Trans. by Harry Lindblom. Chicago: Philadelphia Book Concern, 1945.

Pierson, Arthur T. *The Acts of the Holy Spirit*. New York: Fleming H. Revell Co., 1895.

Pridie, J. R. *The Spiritual Gifts*. London: Robert Scott, 1921.

Quebedeaux, Richard. *The New Charismatics*. New York: Doubleday & Company, 1974.

Ramm, Bernard. *The Witness of the Spirit*. Grand Rapids: Wm. B. Eerdmans Publishing Co., 1959.

Ranagham, Kevin and Dorothy. *Catholic Pentecostals*. New York: Paulist Press, 1969.

Ratz, Charles A. *Outlined Studies in the Holy Spirit*. Peterborough: The College Press, 1963.

Richards, W. T. H. *Pentecost Is Dynamite*. Nashville: Abingdon Press, 1972.

Richardson, Alan. *An Introduction to the Theology of the New Testament*. New York: Harper and Row, 1958.

Riggs, Ralph M. *The Spirit Himself*. Springfield, MO: Gospel Publishing House, 1949.

Rimmer, C. Brandon, and Bill Brown. *The Unpredictable Wind*. New York: Thomas Nelson Publishers, 1972.

Roberts, Richard. *The Spirit of God and the Faith of Today*. New York: Willet, Clark & Colby, 1930.

Robinson, H. Wheeler. *The Christian Experience of the Holy Spirit*. London: Nisbet & Company, 1928.

Ryrie, Charles C. *The Holy Spirit*. Chicago: Moody Press, 1965.

Samarin, William J. *Tongues of Men and Angels*. New York: The Macmillan Co., 1972.

Sanders, J. Oswald. *The Holy Spirit of Promise*. London: Marshall, Morgan & Scott, 1970.

_____. *The Holy Spirit and His Gifts*. Grand Rapids: Kregel Publications, 1971.

Schlink, Basilea. *Ruled by the Spirit*. Minneapolis: Dimension Books, 1969.

Scofield, C. I. *Plain Papers on the Holy Spirit*. New York: Fleming H. Revell Co., 1899.

Sherrill, John L. *They Speak With Other Tongues*. New York: McGraw-Hill Co., 1964.

Simpson, A. B. *The Holy Spirit of Power From on High*. (2 vols.) New York: Christian Alliance Publishing, 1924.

_____. *Walking in the Spirit*. Harrisburg, PA: Christian Publications, n.d.

Smail, Thomas A. *Reflected Glory*. Grand Rapids: Wm. B. Eerdmans Publishing, 1975.

Stagg, Frank; E. Glenn Hinson; Wayne E. Oates. *Glossolalia*. Nashville: Abingdon Press, 1967.

Starkey, Lycurgus M. *The Work of the Holy Spirit*. Nashville: Abingdon Press, 1962.

Stauffer, Joshua. *When He Is Come*. Berne: Light and Life, 1948.

Stemme, Harry A. *Speaking With Other Tongues–Sign and Gift*. Minneapolis: Northern Gospel Publishing House, 1946.

Strauss, Lehman. *The Third Person*. New York: Fleming H. Revell Co., 1927.

Suenens, Leon Joseph, Cardinal. *A New Pentecost*. New York: The Seabury Press, 1975.

Synan, Vinson, ed. *Aspects of Pentecostal-Charismatic Origins*. Plainfield, NJ: Logos International, 1975.

Taylor, Jack R. *After the Spirit Comes*. Nashville: Broadman Press, 1974.

Thomas, W. H. Griffith. *The Holy Spirit of God*. Grand Rapids: Wm. B. Eerdmans Publishing Co., 1975.

Torrance, T. F. *Theology in Reconstruction*. Grand Rapids: Wm. B. Eerdmans Publishing Co., 1965.

Torrey, R. A. *The Holy Spirit*. New York: Fleming H. Revell Co., 1927.

_____. *The Person and Work of the Holy Spirit*. Grand Rapids: Zondervan Publishing House, 1910.

Triplett, Bennie S. *A Contemporary Study of the Holy Spirit*. Cleveland, TN: Pathway Press, 1970.

Turner, Harry L. *The Voice of the Spirit*. Harrisburg, PA: Christian Publications Inc., n.d.

Turner, W. H. *Pentecost and Tongues*. Shanghai: Shanghai Modern Publishing House, 1939.

Underwood, B. E. *The Gifts of the Spirit*. Franklin Springs: Advocate Press, 1967.

Unger, Merrill F. *The Baptizing Work of the Holy Spirit*. Wheaton, IL: Van Kampen Press, 1953.

_____. *New Testament Teaching on Tongues*. Grand Rapids: Kregel Publications, 1971.

Walvoord, John F. *The Holy Spirit*. Wheaton: Van Kampen Press, 1954.

Watson, David C. K. *One in the Spirit*. London: Hodder and Stoughton, 1973.

Wilderman, Joseph E. *A Study of the Plan of Redemption*. Rockford: Interfaith Christian Service, 1971.

Williams, Ernest S. *Systematic Theology* (Vol. III). Springfield, MO: Gospel Publishing House, 1953.

Williams, J. Rodman. *The Era of the Spirit*. Plainfield, NJ: Logos International, 1971.

_____. *The Pentecostal Reality*. Plainfield, NJ: Logos International, 1972.

Wilson, Clarence T. *That Flame of Living Fire*. New York: Richard R. Smith, 1930.

Wisloff, Fredrick. *I Believe in the Holy Spirit*. Minneapolis: Augsburg Publishing House, 1939.

Wood, A. Skevington. *Life by the Spirit*. Grand Rapids: Zondervan Publishing House, 1963.

Wuest, Kenneth S. *Untranslatable Riches From the Greek New Testament*. Grand Rapids: Wm. B. Eerdmans Publishing Co., 1945.

Wunderlich, Lorenz. *The Half-known God*. St. Louis, MO: Concordia Publishing House, 1963.

Yates, J. E. *The Spirit and the Kingdom*. London: S.P.C.K., 1963.

Booklets, Pamphlets, Periodicals, or Manuscripts

Baker, John. "Baptized in One Spirit." Plainfield, NJ: Logos Books, 1970.

Boyd, Frank M. "The Holy Spirit" (Teacher's Manual). Springfield, MO: Gospel Publishing House, n.d.

Brewster, P.S. "The Baptism in the Holy Spirit." Cardiff: City Temple, n.d.

Byrne, James. "Threshold of God's Promise." Notre Dame: Ave Maria Press, 1970.

Caldwell, William. "Pentecostal Baptism." Tulsa: Miracle Moments Evangelistic Association, 1963.

Campbell, R. K. "The Person and Work of the Holy Spirit." n.p., n.d.

Cantelon, Willard. "The Baptism of the Holy Spirit." Springfield: Acme Printing Service, 1951.

Clark, Stephen B. "Spiritual Gifts." Pecos: Dove Publications, 1969.

_____. "Confirmation and the Baptism of the Holy Spirit." Pecos: Dove Publications, 1969.

_____. "Baptized in the Spirit." Pecos: Dove Publications, 1970.

Cockburn, Ian. "The Baptism in the Spirit: Its Biblical Foundations." Plainfield, NJ: Logos International, 1971.

Courtney, Howard P. "The Vocal Gifts of the Spirit." 1956.

Cramer, Raymond L. "The Person and Ministry of the Spirit." Redlands: Published by the author, 1941.

Cunningham, Robert C. "Filled With the Spirit." Springfield, MO: Gospel Publishing House, 1972.

Dorance, Edythe G. "Operation Pentecost." Los Angeles: L.I.F.E. Bible College Alumni Association, 1962.

Evans, William L "This River Must Flow." Springfield, MO: Gospel Publishing House, 1954.

Faupel, David W. "The American Pentecostal Movement: A Bibliographic Essay." Wilmore, KY: Asbury Theological Seminary, 1972.

Frodsham, S. H. "Rivers of Living Water." Springfield, MO: Gospel Publishing House, n.d.

_____. "Spirit Filled, Led and Taught." Springfield, MO: Gospel Publishing House, n.d.

Gaston, W. T. "The New Birth and the Baptism in the Holy Spirit." n.p., n.d.

Gee, Donald. "Proverbs for Pentecost." Springfield, MO: Gospel Publishing House, 1936.

Gillies, George, and Harriet. "A Scriptural Outline of the Baptism in the Holy Spirit." Monroeville: Banner Publishing Co., 1972.

Harper, Michael. "Power for the Body of Christ." London: The Fountain Trust, 1964.

_____. "Prophecy, A Gift for the Body of Christ." London: The Fountain Trust, 1964.

_____. "Life in the Holy Spirit." Plainfield, NJ: Logos Books, 1970.

Hession, Roy. "Be Filled Now." Fort Washington, PA: Christian Literature Crusade, n.d.

Hill, Donald G. "This Is the Refreshing." Toronto: Christian Mission Publishers, n.d.

Hodges, Melvin L. "Spiritual Gifts." Springfield, MO: Gospel Publishing House, 1964.

Hottel, W. S. "Apostolic Signs." Berne: Berne Witness Co., 1955.

Hoover, Mario G. "Origin and Structural Development of the Assemblies of God." Master's Thesis: Southwest Missouri State College, 1970.

Hoy, Albert L. "The Gift of Interpretation." Battle Creek: Grounds Gospel Printing, 1948.

Hunston, Ramon. "Speaking With Tongues—The Initial Evidence." Privately published, n.d.

Kydd, Ronald A. "Charismata to 320 A.D." Doctoral Thesis: University of St. Andrews.

Lewis, L. B. "Believing Is Receiving." Published by the author in Wilmington, California, n.d.

Lillie, D. E. "Tongues Under Fire." Plainfield, NJ: Logos Books, 1966.

Lim, David. "Charismata." Mimeo classroom notes.

Lindsay, Gordon. "Baptism of the Holy Spirit" (1964); "Discerning of Spirits" (1963); "Gift of Faith" (1963); "Gifts of Healing" (1963); "Gift of Prophecy and Interpretation" (1964); "Gift of the Word of Wisdom" (1963); "The Gifts of the Spirit" (1962); "21 Reasons Christians Should Speak in Other Tongues" (1965); "The Word of Knowledge" (1963); "Working of Miracles" (1963). Dallas: Voice of Healing Publishing.

MacDonald, William G. "Glossolalia in the New Testament." Springfield, MO: Gospel Publishing House, n.d.

Maxwell, L. E. "The Pentecostal Baptism." Three Hills: Prairie Press, 1971.

McAlister, R. E. "The Manifestations of the Spirit." Privately published, n.d.

Mjorud, A. Herbert. "Glossolalia." Minneapolis: Mjorud Evangelistic Association, n.d.

Mooth, Verla A. "The Age of the Spirit." Pecos: Dove Publications, 1972.

Ness, Henry H. "The Baptism With the Holy Spirit—What Is It?" Hayward: Evangelism Crusaders Inc., n.d.

O'Conner, Edward D. "Pentecost in the Modern World." Notre Dame: Ave Maria Press, 1972.

_____. "Pentecost in the Catholic Church." Pecos: Dove Publications, 1970.

Paraclete, Vols. 1 through 10, Hardy W. Steinberg, editor. Springfield, MO: General Council of the Assemblies of God.

Paxson, Ruth. "Rivers of Living Water." Chicago: Moody Press, 1941.

Pearlman, Myer. "The Heavenly Gift." Springfield, MO: Gospel Publishing House, 1935.

Pickford, J. H. "The Charismatic Experience." Privately published, n.d.

Price, Charles S. "The Fruit of the Spirit" and "The Gifts of the Spirit." *Golden Grain,* Vol. II, Nos. 7 & 8, Pasadena, CA: Charles S. Price Publishing.

Purkiser, W. T. "The Gifts of the Spirit." Kansas City, MO: Beacon Hill Press, 1975.

Rhodes, D. L. "Power." Fort Worth: Inspiration Publishers, 1961.

Rice, John R. "Speaking With Tongues." Wheaton, IL: Sword of the Lord, n.d.

Ridout, Samuel. "The Person and Work of the Holy Spirit." New York: Loizeaux Bros., 1899 (reprint, 1954).

Sheppard, Arthur E. "A Fresh Wind Is Blowing." Published by the author, n.d.

Shevkenek, Alice. "Things the Baptism in the Holy Spirit Will Do for You." Published by the author, 1972.

_____. "Of the Doctrine of Baptisms." Published by the author, 1972.

Shields, Sidney Guy. "The Moving of the Spirit." Fort Worth: Manney Printing, n.d.

Spirit, Vol. I, James S. Tinney, editor. Washington: Spirit Press.

Stott, John R. W. "The Baptism and Fullness of the Holy Spirit." Downers Grove, IL: InterVarsity Press, 1964.

Stuernagel, Albert E. "Five Sermons on the Doctrine of the Holy Spirit." Sacramento: World's Best Literature Depot, 1928.

Talbot, Louis. "The Baptism in the Holy Spirit." Privately published, n.d.

Tinney, James S. "In the Tradition of William J. Seymour." Washington: Spirit Press, 1978.

Wilson, Walter L. "Ye Know Him or What Is the Holy Spirit to You?" Kansas City: W. & M. Publishers, 1939.

Index